S0-BNC-374

Stamp!

TIPS, TECHNIQUES, AND PROJECTS FOR STAMP LOVERS

DISCARD

QUARRY

First published in the United States of America by
Quarry Books, an imprint of
Rockport Publishers, Inc.
33 Commercial Street
Gloucester, Massachusetts 01930-5089
Telephone: (978) 282-9590
Fax: (978) 283-2742
www.rockpub.com

Library of Congress Cataloging-in-Publication data available

ISBN 1-59253-035-4

10 9 8 7 6 5 4 3 2

Cover Design: Wilson Harvey, London [+44 (0)20 7420 7700]

Grateful acknowledgment is given to Sharilyn Miller for her work from *Stamp Art: 15 Original Rubber Stamp Projects for Cards, Books, Boxes, and More* on page 6 and pages 42–143, and also for her work from *The Stamp Artist's Project Book: 85 Projects to Make and Decorate* on pages 8–39, 144–265, and 292–299; and to Betty Auth for her work from *Stamping Tricks for Scrapbooks: A Guide for Enhancing Your Pages with Stamps* on pages 268–291.

Printed in China

Stamp!

TIPS, TECHNIQUES, AND PROJECTS FOR STAMP LOVERS

GLOUCESTER MASSACHUSETTS

QUARRY BOOKS

contents

introduction

This jumbo *STAMP!* volume is an invaluable resource and tool for anyone interested in the art of stamping. Covering everything from the basic information to get you started to the literally hundreds of applications that stamps have, this book will guide you as you cultivate and expand your stamping style and skills.

The exploding popularity of stamping has encouraged a level of experimentation that has brought stamping in contact with nearly every creative endeavor. Whether you want to work with paper to make cards, embellish clothing or scrapbook pages, or take stamping to the level of fine art, this fabulous compendium will support your efforts. A full array of technique information is provided and inspirational projects will get your creative juices flowing.

HAVE FUN!

stamp basics

Basic Skills

Art stamping is a form of relief printing. It requires some manual dexterity and the ability to choose colors that work well together, but no drawing or painting ability. The skill is easily mastered with practice—the key to success in most endeavors. The best stamp artists understand that stamps are simply tools, much like paintbrushes, paper, and pencils, and the only way to improve is by stamping, stamping, and more stamping!

Before you begin, have your tools ready in hand. Work on a firm, even surface such as a steady tabletop. An inexpensive table can be constructed from a plain wooden door purchased at a hardware store. Sand the surface, paint it to create a nonporous surface (very important), and place it on something sturdy and practical, like metal file cabinets or wire baskets that can hold your art tools and materials. Choose papers, cardstock, fabrics, and miscellaneous materials before each stamping session, have several stamps available, and make sure that all your inkpads, colored pencils, scissors, embossing powders, and other tools are within reach. Once you begin stamping, you won't want to be interrupted.

Commercial and Hand-crafted Art Stamps

When you think of a stamp, the first image that comes to mind may be a commercial rubber image cushioned and mounted on a wood or acrylic block. You can find commercial stamps to suit every taste, from cute-cuddly teddy bears and rainbows to sophisticated art stamps that rival the imagery found in art galleries and museums. Commercial art stamps are available in a vast variety of designs, shapes, and sizes from manufacturers worldwide. Most stamp companies offer catalogs and international mail order service. Rubber stamping magazines and the Internet are also rich sources of rubber stamps and related supplies.

But commercial stamps tell only half the story. As I have explored this fascinating art form, I have found more options. Literally anything that can be used to impress an image onto an object may be considered a stamp. If you can apply coloring medium (ink, paint, etc.) to it, press it against a surface, and thereby create an image, it's a stamp.

In the section "Creative Tools & Techniques," you'll find stamps made from vegetables, plants, textured wallpaper, packing foam, pop-up sponges, even fish—and much more. Soon you'll view the ordinary objects in your home and garden with new eyes; you'll find creative stamping tools all around you, just waiting to be inked!

Ink and Stamp

Select a stamp. Ink the image evenly with dye- or pigment-based ink. Markers may be used to apply several colors to stamps at once. Regardless of which type of ink you use or its application, you must apply it to each stamp evenly to make a successful impression.

When using a raised inkpad, tap the art stamp onto it. If the stamp is large, turn it over, rubber-side up, and tap the inkpad onto the rubber image. Consider using a brayer to cover the stamp surface from edge to edge with an even layer of ink, particularly when a stamp is highly detailed.

Use markers to ink specific areas of the rubber image with the colors of your choice. Because the ink from markers dries faster on a rubber stamp than the dye- or pigment-based inks from pads, you may need to remoisten the ink by holding the rubber stamp near your mouth and exhaling a burst of warm breath. This revitalizes the colors.

Next, press the stamp firmly onto a stamping surface such as paper, cardstock, fabric, or wood. Do not rock the stamp as you press it down because the edges will smudge. Press down firmly and "walk" your fingers around the perimeter of the design. Practice will greatly improve your efforts.

Lift the stamp straight up from the surface with one quick motion. Sometimes pigment ink is sticky, so you may have to hold the paper down with one hand while lifting the stamp with the other.

Practice stamping with different types of ink on various papers and cardstock before beginning an art project. You'll quickly note the difference between soft, absorbent rice papers and glossy cardstock, and find that dye-based ink soaks into porous surfaces while pigment ink rests on top and must be sealed (with heat embossing or an acrylic spray) to keep it from smudging.

Paint and Stamp

My first attempts at stamping with water-based paint were less than satisfactory. Then I learned this easy, foolproof method from art instructor Sherrill Kahn. I've always gotten good results with it.

First, place a stamp image-side up on a paper towel. Pour two or three colors of acrylic or textile paint onto a palette (such as a piece of freezer paper or waxed paper). Dip a small sponge into the paint, stamp the excess onto the palette, and lightly sponge the paint onto the stamp. Using more than one color creates a marbled effect.

When applying paint to a stamp, try for even coverage. Practice stamping on surfaces like cardstock, canvas, fabric, terra cotta pottery, metal, and glass. A blurry impression may be due to too much paint; try applying less next time, and stamp again. If the impression is too light, apply more paint. Practice will help you achieve a good impression every time.

Some commercial stamps are so highly detailed that your paint may clog the engraved lines within the rubber, making a poor impression. In this case, try rolling a foam brayer into the paint then onto the rubber stamp. A rubber brayer will not work well for this technique.

The best stamps for use with paint are deeply etched rubber stamps or hand-carved stamps made from rubber erasers, potatoes, vegetables, or other firm substances. Highly detailed stamps, which resemble fine woodcuts, are almost impossible to use with paint. Reserve these special images for dye- or pigment-based ink. Specially formulated fabric inks also can be used for stamping detailed images on textiles.

Embossing

Thermal embossing is a method used to raise an image above the printing surface. This technique requires an embossing agent, usually a powder, which is heated with an embossing gun (also known as a heat tool) that blows very hot air out of a pointed nozzle. Embossing powder is made of tiny plastic pellets that melt under the heat of the embossing gun.

To emboss, first stamp an image onto a surface using clear embossing fluid or pigment ink. With few exceptions, dye-based inks (including most colored markers) will not emboss.

Sprinkle embossing powder over the inked image, covering it completely while the ink is still damp. Shake off the excess embossing powder and save it for later. Turn on your embossing tool and let it heat for several seconds. Hold the tool a few inches above the powdered image until it melts and bubbles up. (Safety tips: Emboss in a well-ventilated area, and try not to inhale the fumes from the melting powder. The fumes are visible and have a distinct odor.)

When finished, the stamped image will have a raised, dimensional surface. Embossing powders are available in many colors as well as clear. Depending on the type of powder you use, the embossed image may be shiny, matte, glittery, or iridescent. Ultrafine powders are available for embossing finely detailed stamp images and ultrathick powders for deep thermal embossing.

Colored Pencils and Markers

Once your stamped image has dried on the paper, use colored pencils and markers to flesh it out. Stamp with waterproof ink if you are going to color the image in later with water-based markers, or emboss the image first. When an image is embossed, the raised areas form little plastic bumps on the paper, making it safe to color within and around the lines with water-based media.

Masking

Masking allows you to stamp several images over each other without marring the previously stamped prints. This technique is simple and versatile, but the resulting illustration can be amazingly detailed.

First, stamp the image you want to appear in the foreground of your illustration. Next, stamp the same image on another piece of paper. Cut out this stamped image just inside the outer lines.

Place this mask over the original stamped image on your project. Select your background stamp image, and then ink and stamp over this masked image. Use a positioner, if desired. You needn't worry about ruining the foreground image, because it's covered with your mask.

Using a Brayer

Most relief-print artists are familiar with brayers, which are like small rubber paint rollers. Depending on how you ink the brayer, you can achieve varying results including a wash of color, borders, edges, repetitive patterns, and more.

Roll the brayer over an inkpad with a roll-and-lift motion. A back-and-forth motion will ink just one spot on the brayer. Now roll the brayer onto the project as desired. Ink specific areas, lines, or patterns on the brayer with color markers, too.

Use a brayer to ink finely detailed stamps. This will ensure even coverage of the stamp and, subsequently, a more perfect print.

Layering

Stamp artists can achieve dimension in their projects by stamping an image, cutting it out, and then layering it on top of their work, using a spacer of foam tape or silicon caulking to raise the image from the background.

Paper tole, a form of three-dimensional decoupage, is also achieved in this way. Stamp and color one image several times on similar paper. Then cut out the stamped images and layer them onto a cardstock base. Each layer should be smaller and smaller until you are left with the tiniest details in the foreground of your artwork. For added realism, curl the paper cutouts over a pen or pencil before sticking them to the base.

Stamp Positioning

Using a stamp positioner is an easy, helpful skill that will make the difference between sloppy work and elegant, precise stamping. Many positioners are on the market. The best kind includes a stamp positioning tool and a sheet of clear acrylic to stamp on. Tracing paper can be substituted for the acrylic sheet.

First, place the acrylic sheet in the corner of the stamp positioner, and then align the edges of the wood-mounted (inked) stamp with the corner of the tool. Stamp the image firmly and lift off. You now have a template for positioning.

Next, position the template wherever you want to place your stamped image—perhaps right next to another stamped image or in the center of a piece of stationery. Once you are satisfied with the placement, align the corner of the stamp positioner with the acrylic sheet, and then remove the template.

Ink the stamp and align it within the corner of the positioner as before; stamp firmly and lift off. Now you have a perfect impression precisely where you want it.

Stamp Maintenance

With care, your stamps will last for years. It is advisable to store rubber stamps image-side down in a cool, dark place. Sunlight is an art stamp's worst enemy. In a very short time, light and heat from the sun will dry out and crack the rubber, rendering it incapable of absorbing ink.

To prolong their wear, clean your stamps after each impression. The easiest way is to moisten a paper towel with a weak mixture of water and stamp cleaner or household window cleaner. Then pat the stamp onto the paper towel to remove the ink. Pat again on a clean, dry paper towel. Some stamp artists use commercial baby wipes (nonalcohol). The cleansing agent is not only gentle but the moisturizers help keep the rubber supple.

If working with unmounted stamps, simply drop them into a bucket of water and scrub them later with a soft toothbrush. Dry them with a paper towel and they're ready for the next stamping session.

materials

Stamps (rubber stamps as well as stamping tools) are used with many media to create the projects in this book. Before you commence stamping, be sure to familiarize yourself with the necessary tools and materials. Read product labels carefully, particularly noting safety precautions. If you have further questions, consult the glossary.

Many of the stamping tools and materials you will need can be found at your local craft and art supply store, but if they are unavailable in your area, the product manufacturers listed in the resource guide offer mail order services worldwide. Creative stamp artists will also find tools and materials in their local grocery store, hardware store, and home-improvement center.

Art Stamps

Art stamps come in all shapes and sizes. Most are machine manufactured with a wood mount to grip by hand, a soft cushioning material between the wood and the rubber, and the rubber die itself, whose raised image is inked and impressed onto a surface.

Some stamps are made with clear acrylic mounts and clear polymer, making it possible to see precisely where your image will be stamped. Many artists opt to carve their own stamps from potatoes, corks, wood, linoleum, and rubber erasers. Additional stamping tools are explored in the section "Creative Tools & Techniques."

Stamp Cleaner

Keeping stamps clean prolongs the life of the rubber and makes it easier to see the image before stamping. You must clean your stamps between ink applications to avoid muddying the colors. Several commercial stamp cleaners are available; they are generally easy to use, but any gentle household cleaner will work as well. Other options include moist towelettes, baby wipes, and window cleaner sprayed on a pad of paper towels. Whichever product you choose, be sure that it is mild. Never wash wood-mounted stamps or submerge them in water, as this will loosen the adhesive holding the rubber to the cushioned stamp mount. Unmounted and hand-carved stamps may be washed in mild soap and water.

Ink

- **Archival ink:** Ink formulated with a neutral pH level to prevent degradation of the material it is used on, such as scrapbook pages. Archival ink is applied in the same way as any other type.
- **Dye ink:** Water-based, quick-drying ink that penetrates the paper surface and is therefore not the best choice for scrapbooks and other archival materials. Dye inks can be stamped on all types of surfaces, but they often bleed when applied to unsized (absorbent) papers. Dye ink generally cannot be embossed, although new embossing powders specifically formulated to work with dye ink are now available.
- **Embossing ink:** A clear (nonpigmented), slow-drying ink used to emboss, slightly tinted so the artist can see the image long enough to apply embossing powder to it. Embossing ink is most often used when the artist wants to emphasize the color in the embossing powder. Homemade embossing ink is made from glycerin (available at most drug stores) and a few drops of food coloring.
- **Fabric ink:** Ink that is specially formulated for application to fabric. Some kinds must be heat-set with an iron. Read the product label for instructions.
- **Permanent ink:** Also known as waterproof ink. Permanent ink is used when the artist wishes to apply water-based media after stamping, as it will not smear or smudge. Permanent ink can be difficult to clean from rubber stamps afterward.
- **Pigment ink:** Pigment ink dries slowly and is perfect for embossing with clear powder. It lies on the surface of paper and usually must be heat-set or embossed to keep it from smudging. Considered archival, pigment ink is available in a multitude of fade-resistant colors.
- **Rainbow pads:** Inkpads are sometimes packaged in sets of different colors—hence the name. They are available in dye or pigment ink. Try rolling a rubber brayer over a rainbow inkpad, and then applying the ink to paper or cardstock.
- **Re-inkers:** Bottles of dye, embossing, or pigment ink that can be used to add ink to dry inkpads, a moneysaver for stamp artists.
- **Tattoo ink:** Specially formulated for safely stamping images on the human body. Tattoo inks are available in pads and markers. Use only certified nontoxic tattoo ink on skin.

Paint

- **Acrylics:** Fast-drying polymer-based media mixed with pigments. They can be used on both paper and fabric with most deep-etched stamps. Marketed under many brand names, acrylics are widely available in art and craft stores in bottles, jars, and tubes.
- **Applicator-tipped paint:** A wide variety of thick specialty paints—some with glitter, others iridescent or pearlescent—can be purchased in bottles with convenient applicator tips. They are easy to paint with, and can be used to make beautiful accent lines on artwork. Although marketed to fabric painters, the paints work equally well on paper and cardstock.
- **Cel paint:** Used by commercial cartoonists, animators, and illustrators. Cel paints are opaque vinyl acrylic copolymers for use on clear acetate.
- **Fabric paint:** Marketed under different brand names; many can be used with stamps. They are usually water-soluble and permanent when dry. Some must be heat-set before the fabric

can be washed; read the product label before using. Clear textile medium can be added to any acrylic paint to make fabric paint.
- **Gouache:** A water-based opaque pigmented media, available in liquid or cake form, often used by commercial artists and illustrators.
- **Oil paint:** May be used with rubber stamps with care, but this is not recommended due to the lengthy drying time required.
- **Porcelain paint:** A specialty paint made for using on ceramics and glass.
- **Silk paint:** Vivid colors and easy-flow application make silk paint a beautiful option for all types of fabric arts.
- **Watercolors:** A popular choice among stamp artists, watercolors are translucent pigmented water-based media available in liquid or cake form. It's worth the time and effort to take a class in watercolor painting to understand the properties and potential of this paint. Watercolors can be painted directly to a rubber stamp prior to stamping, or an image can be stamped with permanent ink and then painted over with watercolors.

Markers and Pens

- **Embossing pens:** Filled with embossing fluid in place of ink, available in many colors. Artists write with embossing pens and then emboss their graceful handwriting with clear or colored powders.
- **Fabric ink pens:** Specially formulated to work on fabric without bleeding. Fabric ink pens can be used to color in stamped images on fabric.
- **Gel pens:** Ideal for dark and black papers and cardstock. Gel pens are useful for adding pretty accents to stamped artwork.
- **Markers:** All types of markers are available, some water-based, in a multitude of colors and nib widths. They can be used directly on stamps, and the water-based markers can be blended with a paintbrush dipped in water.
- **Metallic ink pens:** Filled with opaque metallic ink. Available in silver, gold, copper, and metallic blue, green, purple, and pink, they are used for a variety of purposes, including faux marbled backgrounds.
- **Opaque ink pens:** Also known as opaque paint markers and available in many colors. They are used on clear acetate and other surfaces when an opaque application of color is desired.

Pencils and Crayons

- **Colored pencils:** Found in just about any art and craft store under a variety of brand names. They are used in stamp art after an image has been impressed.
- **Pastels:** Similar to chalk, pastels can be hard or soft, powdery or oil-based. They are easy to incorporate into stamp art, and may be rubbed into papers before stamping to give an antique look to the surface. Soft pastel artwork must be sealed with acrylic spray to keep it from smudging.
- **Watercolor pencils and crayons:** Can be used to add color to images stamped with permanent (waterproof) ink. A paintbrush dipped in water is applied next to blend the pigments.
- **Children's crayons:** Crayons marketed for children have a wide variety of applications for stamp artists. Skillful coloring and blending techniques work well with stamp art paper and cardstock, and crayons are ideally suited for making rubbings on fabric (see "Creative Tools & Techniques").

Powders

- **Embossing powder:** Made of tiny plastic pellets—too small for the human eye to discern. They are available in hundreds of colors, including metallics and gorgeous color blends, and in various types such as ultrafine powders for detail stamping and ultrathick for deep embossing. Clear powders are popular for adding a thick glaze to artwork and paper jewelry.
- **Interference pigment:** Marketed under various names, including PearlEx. Interference pigments are metal oxides or powdered mica available in many colors. They add sparkle to artwork, and can be mixed with white glue or acrylic medium to create iridescent acrylic paint, or with gum arabic and water to create shimmery watercolors. They can also be brushed or sponged on dry and sealed with acrylic spray.

Clays

- **Air-dry:** Available in black, terra cotta, and white. This clay is ideal for many decorative stamping projects. Most types air dry within 24 hours to a rock-hard finish, but they are not suitable for serving food and cannot be submerged in water.
- **Ceramic:** When working with greenware (unfired, unglazed ceramics) or when stamping into raw ceramic clay, have your project fired and glazed as necessary in a proper kiln. Access to kilns can be expensive; consider enrolling in a ceramics course at your local college or university to save money.
- **Modeling compound:** Marketed for children. Modeling compound can be stamped into and air dried in approximately one week. It can then be painted and used to embellish many stamping projects, and it makes beautiful beads and jewelry.
- **Polymer:** This modern-day clay is a favorite medium of stamp artists. It is available in many colors, including metallic, pearlescent, and glow-in-the-dark types, and can be stamped into easily once it is conditioned properly with a pasta machine. Once stamped, it bakes to a hard finish in a conventional toaster oven and can then be sanded, drilled, glued, painted, and embellished with just about anything.
- **Terra cotta:** Most pottery can be safely stamped and painted if prepared first with a primer coat of paint and sealed afterward with pottery sealant or acrylic spray.

Tools

- **Brayer:** A soft rubber roller used to apply ink in a smooth layer to detailed art stamps and to apply an even layer of ink to smooth surfaces such as glossy cardstock. When applying ink to a brayer, roll it over the pad in short strokes, not a back-and-forth motion, which coats just part of the roller.
- **Craft knife:** Also known as an X-Acto knife. Indispensable to the stamp artist. Use it to cut stamped images for paper tole and for trimming cardstock and papers. A self-healing cutting mat will protect the table surface as you cut.
- **Embossing (heat) tool:** Also known as a heat gun. This is the best hand-held tool for embossing stamped images. A highly concentrated heat source, embossing tools melt the embossing powder as it adheres to the ink on the stamped surface. I do not recommend using a toaster oven, hot plate, or light bulb with embossing ink because these can be dangerous. A hair dryer won't emboss because it doesn't get hot enough.

- **Fabric:** For most rubber stamping projects, better-quality fabrics with a tight weave are recommended. Loosely woven fabrics with rough, nubby surfaces will not take a detailed impression. Washing the fabric before applying paint and stamped images is an option. The advantages are that the fabric will be clean and preshrunk. The disadvantage is that prewashing removes fabric sizing, which adds a nice sheen to the surface. Always iron fabric well before stamping it for best results. Try using both plain white fabrics (quilters' muslin, rayon, cotton sheeting material) and colored fabrics—black is especially dramatic when stamping with metallic paints.
- **Iron-on fusibles:** Material used to fuse fabrics together; helpful for all types of art and craft projects, particularly fabric motifs.
- **Linoleum cutter:** Used to carve stamps from linoleum, soft rubber erasers, potatoes, and other soft materials to make custom stamps.
- **Paintbrushes:** Brushes in various sizes, both round-tipped and flat-edged, will add greatly to your repertoire of stamping skills. Expensive natural-hair bristled brushes are not necessary except for fine watercolor painting; good-quality synthetic-bristle brushes made for acrylic painting should suit just fine. Avoid cheap brushes, however, as they will not last and waste money in the long run.
- **Paper palette:** An inexpensive painter's palette can be made by taping a sheet of freezer paper or waxed paper on a stamping surface. Water- and oil-based paints can be mixed right on the paper, and it is easily discarded after a stamping session, which cuts down on cleanup.
- **Paper towels:** An absolute essential for cleanup after a stamping session. Torn paper towels can also be used to create lovely soft edges for stenciling applications. Papers used to wipe excess paint can be torn into strips, stamped, rolled, and glued to make paper roll-up beads.
- **Ruler:** A good-quality ruler is indispensable to the artist and will be used over the years for many projects. A clear plastic ruler is a good choice; it allows you to see the artwork beneath it.
- **Salt:** Both table salt and rock salt can be used with water-based inks and paints to create starbursts and other interesting textured effects.
- **Scissors:** Now made with a variety of decorative edges, including scallops, waves, postal notches, and curves. They can be used in stamp art when crafting a special greeting card, but they must be kept sharp for ultimate performance.
- **Sponges:** All types may be used to add color to paper and cardstock prior to stamping, or to add paints and dyes to stamps. Collect an array of sponges with different textures—sea, makeup, and pop-up sponges are just a few—and wash them thoroughly before and after use. Cut the sponges into geometric shapes to create stamps; these are especially effective when stamping on fabric. For applying paint to rubber stamps, the best type of sponge is big and soft, made for washing cars and boats. Cut it into manageable 1" x 1" (3 cm x 3 cm) squares.
- **Spray bottle:** Bottles in various sizes can be used to spray on paint or ink. A water bottle is helpful for diluting paint already applied to a surface, and for cleanup.
- **Stamp positioner:** Used to prepare for stamping. Allows the artist to position each image precisely. Instructions for its use are included in the packaging.

- Stencil: Shaped holes cut out of acetate or cardstock. The artist uses stencils to apply color to an area while protecting the surrounding area from its application. Stencil arts and art stamping go hand in hand; sometimes it's fun to stencil first then stamp over the stenciled area.
- Toothbrush: Essential for cleaning stubborn acrylic paints from unmounted rubber stamps, toothbrushes are also used to spatter paint onto a surface before stamping.
- Water containers: Have at least two on hand at all times when working with paint—one to remove most of the paint from your brushes, the other for removing the last bits.

Adhesive

- Dry: Try double-sided adhesive tape, glue sticks, foam tape, and spray adhesive for most projects. Another option is the popular Xyron machine, which applies various types of adhesive to flat items when you turn a hand crank. Masking tape and artists' tape (which looks like masking tape but is less tacky) are essential tools for stamp artists and crafters.
- Wet: Wet adhesives are fine for most papercrafts, but they can buckle the paper if used improperly. Try using small amounts of PVA (white glue), Perfect Paper Adhesive, or wheat paste, all of which are acid-free. For fabric projects, glue that is specially formulated for using with fabric is recommended. Also try thick, tacky glues with fabrics.

Paper

- Cardstock: A heavyweight paper used to craft greeting cards and business cards. Cardstock is a common material used by stamp artists. If the colors and metallics you are looking for are unavailable, try painting plain cardstock with the spray paint of your choice.
- Decorative: Giftwrap, decoupage paper, marbled paper, printed paper of all types—these are known as decorative papers. You can make your own with paints and other media. Some artists create collages and have them color-copied to use as decorative paper in other projects.
- Envelopes: Envelopes are available in many colors and sizes, but you can make your own with a template. Many stamp artists consider the humble envelope the perfect canvas, often sending mail art through the postal system to their friends.
- Handmade: Handmade paper is used for collage elements in compositions, but it can also be stamped as long as sizing has been added to prevent the ink from bleeding. A full range of handmade papers is available through art and craft suppliers, and many companies listed in the resource guide provide mail order services.
- Machine-made: Stationery, business cards, and commercial cardstock are most often machine-made and perfect for stamping. Such papers provide a smooth surface, either porous or nonporous, and are available in a variety of colors.
- Templates: Templates are used to make custom envelopes, notecards, gift boxes, and other items. They can be purchased through art and craft dealers, or you can make your own by taking apart an envelope or a box of the right dimensions and tracing it onto decorative paper. Discarded magazine pages and calendars are wonderful sources of paper for these projects.

Other Stamping Surfaces

- Candles: Stamping on candles is most easily achieved by stamping first on white tissue paper, embossing the images, and then wrapping the tissue around the candle. Apply heat from the embossing tool to the candle surface, and the wax will melt slightly, causing the tissue to adhere to the candle and then disappear, leaving behind the stamped images.
- Glass: Stamping on glass and ceramics can be tricky. Use acrylics or porcelain paint, and follow the manufacturer's instructions regarding oven baking.
- Velvet: Stamping on velvet is popular and the results are exquisite, but care must be taken not to ruin your stamps. Not all art stamps were made to withstand the heat of an iron; when in doubt, consult the manufacturer. When choosing velvet, use silk, rayon, rayon-acetate, or any combination of these fibers. Rayon-acetate gives the most dramatic results, and the embossed images will be more stable than with other fabrics. Avoid nylon, polyester, and washable velvet.
- Wood: Stamping on wood is similar to stamping on paper. Dye inks soak into porous wood, but pigment ink dries more slowly and can usually be embossed. Some stamp artists purchase thin sheets of plywood and have it cut to postcard size before stamping and mailing their artwork to friends.

Embellishments

- Beads: Beads are available in thousands of shapes, colors, and sizes. They can be glued onto stamped artwork, threaded and sewn in place, or used as dangling embellishments on art books or greeting cards.
- Buttons: Tiny antique buttons beautifully complement stamp art. Note that large buttons can be difficult to work into a composition successfully as they tend to overwhelm the artwork.
- Charms: Small metal and paper charms are available in many shapes and colors from a multitude of sources, including art and craft stores. They can be used to embellish cards, art books, jewelry, and giftwrap.
- Found items: Organic and inorganic materials—what some may call litter—can be found in every neighborhood. Scraps of paper, ticket stubs, bits of wire and twisted metal, soup can labels, discarded greeting cards, foreign newspapers, seed catalogs, leaves, feathers, rocks, twigs—from these humble materials, great art has been made.
- Ribbon and lace: Stamp artists often embellish their artwork with various types of ribbon and lace. Antique ribbon is a favorite; so is sheer organdy. Narrow ribbon can be used to bind simple books. Wide ribbon made of natural materials can be stamped, heat-set, and wrapped around gifts.

creative tools & techniques

"Stamps" are all around us. Which leads to the question: Just exactly what is a stamp? Any object can be used to transfer an image to a surface, usually with some type of water-based colorant such as ink or paint.

Stamping tools can be roughly divided into two types: hard and soft. Hard stamps such as rocks, shells, fossils, wood blocks, and metal implements work best when impressed into soft materials such as thin printing papers, paperclay, and children's modeling compound. Soft stamps, such as leaves, bubble wrap, sponges, felt, and even fish, can be stamped on most surfaces but leave the best impressions on surfaces with a sturdy support such as cardstock, matboard, wood, ceramic, and metal.

Commercial rubber stamps and hand-carved eraser stamps fall somewhere between hard and soft. A rubber stamp can be used to impress into many surfaces including clays or cardstock. Experiment at home with the variety of stamping tools lying about the house or in your own backyard. When looking for unusual stamping tools, make a habit of asking yourself, "What if?" You'll be surprised by the multiplicity of answers you come up with.

commercial
rubber stamps

A section on stamping tools and techniques would be incomplete without a discussion of commercial rubber stamps. Although these stamps can be expensive, their popularity has never waned. There are many advantages to using commercial rubber stamps (also known as art stamps) in your arts and crafts—and a few disadvantages as well.

Commercial rubber stamps are popular primarily because they are so easy to use and are available in so many shapes, sizes, and designs. Literally thousands of stamp designs exist and more are being made and marketed every year. The best art stamps are hand-drawn by professional illustrators and graphic artists, but many catalogs specialize in clip-art designs as well. You can even have custom rubber stamps made from copyright-free clip-art or from your own original line-art drawings.

Another key to the popularity of commercial art stamps is their versatility. Rubber stamps are ideally suited for stamping on paper and cardstock, but they also can be used to print on fabrics, wood, metal, and into soft clays. Artists use rubber stamps in their fine-art prints, collage compositions, artists' books, jewelry, clothing, home decor items, and myriad other projects. Because rubber stamps are available in so many images and styles, one exists to suit every taste—cute bunny rabbits, clowns, and flowers through sophisticated collage imagery, Asian designs, and artwork patterned after ancient artifacts.

The disadvantages of commercial rubber stamps are few but important. One obvious disadvantage is that the design is not your own, and it cannot be altered easily without destroying it. Rubber stamps may be cut apart, but they are so expensive that most artists and crafters cringe at the thought. Another disadvantage to commercial stamps is their high cost, typically between $5 and $20 for a single stamp. Rubber stamps are not widely available in every country. Fortunately, most stamp companies now offer mail order catalogs and online purchasing options.

Finally, one must take special care when using commercial rubber stamps in artwork intended for resale. With few exceptions, these stamps are vigorously protected by copyright law and may not be used for such purposes. Some stamp companies allow this practice; they are referred to as angel companies. Before using stamps on artwork intended for sale, please consult the individual stamp manufacturers and inquire into their angel status. Try to obtain their permission in writing.

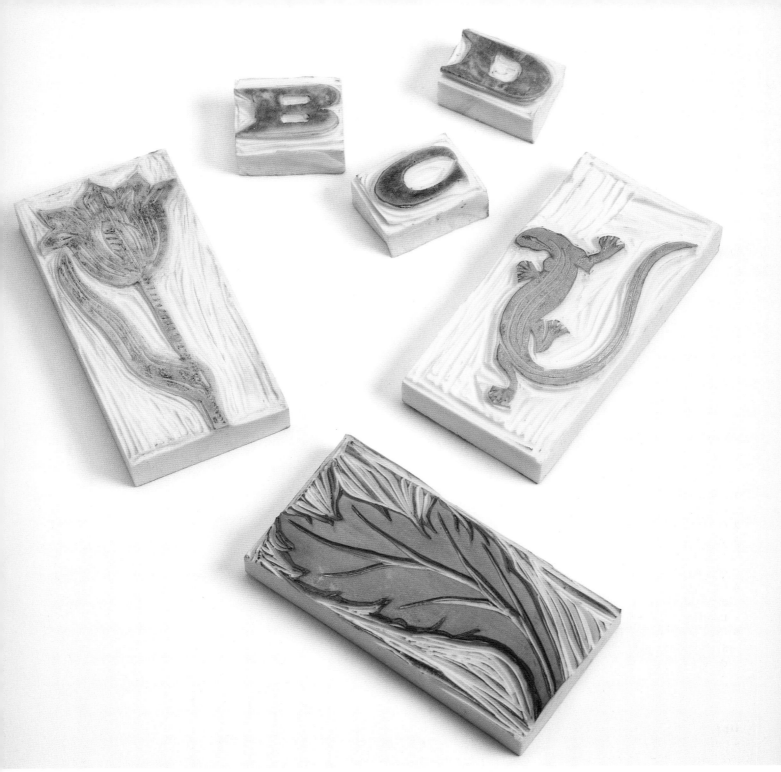

Carving your own art stamps from rubber erasers is a great way to add images to your collection, especially if you live in an area where commercial rubber stamps are not widely available. This approach has many advantages. Stamps made from rubber erasers are usually durable and last for many years. You can make stamps that are uniquely your own—no one else will ever fashion quite the same images. By making stamping tools from your own designs, you will never violate copyright laws selling hand-stamped artwork.

Carving stamps from rubber erasers is similar to woodblock cutting, but it's much easier and faster. The basic skills can be learned in just a few minutes. Once you have carved a few simple designs, you may want to expand your skills by carving large-scale images from soft printmaking blocks, which are available in many shapes and sizes. When choosing material for carving, look for large, flat erasers that don't crumble easily. The best erasers for carving have the consistency of firm cheese. Also, consider the end of your pencil: Chances are, it's capped with an eraser tip that can be carved into a miniature heart, coffee bean, star, or similar image. Ministamps are versatile, and children enjoy using them to stamp pen-pal letters and school assignments.

erasers

1 Select a design, then use a carbon-based photocopier to enlarge or reduce the image to a manageable size. Remember that the image must fit within the parameters of the rubber eraser.
2 Cut out the photocopied image and place it face down on the back of a smooth, clean eraser.
3 Soak a cotton ball with nail polish remover, and rub it over the back of the paper. Rub in one direction only to avoid distorting the image. The nail polish remover interacts with the carbon on the photocopy, causing it to transfer permanently to the eraser.
4 Lift one corner of the paper away from the back of the eraser to see if the image has transferred properly. If not, replace it and continue soaking the paper with nail polish remover. It should transfer within seconds; once it has, remove the paper and discard it.
5 Use a linoleum cutting tool with interchangeable blades to carve out the white areas of the eraser. Starting with the finest blade, trim carefully around the image. Use the same blade to carve out tiny detail lines and dots. As you carve farther from the design area, switch to larger blades.

MATERIALS
• Source image
• Photocopier
• Rubber eraser
• Cotton balls
• Nail polish remover
• Linoleum cutters
• Ink
• Paper

tips

• Use wider blades to carve away large portions of the eraser, but take care not to undercut the design area, as this will weaken the stamp. When carving curved lines, it's easier to turn the eraser than the blade.

• Test the carved image by inking it well and stamping it onto scrap paper. Some artists prefer a rough-cut look, reveling in the stray lines and jagged areas of the image. Others prefer clean lines for perfect repeat stamping. Just continue carving away unwanted areas until the image is satisfactory.

• Source material for creating hand-carved imagery is easy to find. Bookstores and libraries often carry clip-art books, the best sources of copyright-free imagery. The black and white illustrations can be photocopied and used for any purpose. Geometric shapes such as circles, squares, and stars are good designs for a first attempt. Try carving a pear or an apple shape.

• Most erasers are 3/8" (.5 cm) to .5" (1 cm) thick, so they can be carved on the front and back. Some artists also carve tiny border images along the sides of the eraser.

• Those with drawing skills may use a ballpoint pen or laundry pen with permanent ink to draw an image directly on the eraser, thus avoiding the trouble of transferring a photocopied image.

• When creating stamps with letters or words, write them out normally and they will transfer backward to the printmaking block. Once the letter(s) have been carved, the stamp itself will print a correct image. If drawing letters directly onto the printmaking block, be sure to write backward.

• Stamps carved from rubber erasers or printmaking blocks can be washed in warm soapy water and dried after use.

The ancient art of gyotaku (fish printing) was first practiced—as far as we know—when a Japanese lord had direct prints of his prize catches made to preserve them for posterity. The earliest known example dates from 1862. Fish prints are a type of nature print, and the same fish can be used many times over to stamp everything from T-shirts to stationery. Water- and oil-based inks and paints may be used to create these prints. In either case, it is important to discard the fish afterward. It is not safe to eat! Gyotaku is not difficult, but it is important to follow each step carefully. In particular, take care to clean the surface of the fish and to prop the fins to ensure a clear print. Note: The fish images below are actually rubber stamps made from actual fish prints.

fish

1 Clean and dry a fish carefully. Arrange it on a worktable and support the fins with clay to bring them up to the surface level of the body. Be sure the fish is clean and dry to the touch, otherwise the colorant may not cling to its scaly surface.
2 Close and seal all openings (mouth, gills, and anus) with absorbent tissue paper to prevent leakage of bodily fluids.
3 Apply oil- or water-based ink or paint to the top surface of the fish.
4 Cover the fish with soft, pliable Japanese or sumi-e sketching paper and rub it gently to transfer the ink from the fish to the paper.
5 Peel off the paper and allow the print to dry. Add color to the image with markers, watercolors, or colored pencils.

MATERIALS
• Fish
• Clay
• Absorbent tissue paper
• Ink or paint
• Thin paper
• Colored markers, pencils, watercolors

tip
• *Your first attempts at gyotaku may be smudged and messy, but don't get discouraged. Keep trying, and save your misprints for collage projects.*

A surprisingly versatile stamping tool, bubble wrap is available just about everywhere. Usually offered in two sizes, large and small, each air-filled plastic pillow offers printing possibilities to the stamp artist. Bubble wrap can be colored with dye- or pigment-based inks, acrylics, gouache, watercolor, textile paints, and even oil paints. The transferred prints make lovely backgrounds of irregularly shaped circles. Consider using this stamping tool for greeting cards, wall stamping, decorated furniture, quick and easy giftwrap, and fabric stamping.

bubble wrap

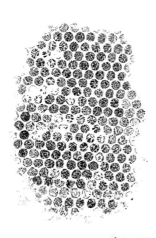

1 Prepare a stamping surface (cardstock, ironed fabric, painted furniture, plain paper for giftwrap, etc.). Place it nearby before preparing the bubble wrap.

2 Cut out a manageable piece of bubble wrap, taking care not to cut through the air-filled plastic pockets.

3 Apply colorant to the bubble wrap. If using dye ink, cover the surface quickly before it dries. Pigment-based inks, acrylics, watercolors, gouache, and especially oil paints will take much longer to dry, allowing greater flexibility.

4 Flip the bubble wrap over, and place it on the stamping surface from step 1. Holding the wrap firmly in place with one hand, use the other to press it down, transferring the coloring medium to the stamping surface.

5 Quickly remove the bubble wrap and repeat steps 1–4 as desired.

MATERIALS
- Stamping surface
- Scissors
- Bubble wrap
- Coloring medium

tips
- *Choose the type of paint or ink according to the project you have in mind. For example, textile paints and inks are made for stamping on fabrics, oil paints for canvas, watercolor, gouache, and pigment- and dye-based inks for paper and cardstock, and acrylics for just about any surface.*
- *When choosing colors, two or three will usually work well together and create a marbled effect when applied simultaneously. Metallic paints are beautiful.*
- *If a few of the air pockets in your bubble wrap have deflated, don't let that concern you. They can still be colored and stamped on most surfaces.*

Nature provides a superabundance of stamping tools in the form of fruits and vegetables. Yes, you can stamp with a celery stick, a cabbage, a pear, or a peach! Also try carving designs into the cut surface of firm vegetables such as carrots, pumpkins, potatoes, and turnips. You are limited only by your imagination and the produce available in your region. One important consideration when creating stamps from fruits and vegetables is time: These stamps will not last long. You may refrigerate them to extend their usefulness, but it's best to stamp as soon as possible after slicing or carving into them. The best fruits and vegetables for stamping are firm and relatively dry; wet, mushy items will not produce satisfactory prints. When using damp fruits such as peaches and pears, lay the cut side down on paper towels and allow them to absorb some of the moisture before you apply a colorant.

The lists on the right will help you select appropriate fruits and vegetables for this project, but you are by no means limited to them. Experiment with the produce you find in your area.

RECOMMENDED
FRUITS AND VEGETABLES

Apples	**Okra**
Broccoli	**Onion**
Cabbage	**Peach**
Carrots	**Potato**
Celery	**Pumpkin**
Gourd	**Radish**
Lettuce	**Star fruit**
Mushroom	**Turnip**
Nectarine	**Yam**

FRUITS AND VEGETABLES TO AVOID
Banana
Grape
Lemon
Orange
Pomegranate
Strawberry

fruits and vegetables

1 Here is the first of two approaches to using fruits and vegetables as stamping tools. Find produce with an appealing shape, cut it in half, and apply a water-based colorant to the cut surface. Stamp the item, allowing the fruit or vegetable itself to dictate the design. The star fruit coasters are an excellent example of how lovely an impression nature can make, and I have seen beautiful prints made from a cabbage sliced in half.

2 The second approach is to cut a firm fruit or vegetable in half and then draw or inscribe a simple design on it. Use a sharp craft knife to remove the unwanted background material to create a stamp design, similar to carving images into rubber erasers. Apply water-based colorant to the carved design and stamp it.

MATERIALS
- Fruits and vegetables
- Sharp craft knife
- Water-based colorant

tips
- *When carving into produce, simple geometric motifs such as triangles and stars work best.*
- *Accidents are more likely to occur when using a dull knife, so use fresh blades for this project.*
- *Some produce can be difficult to cut, so carve away small bits at a time until the design is revealed.*
- *Individual lettuce leaves may be used to make lovely prints by applying water-based media to the convex side of the leaf. Lay the leaf on a stamping surface and gently burnish the top with your fingers, transferring the veined designs to the stamping surface.*
- *If you create a lovely design that you want to preserve, consider stamping the vegetable or fruit print onto a rubber eraser with permanent ink. Once the ink is dry, carve out the image as described in the section on eraser carving.*

A stamp in your hand—that's what you have, literally! Yes, you can apply nontoxic colorants such as watercolor, pigment ink, acrylic paint, and gouache to your hands, fingertips, feet, and toes to make stamped paper or fabric with a personal touch. The resulting prints can be used for a variety of projects, from art books to fabric painting, giftwrap, and greeting cards. If you have a cooperative cat, her paws can be inked or painted with nontoxic materials and used to print small projects. Please take special care to wash her paws thoroughly with soap and water immediately afterward.

Children can safely stamp with their hands and feet, noses, chins, and elbows, if they use nontoxic colorant under adult supervision. Fill a bowl or sink with warm soapy water, and have washcloths and scrub brushes available for cleaning immediately after each stamping session.

handprints,
footprints, & pawprints

1. Apply a nontoxic colorant to fingertips, hands, feet, etc.
2. Press the inked or painted body part to a stamping surface. If printing with a cat's paw, gently hold her upper leg with one hand and use the other hand to press her paw firmly onto the stamping surface.
3. Allow the prints to dry completely before incorporating them into a final project.

MATERIALS
• Nontoxic colorant

tips

• *Using certified nontoxic colorant is critically important to your health and safety. Read product labels carefully, including safety precautions and consult manufacturers if you have any questions about the toxicity of their pigmented products. Never apply permanent ink to bare skin.*
• *Choose the type of paint or ink according to the project you have in mind. For example, the cleanest fingerprints are obtained with dye inks. Textile paints and inks work well with high-quality fabrics. Watercolor, gouache, and pigment- and dye-based inks are made for paper and cardstock; acrylics can be applied to just about any surface.*
• *When choosing colors, two or three will usually work well together and create a marbled effect when applied simultaneously.*
• *If your cat's pawprints come out smudgy, clip the hair between her footpads before applying color to them.*
• *Try using pigment ink or embossing ink, then emboss the image with powder for greater impact. For information on embossing techniques, see "Stamp Basics."*

Heat & Mold stamps are made by applying the heat from a light bulb to a special material for fifteen seconds, then pressing the heated material against a textured object. In two or three seconds, the material cools and takes on the texture from the object and can be coated with ink or paint and used for stamping. The material is surprisingly durable, holding up to numerous stampings, and is particularly well suited for creating repeat patterns.

You can make fascinating stamp designs by pressing the heated material against a large rubber stamp and picking up a portion of the overall design. The best thing about this material is that it can be reheated and molded to make many more stamp impressions, over and over again. Heat & Mold material is a specialized stamp tool available through retail stamp stores. For more information, please see the resource guide.

heat &
mold stamps

1 Insert the material into the plastic handle provided.
2 Press the material against a lit light bulb for approximately fifteen seconds.
3 Immediately press the heated material firmly against a textured item. Hold it in place for a few seconds.
4 Apply dye ink, pigment ink, or water-based paint to the molded material—now a stamp—and press the stamp onto cardstock, fabric, wood, metal, or ceramics. Heat & Mold stamps are used in precisely the same way as commercial rubber stamps.

MATERIALS
- Heat & Mold material
- Art stamps and other textured items
- Colorant

tip
- *Create many new stamps by pressing Heat & Mold material against various areas on a single rubber art stamp. And virtually any clean, firm surface with texture can be used to create new stamps. Try pressing the heated material against a textured wood surface, leaves and plants, stucco, brick, rocks, tree bark, metal objects, ornamental objects, or anything with lots of surface texture.*

You can make a wide variety of stamping tools with instant pop-up sponges, available in sheets 1/16" (1.5 mm) thick that expand in water to 5/8" (1.5 cm) thick. Trace a shape on the sponge, cut out, then immerse in water—and watch your new stamp expand! The great thing about these sponges is that they can be reversed, providing you with two stamps in one! Because they are soft and flexible, they're perfect for stamping rounded surfaces such as drinking glasses and furniture.

instant
p o p - u p   s p o n g e

1 Lay a small- to medium-sized stencil on the pop-up sponge. Use a pen to trace the stencil on the sponge. For example, a diamond-shaped stencil may be used to draw a diamond shape on the sponge.
2 Remove the stencil and cut out the shape. Drop it in water then squeeze out the excess water. Apply acrylics to one side of the damp sponge stamp. Try using two or three complementary colors together for a marbled effect.
3 Print paper, cardstock, fabric, wood, plastic, or virtually any other surface with the new stamp, including walls and furniture, pillowcases, table runners, placemats, and unglazed terra cotta pottery.

MATERIALS
- Stencils
- Instant pop-up sponge
- Pen
- Water
- Scissors
- Acrylics

tips
- *Once the sponge expands in water, it cannot be compressed again, so take care that unused sponge material is always protected in a sealed plastic bag.*
- *It isn't necessary to use a stencil to create sponge stamps; any closed shape may be drawn freehand with a pen. Stencils do provide great outlines, however. Bold images without much detail are the best choice; try diamonds, hearts, circles, and geometric designs. Another option is to use a commercial rubber stamp to print an image on the pop-up sponge sheet, then cut it out as described above.*
- *When choosing paint, the two important considerations are type and color. Choose the type of paint according to the project you have in mind. For example, acrylic glass paints are made for stamping on glass plates and drinking glasses, and patio paint for stamping on unglazed terra cotta. When choosing colors, two or three will usually work well together. Metallic paints are a nice accent.*
- *Seal the completed project as necessary. For example, products are formulated especially for sealing unglazed terra cotta, and a garment stamped with acrylic paint should be sealed with a light application of textile medium so that it may be laundered.*

Model Magic® is a malleable, spongy material that air dries in 24 hours, yet retains a soft, marshmallow-like texture. Although this product is currently marketed as a children's craft item, the home crafter with a limited range of rubber art stamps can also greatly expand her repertoire by making Model Magic® stamps.

Model Magic

1 Pinch off a piece of Model Magic® and roll it into a smooth ball.
2 Press the ball of Model Magic® against a rubber art stamp or any firm surface with interesting texture. The material will be impressed with a reverse image.
3 Allow the molded material to dry for 24 hours on a nonstick surface.
4 Apply dye ink, pigment ink, or water-based paint to the molded material—now a stamp—and press the stamp onto surfaces such as cardstock, fabric, wood, metal, and ceramics. Model Magic® stamps are used in precisely the same way as commercial rubber stamps.

MATERIALS
- Model Magic
- Art stamps and other textured items

tips
- *Sometimes Model Magic® sticks to rubber stamps and isn't easy to clean off. In that case, it's best to scrub the stamp with a soft toothbrush. If the material is very sticky, apply a little clear embossing ink to the stamp before impressing it, and it will release without difficulty.*
- *Many, many new stamps can be made from pinched-off pieces of Model Magic® pressed against various areas on a single rubber art stamp. Other textures to try include natural leaves (watch Model Magic pick up the veins and subtle surface variations!), dried plants, rocks, wood (try tree trunks!), and architectural elements. Virtually any clean, firm surface with texture can be impressed into Model Model Magic® to create a new stamp.*

Leaf printing (also known as nature printing) is perhaps one of the easiest and least expensive forms of stamping available to artists and crafters. Virtually any leaf or herb may be used to create an acceptable print, and many flowers work as well. The best specimens are soft and malleable; dried leaves are often too brittle to withstand the printing process. Look for plump green leaves with veins clearly visible. Leaves, flowers, and herbs may be gathered in your own backyard or neighborhood, or take a nature walk and gather specimens on your way. Some artists enjoy keeping nature journals, taking notes while hunting and gathering, and later printing samples by their notes. Children particularly enjoy this aspect of nature printing, but keep a few points in mind as you collect nature stamps for your artwork. When on public property, avoid picking fresh plants or stripping trees of their leaves. Many fresh leaves can be found lying on the ground. If you must pick leaves off trees or shrubbery, be kind. Pick sparingly! Always obtain permission from park personnel before taking any vegetation, because many plants in public parks are on endangered species lists. Sometimes, if you explain your project convincingly enough, a park ranger will allow you to remove a few fresh leaves. Also, beware of poisonous plants. No matter how tempting it might be, never pick a leaf or plant that you are unfamiliar with. Obtain the advice of park personnel before stamping with exotic specimens.

leaves, flowers & herbs

1 Once you have collected a batch of leaves, herbs, or flowers, separate them into small piles and clean the surfaces with a damp cloth. Take care not to bruise or tear the plant. Some plants should stand in a bucket of water to preserve their lovely surface texture.

2 Apply ink or paint (watercolors, acrylics) to the convex side of the leaf (the side with raised texture from veins) with a makeup sponge. A light layer of color will print much better than a heavy application.

3 Turn the leaf over onto a stamping surface and gently lay it down. Small, fragile items may require handling with tweezers.

4 Press the back of the leaf with your fingers, walking them up and down over all areas of the leaf rather than rubbing them, which may smudge more delicate prints. Experiment with this technique on scrap paper before committing yourself to a more permanent project.

MATERIALS
- Leaves, flowers, and herbs
- Makeup sponge
- Water-based colorant
- Tweezers

tips
- *When selecting leaves and plants for nature printing, don't automatically reject torn or damaged specimens. The random torn edges and areas that insects may have eaten away add to the charm of nature prints.*
- *Herbs such as parsley, sage, rosemary, and thyme make lovely nature prints. Ink and stamp with them the same way as you do leaves and flower petals.*
- *Many surfaces besides paper and cardstock may be successfully printed with leaves and flowers. Try stamping on fabric to make clothing or home decor items. Create nature prints on ceramic plates or tiles. Decorate your walls with nature prints. The possibilities are almost endless.*
- *Oil-based colorants may be substituted for water-based, but they are messy and take a long time to dry. Apply the colorant sparingly to avoid smudges.*
- *In some cases, no colorant is needed to make nature prints, as many plants have natural dyes embedded in their tissue structure. The dyes can be released by laying the plant on a porous surface (paper, fabric), taping it in place, and hammering it sharply. Beat the entire leaf with the hammer, then gently peel it away. Some natural dyes are permanent; if creating a washable fabric item, heat-set the dye with an iron.*
- *If you create a lovely nature print that you want to use again, consider having a custom rubber stamp made from it. Print the leaf with black permanent ink on plain white paper; your local stationery or office supply store can make the stamp from the print.*

If you work in a shipping department, you are very fortunate indeed. A unique type of stamping material surrounds you: packing foam! Puffy plastic-based foam peanuts are available in many shapes and sizes, and they make terrific tools for stamping on many types of surfaces. The small shape and flexibility of this material suit it particularly for stamping small objects.

packing foam

MATERIALS
- Colorant
- Packing foam

1 Apply colorant to a packing foam piece. If using dye ink, coat the surface quickly before the ink dries. Pigment-based inks, acrylics, watercolors, gouache, and especially oil paints will take much longer to dry, allowing greater flexibility.
2 Quickly stamp the foam piece onto a surface. Repeat this process as desired.
3 Allow the stamped project to dry completely and seal it, if necessary, with acrylic spray.

tips
- *Dye-based ink picks up the most detail in foam pieces, but acrylic paint also can be used effectively on most stamping surfaces when applied sparingly. Choose the type of paint or ink according to the project you have in mind. For example, textile paints and inks are made for stamping on fabrics, oil paints for canvas, watercolor, gouache, and pigment- and dye-based inks for paper and cardstock, and acrylics for just about any surface.*
- *Practice stamping repeat patterns with black ink on plain paper, experimenting with design and shape before introducing color. Once you have a satisfactory composition or repeat design perfected, transfer your ideas to an art project.*
- *Repeat patterns are particularly well suited for fabric stamping and for painting plates and glassware, tablecloths, napkins, and other home decor items.*
- *Try using a hot needle to inscribe a simple design on the foam before stamping.*

Amazing designs and textures can be created with an ordinary kitchen item: plastic wrap! For a crackled surface effect or batik look, nothing beats this product. Plastic wrap can be folded, squeezed, squished, and smooshed into just about any shape, held together, if necessary, with strong adhesive, and used as a stamp. Once you're finished with it, simply discard it.

plastic wrap

1 Tear off a generous sheet of plastic wrap.
2 Fold, squish, or pleat the wrap into a desirable shape. Try folding it lengthwise to create a plastic rope before wrapping it into a circular shape, or tie it into knots. Once you have a pleasing molded shape, glue it together with strong adhesive (this may not be necessary; you might be able to hold the shape together with your hand).
3 Prepare a stamping surface (paper, cardstock, fabric, clay, etc.).
4 Apply colorant to the shaped plastic wrap, stamp the surface, and repeat as desired.

MATERIALS
- Plastic wrap
- Adhesive
- Stamping surface
- Colorant

tips
- *Experiment with a variety of plastic wraps. They are available under different brand names and you may prefer one type over another.*
- *Before commencing a large project, practice stamping with plastic wrap on a sheet of white scrap paper. A shape that appears to be pleasing in your hand may actually not stamp as nicely as you anticipated. Keep experimenting with different shapes, allowing the natural texture of the crinkled wrap to dictate your design.*

You've heard the expression, "hard as a rock." Can you stamp with a rock, a fossil, or even a seashell? Yes—provided the type of material you stamp into is soft and malleable. Because rocks, fossils, and seashells are hard objects, they are ideally suited for making impressions in pottery, polymer, and air-dry clays. The rich texture leaves behind a beautiful print impossible to duplicate with any other method. Seashells and fossils in particular are abundantly available in so many shapes and textures, you will never run out of stamping tools. The best thing about rocks, fossils, and seashells is that they are free for the picking. Stamping with them can be an educational exercise as well as an artistic one. It's a great craft for children and adults alike.

rocks, fossils, & seashells

MATERIALS

- Rocks, fossils, seashells
- Soft toothbrush
- Soft clay
- Paint or dye
- Acrylic spray

1 Clean the rock, fossil, or seashell with a soft toothbrush and allow it to dry completely.
2 Roll out a piece of clay to the desired size and shape.
3 Press the rock, fossil, or seashell into the clay; remove it quickly. Continue stamping into the clay until the project is complete.
4 Allow the clay to air dry, or bake it per the manufacturer's instructions.
5 Paint or dye the finished artwork as desired and seal with an acrylic spray if needed.

tips

- If the rock, fossil, or seashell sticks to the clay, apply a little clear embossing ink to it before making an impression, and it should release without difficulty.
- Make a hard-baked polymer clay mold of the rock, fossil, or seashell by impressing it into polymer clay and baking as usual. Once the mold is hardened and cooled, press any type of clay into it, and air dry or bake as required. You now have a duplicate of the rock, fossil, or seashell that can be incorporated into a variety of artwork pieces or used as a bead or pendant.

A common household item, nubby textured shelf liner is ideal for stamping backgrounds onto paper, cardstock, wood, metal, and fabric. It can even be impressed on soft clays. To apply an even layer of paint, use a rubber brayer. Alternatively, try sponging on several colors of acrylics, watercolors, or metallic paint for an even more interesting textured effect. You can find shelf liner in most grocery stores, home improvement centers, and some hardware stores. It's available in different styles and weights; each type of shelf liner leaves a different impression.

shelf liner

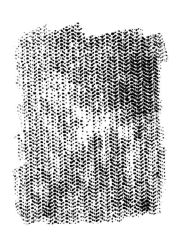

1 Cut out a piece of shelf liner.
2 Apply watercolor paints, diluted acrylics, or liquid inks to the surface of the shelf liner in a random pattern, using a foam brush, brayer, or sponges. Allow the paints to mingle, but avoid overmixing them.
3 Turn the shelf liner over onto a stamping surface. Practice with paper or scrap fabric.
4 Press the shelf liner into the stamping surface to transfer the colorant.
5 Gently peel back the shelf liner and remove it from the stamping surface. Repeat as desired.

MATERIALS
- Shelf liner
- Scissors
- Colorant
- Brayer, foam brush, or sponge
- Stamping surface

tip
- *Rolling the brayer over the back of the liner may yield a clearer print.*

Don't overlook the common household sponge. Not only are they indispensable for applying paint to rubber stamps for fabric stamping, they also make terrific stamps in their own right. The natural texture of kitchen sponges, sea sponges, boat-washing sponges, even makeup sponges transfers lovely prints to just about any surface. Sponges are foolproof tools for both children and adults, requiring very little talent, just a lot of imagination. The secret to stamping with sponges is to avoid over-saturating them with paint. For this reason, it's a good idea to tap off excess paint on a paper towel before applying a sponge to the final project. Practice pressing the sponge down onto a white piece of paper. Note how the areas you pressed most firmly against the stamping surface are dense in color, while the rest of the image has a fascinating textured appearance. You should be able to get three to five "stampings" from a paint-saturated sponge before it requires more paint. It's fun to watch the beautiful impressions appear as you stamp.

sponge

1 Cut up a large boat sponge into manageable pieces about 1" (3 cm) square, or use sea sponges and makeup sponges as is.
2 Squirt out a puddle of watercolor paints, acrylics, fabric paints, or liquid inks onto a piece of freezer paper or non-stick working surface. Dip the sponge into the colorant, and tap off the excess on a paper towel.
3 Stamp the sponge several times onto a fabric, paper, wood, metal, cardstock, or other surface. Reapply paint or other colorant when necessary, and repeat stamping.

MATERIALS
- Sponges
- Colorant
- Stamping surface

tips
- *Remember to save paint-saturated paper towels to make rollup beads (please see the related chapter).*
- *Mix two to three similar colors for a marbled look.*
- *Use commercial rubber stamps over a sponge-stamped background.*
- *Allow paint to dry before applying a wash of diluted acrylics, watercolors, or other transparent colorants to it.*
- *Find sea sponges at hardware and home-improvement stores. Makeup and kitchen sponges can be found in groceries and drugstores, and common boat-washing sponges are available in auto parts stores as well as hardware department stores.*

Rubber stamps and hard stamping tools such as rocks, fossils, tree bark, and seashells can be used to make beautiful rubbings on paper or fabric. Instead of stamping a surface, the surface is pressed or wrapped tightly against the stamp and a crayon or colored pencil is rubbed against it. The technique is similar to gravestone rubbings. As you pass the colorant over the rough texture of the stamp, the surface picks up a pattern of color. This technique is particularly well suited for thin papers and fabrics with a tight weave. Thick cardstock and canvas-type fabrics will not render the same results.

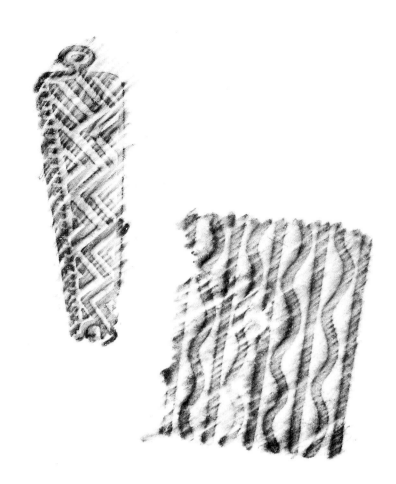

stamp rubbings

1 Place the stamp rubber-side up on a worktable.
2 Press a thin sheet of paper or fabric against the stamp, holding it taut with one hand.
3 Rub the surface of the paper or fabric with a solid colorant such as a wax crayon or colored pencil. Rub vigorously in one direction.
4 Remove the fabric or paper, and repeat as desired until the project is complete.

MATERIALS
• Art stamps
• Paper or fabric
• Solid colorant

tips
• *When using crayons for rubbings, the best results are obtained by laying them flat against the taut fabric or paper and rubbing sideways. Try placing two or three crayons side by side on the surface and rubbing hard to transfer more than one color at a time.*
• *Try applying a thin wash of acrylic or watercolor paint to the rubbing. The wax in the crayon or colored pencil will resist water-based media, creating a batik look.*

Stamps can be used for more than just stamping; you can actually make lovely stencils with them, too. The key is to look at your art stamps with fresh eyes, finding design possibilities in their outline shapes. The first of two basic methods for creating stencils from rubber stamps utilizes freezer paper, which can be ironed onto fabric. The other method requires the use of acetate. A wood-burning tool may be substituted for a craft knife when cutting acetate.

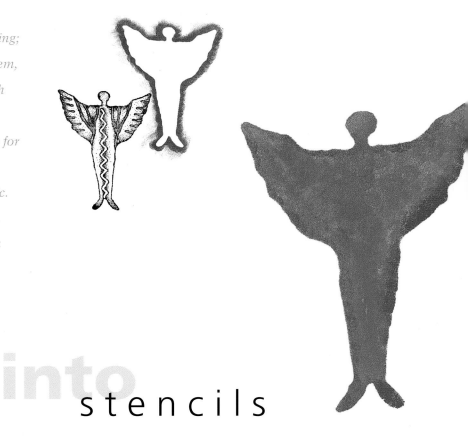

stamps into
stencils

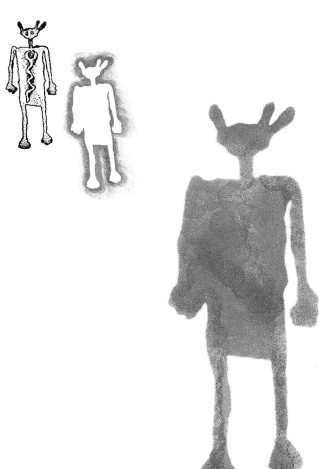

1 Stamp an image onto freezer paper or acetate with permanent ink that won't smudge.
2 When the image has dried, cut around the perimeter with a craft knife; remove the shape.
3 Place an acetate stencil on any surface—walls, furniture, paper, cardstock, fabric—and sponge color through the opening. If using a freezer paper stencil, place it shiny-side down on a piece of fabric and iron it in place. Sponge color through the opening.
4 Remove the stencil, and repeat the process as desired. If using a large or intricate stencil, it may be necessary to tape it or apply spray adhesive to the back to hold it firmly in place.

MATERIALS
• Art stamps
• Freezer paper
• Acetate
• Permanent ink
• Sharp craft knife
• Sponge
• Acrylic or fabric paint

tips
• *Craft stores that specialize in stenciling supplies often carry acetate made specially for creating custom stencils, but you can use any type of acetate for this project. In a pinch, try using file folders or thick cardboard.*
• *Option: After removing the stencil, stamp over the painted area with a contrasting color.*

This ordinary picnic product is fantastic material for stamping. You can cut it into various shapes and inscribe a design on it with a sharp object such as a ballpoint pen. Once coated with ink or paint, the plate can be stamped on any flat object. Inexpensive and readily available, Styrofoam plates will provide you and your children with hours of fun. Look for Styrofoam meat trays the next time you're grocery shopping. Clean and store the trays until it's time for your next stamping project. Children love making stamps from Styrofoam plates. Their simple designs are charming and make successful prints every time. If you use top-quality ink or paint and print onto equally fine fabric, paper, or cardstock, the design is almost guaranteed to please you.

styrofoam plate

1 Draw a simple design onto the back of a Styrofoam plate or meat tray. Use a sharp implement such as a pencil or a ballpoint pen to dig into the plate, taking care not to pierce all the way through it.
2 Apply a colorant such as acrylic paint, watercolor, ink, or oil paint to the inscribed surface of the plate.
3 Prepare a stamping surface (paper, cardstock, fabric, wood, metal, etc.) and stamp it with the plate. Reapply paint or ink, and repeat stamping until the project is complete. Seal it as necessary with acrylic spray.

MATERIALS
- Styrofoam plate
- Ballpoint pen or other sharp implement
- Colorant
- Acrylic spray

tips
- *Use a brayer for a more even application of colorant.*
- *An application of two or three paint colors will produce a lovely marbled effect.*
- *Styrofoam is somewhat fragile, breaks easily, and will eventually fall apart. If you've designed a beautiful image and want to preserve it, print it with black ink on white paper and have a custom rubber stamp made from the print.*

Stamping with textured wallpaper is easy, but it renders amazing results. This type of wallpaper is textured with blind-embossed patterns, and because it's thick and meant to be used for home decor, it's sturdy enough to use for making relief prints on most surfaces. Just as in rubber stamping, a colorant is applied to the raised surface of the wallpaper. The paper is then turned over onto a printing surface (such as soft paper, ceramic tile, or fabric) and pressed to transfer the print to the item being stamped. The paper peels away easily and can be reused many times. A caveat: Allow the textured paper to dry somewhat between applications of water-based color, as the moisture from the ink or paint will eventually soak through the surface of the wallpaper and soften it.

You can find textured wallpaper sample books at home-improvement stores and through interior designers, who discard outdated books each season. The designs in wallpaper books are vigorously protected by copyright, so always obtain permission before selling artwork that features them prominently.

textured wallpaper

1 Cut a square or rectangle of textured wallpaper to the desired size.
2 Apply watercolor paints, diluted acrylics, or liquid inks to the raised side of the textured wallpaper in a random pattern, using a foam brush, sponges, or paintbrush. Allow the paints to mingle, but avoid overmixing them.
3 Turn the textured wallpaper over and apply it directly to the center of the stamping surface. For your first attempt, hot-press watercolor paper is recommended. Lightly burnish the back of the wallpaper with your fingers or with the bowl of a spoon to transfer the image to the stamping surface.
4 Gently pull back the wallpaper, leaving behind a colored print. Save the wallpaper for other projects. Allow the painting to dry completely.

MATERIALS
• Textured wallpaper
• Scissors
• Water-based colorant
• Foam brush, sponge, or paintbrush
• Stamping surface

tips
• *For a blurred effect, spritz the watercolor paper with water before applying the textured wallpaper to it.*
• *If you are dissatisfied with your first attempt, keep trying. Print multiple images until you are successful, then mat and frame the piece. Prints that don't make the cut can be used for greeting card background papers or for collage projects.*
• *Option: Use a metallic marker to enhance and embellish areas of the print. A light application is best. Once finished, the print is ready to mat and frame.*
• *Textured wallpaper may not be suitable for pressing into soft clays because the clay could cling to the paper and lift off. This is because textured wallpaper is somewhat absorbent, and clays have moisture until they are air dried or baked. Experiment with clay stamping before committing yourself to a large project.*

Beautiful prints abound throughout Indonesia, Thailand, India, and most tropical islands because, for several millennia, the indigenous peoples have used carved woodblocks to print colorful fabrics and tapa cloth (a type of handmade paper made from beaten tree bark) for clothing and home decor items. The designs are specially made for repeat stamping to create textiles suitable for many purposes. You can carve your own woodblocks from soft wood if you have a sharp knife and a bit of know-how. Woodcarving is beyond the scope of this book; it is advised that you consult an expert before attempting it. Look for carved woodblocks in stores that specialize in ethnic products. Some rubber stamp stores also carry them and, if you're lucky, you may find discarded woodblocks at flea markets and yard sales. The best stamping surface for woodblocks is tightly woven fabric. Cotton, rayon, muslin, and some silks are all good candidates. Prewashing the fabric is optional. Paper and cardstock also may be stamped with woodblocks, but because so much pressure is required to transfer the colorant to the paper, the process might damage it.

woodblocks

1 Stretch a piece of fabric on a worktable.
2 Apply paint to the woodblock with a sponge. Try mixing two or three colors together for a marbled effect.
3 Firmly press the woodblock into the fabric surface. It may be necessary to tap the woodblock with a hammer to transfer the image to the fabric.
4 Lift the woodblock; repeat stamping until the fabric is finished. Add a wash of diluted paint if desired.
5 Allow the painted fabric to dry completely. Heat-set it with an iron on the highest setting.

MATERIALS
- Fabric or other stamping surface
- Sponge
- Acrylics or fabric paint
- Woodblock
- Hammer
- Iron

tips
- *Experiment with various types of colorant, but acrylics and fabric paints are both highly recommended.*
- *Padding the table with newsprint prior to stamping may result in sharper prints.*
- *To make some areas of the woodblock designs stand out, outline them with dimensional fabric paint after heat-setting the fabric. Wait at least 24 hours before laundering.*

ALTERED SURFACE TREATMENTS

Before most stamp artists set rubber to paper, they consider the printing surface. A marvelous selection of commercially made paper is available today. Nonetheless, many artists prefer to make their own background papers to complement their work.

Janet Hofacker prepares her nature journals with a random sponging of inks, thin acrylic washes, and metallic paints, while Lynne Grant Mohr takes meticulous care applying layers of pigment ink to glossy cardstock. Marbled backgrounds are Lea Everse's specialty. She likes nothing more than a surprise to reward her efforts, often allowing the media its own way—with stunning results.

Hélène Métivier makes patterned papers by applying pigment ink pads directly to cardstock. In her easy, elegant way of transforming ordinary paper into something special, she then stamps images in a random fashion. Nathalie Métivier uses a similar but more complicated technique, employing a series of masks and stencils to create intricate layers of color.

Nature Stamping

Janet Hofacker's nature journal allows her to experiment with background surface treatment and new color combinations, while also providing a safe place to experiment with mixed media. On each journal page, she blends stamped images with collaged elements such as cutouts from catalogs or bits of tree bark, leaves, and flowers gathered on nature walks. In addition to using manufactured stamps, she also makes imprints of leaves and feathers. Yes, it's possible to stamp using materials found in nature. Leaves, bark, lichen, rocks, seashells—virtually anything with texture can be inked, printed, and preserved on paper.

ARTIST: **Janet Hofacker**

Materials

Stamps

Blank, unlined journal

Feathers, bark, and/or dried vegetation

Ink pads in assorted colors

Acrylic glazes (or acrylic paints)
in assorted colors and metallics

Colored pencils and pastels

Sea sponge

Dry adhesive

Getting Started

Nature journals require artists to exchange the quiet confines of the studio for a walk outdoors. When possible, seek out new vistas—perhaps a mountainside trail frequented by bird watchers or a stream bed in a park you've never visited before. As you walk, make note of the surrounding colors, textures, and scents. Pick up leaves, feathers, and other natural elements with which to stamp. However, take some precautions: Avoid poisonous vegetation and plants on your local conservation list.

1 Prepare a blank, unlined journal by sponging or painting each page using thinned-down acrylic glazes or paints. Glazes are preferable since they do not need to be thinned down too much and are less likely to buckle the paper. To add interest, layer the background colors, allowing each application to dry before further additions.

2 To print with natural elements such as feathers or leaves, clean them, if necessary, with a lightly dampened sponge and allow them to dry completely. Apply a little color to one side of the specimen by pressing it onto an ink pad or sponging it lightly with acrylic paint. Press the specimen gently but firmly onto the journal page, taking care not to move it. Carefully lift the specimen and let the stamped image dry. Lightly accent the page with metallic gold wash.

Journal Tips

- For a unified look, use the same color scheme and background paint on the facing pages of each spread of your journal.

- The same leaf often can be reused if handled gently. Immediately remove the paint or ink with a damp sponge, and pat the leaf between paper towels to dry.

- Lightly coat the finished pages with protective acrylic spray, allowing each spread to dry thoroughly before spraying the next.

3 Continue adding interest to the page. Apply another metallic wash, such as copper. Adhere collage elements—a feather, as shown here, or bits of torn paper, pressed flowers or leaves, or thin layers of tree bark.

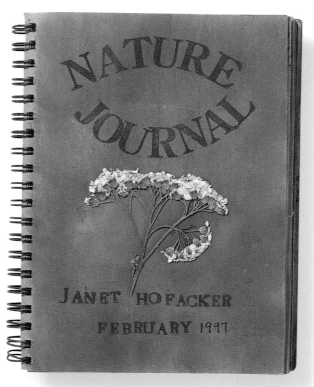

Variation

Hand write or use alphabet stamps to print brief inspirational quotes, poetic phrases, or field notes describing the origin of a specimen. Introduce fauna into your composition with manufactured stamps of bird and insect images. Create soft backgrounds with pastels or colored pencils.

Faux Finishes

Lynne Grant Mohr's delicate manipulation of pigment inks on glossy cardstock easily achieves the luxurious appearance of marble and stone. The resulting sensuous, textured background is perfect for stamping. Mohr's approach is careful and deliberate; her method will appeal most to those artists who prefer a controlled application of color and design. Use pigment inks for this project—dye inks will not work with the technique. Generally, dye inks permeate the surface of most papers and cardstock, while pigment inks lay on the surface and must be heat set or sealed with an acrylic spray.

ARTIST: **Lynne Grant Mohr**

Materials

Stamps: leaf, texture

White glossy cardstock

Pigment ink pads in beige, deep pink,

ocher, brown, terra cotta, light green

Soft rubber brayer

Sea sponge

Acrylic protective spray

Getting Started

Assemble the materials and prepare your work area by laying down some newsprint, as pigment inks are messy and may stain some surfaces. You will need several pieces of glossy cardstock to practice with. Remember that if you make a mistake at any time during the process, you can start over by re-wetting and rubbing off the pigment ink.

1   Starting with the lightest color, roll the brayer over the beige ink pad several times to thoroughly coat it with pigment ink. Bray the cardstock with short strokes in a random pattern. Then roll the brayer over the deep-pink ink pad, and bray the cardstock again in the same manner. Continue as above with the ocher ink, massaging and blending the colors together with firm, short strokes.

2 To create darker values, use a soft sea sponge to dab on more deep-pink and ocher ink. Sponge on brown ink in a few select areas. Then roll the brayer over the cardstock again, this time with a little less pressure, being careful not to smooth out too much sponged-on texture. To add interest to the composition, use an accent color such as terra cotta. Dab it on lightly, and feather it a bit with the sea sponge.

3 To add veins, use the edge of torn cardstock. Lightly scrape the edge back and forth through the layers of ink until you reveal a light streak. Feather the edges with a sponge. Allow the ink to set for about 30 minutes before proceeding. For added interest, stamp the entire surface with a texture stamp and brown ink.

Ink Tips

- Try adding a little color to the leaf veins by moistening the scrap paper with dark ink such as dusky brown.

- Coated glossy cardstock will not absorb pigment ink, so you can continue to manipulate the surface until it is sealed with acrylic spray. Be careful not to smudge foreground images before sealing the artwork. If a design is less than successful, feel free to remove all of the color and return to the original glossy paper surface; simply re-moisten the color with additional pigment ink and firmly rub it off.

4 To add foreground images, create a mortise mask the same size as the image area by tearing a piece of paper to form a hole or frame. Lay the mask on the finished cardstock, and buff off some of the ink within the framed area. For an antique look, rub very lightly to remove just the top layers of ink. Try sponging on a bit of light-green ink through the mask.

5 Now stamp the foreground decorative images using a dark, contrasting color. If you have a stamp positioner, use it to stamp over the light-green ink design. To protect and seal the artwork, spray it with several light coats of acrylic protective spray. Allow it to dry, and adhere the artwork to a folded card or frame it for display.

Variation

Using the same faux background and leaf colors, vary the design with a different leaf stamp—in this case, bamboo leaves. Stamp over the light-green leaf image with gold ink instead of red to add depth and shimmer to the leaves. For a middle-ground image to add interest to the faux background, stamp terra-cotta Chinese calligraphy characters in loose columns.

Marbled Surfaces

Luscious, marbled background papers are easy to make with just a few materials. While the process may appear to be difficult and time-consuming, Lea Everse's marbled background technique is actually quite simple. Beautiful, saturated colors of wet ink flow gracefully together on black glossy cardstock when the artist tilts the surface. Voila! Marbled backgrounds, which can be used to create attractive greeting cards such as the one shown here.

ARTIST: **Lea Everse**

Materials

Stamps: background, bird

Glossy cardstock

Card base

Metallic pigment ink markers in gold, pink, blue, purple

Black pigment ink

Black embossing powder

Gold thread

Two-sided tape (or other dry adhesive)

Foam tape

Spray mister

Distilled water

Sea sponge (or crumpled plastic wrap)

Embossing tool

Scissors (straight or decorative edge)

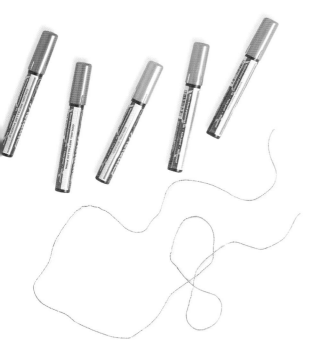

Getting Started

Only a few materials are needed for this project, but metallic pigment ink markers are absolutely essential. Black glossy cardstock will render the most dramatic effects, but white cardstock is another option. Stamp artists are very particular about the cardstock they use, but if a specific color or finish is unavailable, it's easy enough to spray ordinary cards with glossy paint.

1 Trim the cardstock to 4.25" x 5.5" (10.5 cm x 14 cm). Using a spray mister, lightly spritz the surface with distilled water until lightly dampened. Color the middle of the card with gold metallic pigment ink. Quickly, before the water evaporates, cover the surface completely with additional colors of metallic pigment ink.

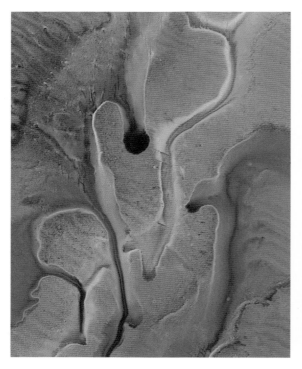

2 Tilt the card, which causes the wet metallic inks to flow and gives the piece its distinctive marbled look. Once the entire surface is colored, spritz again with water and touch lightly with a sea sponge.

3 When the card is completely dry, stamp and emboss the marbled surface using a background stamp, black ink, and black embossing powder. Heat with an embossing tool.

Marbling Tips

- When covering the dampened card surface with metallic pigment ink, try braying the ink together or creating patterns by dragging a feather, small paintbrush, or cat's whisker through the wet ink.

- Use an embossing tool or hair dryer to hasten drying of the marbled background before stamping.

- If an attempt at marbled paper is less than satisfactory, cut the cardstock into strips to be used later for paper weaving or assembling a unique modern-art design.

4 Use two-sided tape to mount the marbled background card onto coordinating layers of black and gold cardstock, graduated in size and cut with straight or decorative-edge scissors. For the card's central imagery, prepare decorative cutouts such as the birds shown here, which were stamped and embossed on prepared marbled paper.

5 Mount the central images to the background paper with foam tape and embellish with gold thread. Adhere the design to a card base with two-sided tape.

Variation

To reveal more of the marbled background, use a single figurative stamp, such as this woman with a fish, instead of an overall pattern.

Patterned Backgrounds

Making beautiful papers for stamping backgrounds is much easier than it looks. With pigment inks, stamp artists can transform ordinary cardstock or paper into beautifully patterned, undulating surfaces.

Canadian artist Hélène Métivier begins with ordinary beige cardstock and, with a few strokes of pigment ink pads, creates papers perfect for stamping. In this project, a range of stamps decorate richly colored squares of paper which are arranged to make an intriguing cover for a scrapbook.

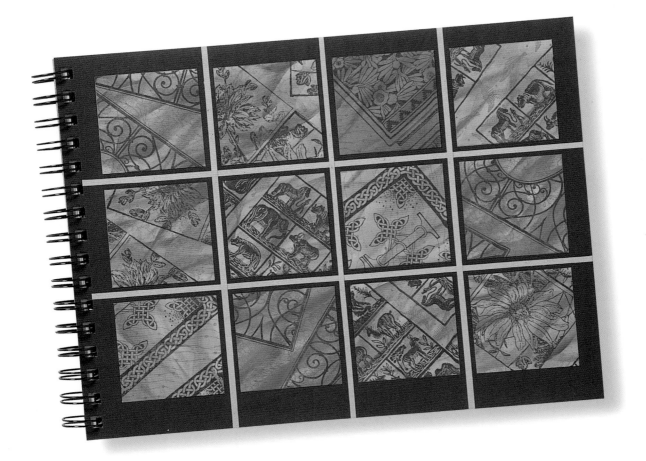

ARTIST: **Hélène Métivier**

Getting Started

For this project, use pigment inks—which lie on the paper's surface and dry very slowly—to achieve the subtle look of brushed-on pastels. Dye ink pads also may work, but they make the desired effect more difficult to attain. When choosing inks for each surface, consider analogous color combinations such as yellow, green, and yellow-green, or red, violet, and orange.

Materials

Assorted stamps

Light-color cardstock (or paper)

Pigment ink pads in black, gold, assorted colors

Scrapbook
(approximately 10.75" x 8.25"
[27.5 cm x 21 cm])

Two-sided tape (or other dry adhesive)

Scissors (or craft knife and cutting mat)

Ruler

Acrylic protective spray

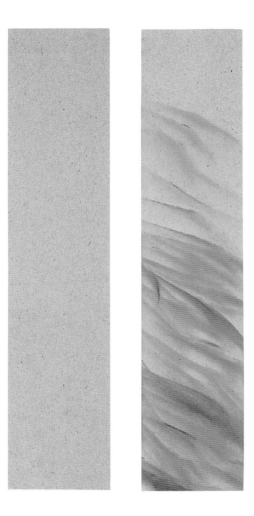

1 Measure and cut the cardstock into three 2" (5 cm) strips at least 8" (20 cm) long. Gently brush each strip with pigment ink pads, choosing analogous colors and applying each pad directly to the surface using soft, S-shaped strokes. Spread on the lightest hues first.

2 Continue layering pigment ink in a swirling pattern, ending with the darkest colors. Allow the ink to dry.

Pigment Application Tips

- For each background, restrict the number of pigment inks to two or three to avoid muddied colors.

- As an alternative approach, apply pigment ink to a sponge, and sponge the paper with soft, gentle strokes.

3 Use various stamps to cover the strips with random patterns. Stamp with ink that contrasts well with the background—black and gold pigment ink are good choices. Finish the surface with acrylic protective spray.

4 Cut the strips into 2" (5 cm) squares, and arrange them in a pretty pattern on the scrapbook's front cover, leaving .25" (.5 cm) between the squares. Adhere them with two-sided tape. Add interest by applying a grid of narrow strips of contrasting paper between the squares.

Masking, Layering, and Stenciling

This project calls for the basic skills necessary to every stamp artist desiring to increase the complexity of his or her work. Stamping, of course, comes first. But masking and stenciling skills are no less important. Finally, layering images is key to creating a multidimensional pattern. The following piece's appealing design incorporates all of these techniques. Canadian artist Nathalie Métivier limits her color palette to emphasize the butterfly stamp, which she also designed.

ARTIST: Nathalie Métivier

Getting Started

This is a complex project requiring several intricate steps, so gather all the needed materials and have plenty of repositionable glue and correction tape on hand before you begin. Read the instructions through at least once before commencing the project to avoid confusion. Foreground images will be stamped in warm colors, contrasting with cool-color backgrounds that appear to recede.

Materials

Stamps: butterfly, leaf, flower

Tan cardstock

Paper

Pigment ink pads in greens, oranges, assorted light colors

Permanent black ink

Two-sided tape (or other dry adhesive)

Repositionable glue stick

Correction tape

Scissors (or craft knife and cutting mat)

Acrylic protective spray

1 Trim tan cardstock to 8.5" (22 cm) square and use permanent black ink to stamp a butterfly three times along the center vertical axis. On a piece of thin paper, prepare paper masks by stamping the same butterfly three times and cutting out the images. Apply a thin layer of repositionable glue to the back of the masks, and place them as shown over the stamped butterflies. Begin coloring in the background by gently rubbing pigment ink pads directly on the cardstock.

2 Using correction tape, mask off the edges of the cardstock. Cut a rectangular piece of paper to mask the center, and adhere as shown. Use permanent black ink to stamp four leaves onto the cardstock, and then make eight paper leaf masks. Adhere masks onto the stamped leaves, and artistically position and adhere the other four masks to create silhouettes.

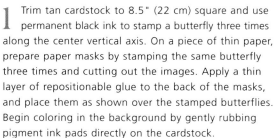

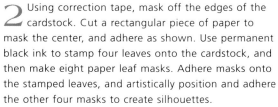

3 Apply pigment ink to both sides of the design, rubbing it in liberally and using various shades of green or similar colors. The masks will protect the foreground images and borders from ink.

4 Remove the rectangular mask from the center, cut it in half lengthwise, and adhere the pieces to the design as shown. Apply pigment ink pads to the center of the design, including orange and green. The butterfly masks will protect the stamped images beneath them.

5 Remove the two narrow rectangular masks and the masks of the silhouette leaves. Rub on a bit of orange or red ink for contrast. Remove the outermost row of correction tape and stamp a series of small leaves to create a narrow border.

6 Remove all remaining masks and tape, and stamp a little flower in each corner of the masked-off frame. Now create stencils by stamping three butterflies on paper and carefully cutting them out. Discard the stamped centers and separate the stencils.

Masking and Stenciling Tips

- Accurate paper masks and stencils are critical, so be sure your scissors or craft knife blades are extra sharp.

- Begin your own designs by deciding which stamps will ultimately predominate. Stamp and mask these images first, and cause them to advance by filling them in with colors that are in contrast with and darker than the background.

- Masking and stenciling techniques also work well for airbrushing. Instead of applying pigment ink to cardstock, lightly airbrush paint over the masks and through the stencils.

7 Apply glue to the stencils and lay each one over a stamped butterfly on the cardstock. Gently apply contrasting pigment inks to the stamped butterflies through the stencils. Remove the stencils and finish by randomly stamping a few small images in very light ink (pink, light blue, gold) onto the overall design. Coat lightly with acrylic protective spray, and mount the finished artwork on graduated layers of cardstock.

Variation

By using lighter colors to advance the foreground image, a single flower, surrounded by darker leaves, appears to pop out of this masked and layered composition.

GALLERY OF
Altered Surface Treatments

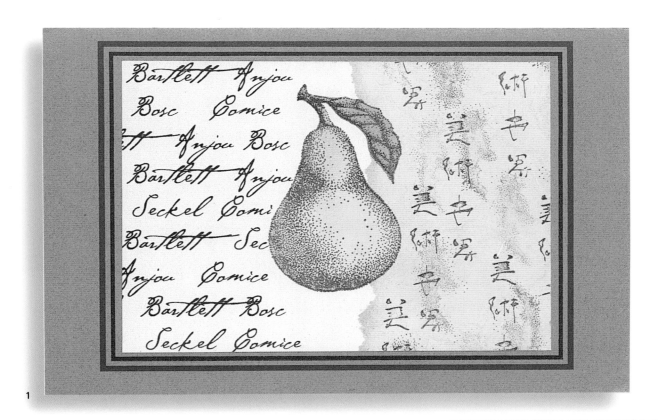

LYNNE GRANT MOHR

1 *Pear*
   Chinese calligraphy, rubber stamped

2 *Collage*
   text, postage stamp, metallic ink

3 *Feather*
   cardstock, script, stamp images

4 *Snapshots*
   sponge, computer-generated border

3

4

1 **JANET HOFACKER**
painted, stamped wooden
box with found items

2 **NATHALIE MÉTIVIER**
stamping, masking, layering,
and stenciling on cardstock

3 **MARYSE CARRIER**
collage of strips of
stamped cardstock

4 **JANET HOFACKER**
wood, metallic paint

1

2

3

Dream
no small dreams.

4

1 **LEA EVERSE**
cardstock, beads

2 **MARYSE CARRIER**
collage of strips of stamped cardstock

3 **LYNNE GRANT MOHR**
rubber stamps, pigment ink,
glossy cardstock

4 **LEA EVERSE**
stamped, embossed image on
marbled cardstock

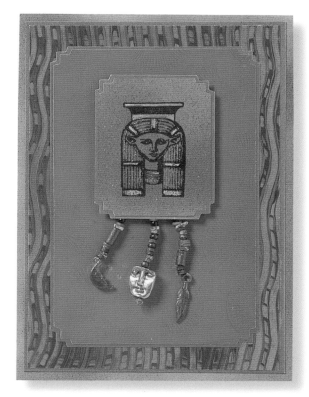

1

2

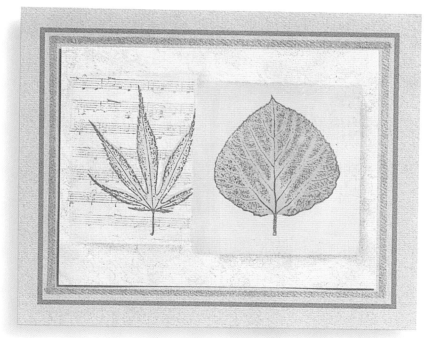

3

4

ARTISTIC STAMPING

Stamping artistically means using rubber stamps in unusual ways, combining stamp images with handmade papers, or creating artist books, faux postage, and mail art. The traditional use of stamps to make simple greeting cards is fine, but many more options are available to artists who use stamps in their artwork.

Lea Everse's reverse-stamping technique cleverly mimics the look of monoprinting with far less time and effort. If miniature artwork is your passion, consider making faux postage (also known as arti-stamps) with help from Moya Scaddan. Diane Lewis's technique of deep thermal embossing is popular with stamp artists everywhere; no wonder, when it's so easy and the results are so gorgeous.

Custom-designed, hand-carved art stamps also fall into the realm of artistic stamping. I learned to make rubber stamps from master carver Julie Bloch of Hurleyville, New York. Using ordinary erasers and linoleum cutters, you, too, can make your own custom stamps.

Finally, Linda Yang-Wright stamps on acetate and applies opaque markers and cel-vinyl paint (traditionally used by cartoon artists) to transform the images into striking three-dimensional works of art.

Reverse Stamping

Reverse stamping is very similar to monoprinting, an age-old technique requiring the artist to ink a smooth glass surface, remove portions of the ink from the glass, and transfer the inked design to paper. Monoprinting is beautiful, but the procedure is messy and can be difficult to master.

ARTIST: **Lea Everse**

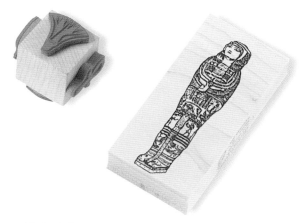

Materials

Stamps: lotus and Egyptian woman

Glossy cardstock

Matte cardstock

Card base

Liquid pigment inks in blue and black

Clear embossing powder

Decorative thread

Two-sided tape
(or other dry adhesive)

Foam tape

Brayer

Embossing tool

Scissors (or craft knife
and cutting mat)

Ruler

Getting Started

Begin this project by assembling the necessary materials in a protected work area with easy access to soap and water for quick cleanup. Be prepared to wash the brayer before the ink dries on the roller after inking the cardstock surface. In addition, stamps must be cleaned thoroughly after each impression in the wet ink. Since reverse stamping uses liquid pigment ink, beware of staining clothing or other items.

1 Squeeze blue liquid pigment ink directly onto a piece of black glossy cardstock. A little ink goes a long way, so start with a very small amount, adding more as needed. Use a large brayer to smooth out a thin, even layer of ink to cover the card surface.

2 Press the clean (un-inked) lotus stamp firmly onto the inked surface. Twist the stamp slightly (about 1/16" [1.5 mm]) to cut through the ink down to the card-stock. Lift the stamp and clean it. Continue stamping the inked surface, cleaning the stamp after each impression. Sprinkle the surface with clear embossing powder, tap off the excess, and heat set with an embossing tool.

3 When the blue lotus-stamped card is dry, trim it to a 4.5" (11 cm) square. Cut three additional layers of cardstock for the finished greeting card: a 3.5" (9 cm) rust-colored square, and a 3.75" (9.5 cm) square and 4.75" (12 cm) square of black glossy cardstock.

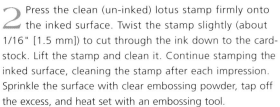

Reverse-Stamping Tips

- When choosing commercially made stamps for this technique, select images with few details or fine lines. Reverse stamping works particularly well with hand-carved stamps, since they typically have straightforward designs.

- As an alternative to non-absorbent, glossy cardstock, try reverse stamping on handmade paper, stationery, watercolor paper, or professional-grade printmaking paper. Also experiment with numerous color combinations. For instance, try spreading red pigment ink on gold cardstock.

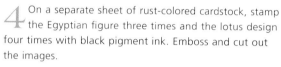

4 On a separate sheet of rust-colored cardstock, stamp the Egyptian figure three times and the lotus design four times with black pigment ink. Emboss and cut out the images.

5 Assemble the layers of square cardstock according to size, beginning with the largest piece and ending with the rust-colored square on top. Adhere the layers together with two-sided tape and embellish the top square with a border of decorative thread. Use foam tape to mount the cut-out images. Adhere the design to a card base with two-sided tape.

Variation

Make another background layer for the card using the same technique with slight variation. Here, a wavy background design is reverse stamped on cardstock on which two colors of pigment ink—blue and rust—are blended together.

Faux Postage

Anyone who has ever admired the diminutive art of postage stamps will understand the prevailing popularity of faux postage, that is, stamped designs on perforated paper mimicking the size and shape of government-issued postage stamps. Also known as artistamps, faux postage obviously cannot be used in lieu of paid postage. Artistamps are a recognized art form, most often applied to envelopes as a decorative element or purchased in numbered sheets by avid collectors. Moya Scaddan of Sorrento, Western Australia, uses beautiful stamps made especially for creating faux postage. Another option is to use any stamped design that fits within the parameters of a typical postage stamp.

ARTIST: **Moya Scaddan**

Materials

Stamp: Cave of the Bulls faux postage

Cardstock

Paper

Ink pads (dye or pigment ink) in black, brown

Pencil, pastels, and watercolor markers

Two-sided tape (or other dry adhesive)

Perforating (tracing) wheel

Sea sponge

Scissors (or craft knife and cutting mat)

Ruler

Getting Started

Creating a sheet of artistamps requires lightly sketching a regularly spaced grid, so select an accurate ruler and a sharp pencil or fine-line pen. Some artists prefer using a computer with a drawing program to lay out uniform sheets of stamps or to design faux postage from scratch.

Simulating the look of commercially produced stamps, artistamp projects involve perforating the paper. Inexpensive perforating or tracing wheels with serrated edges are available in most fabric stores.

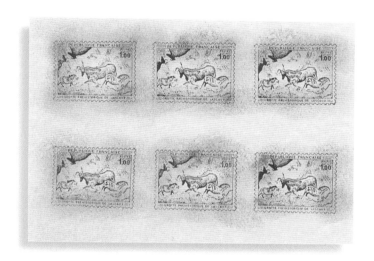

1 Stamp the faux-post image six times onto buff-colored paper. Sponge around the edges of the stamped images with a sea sponge and some dye ink, or rub pastels in natural earth tones onto the paper.

2 Cut out the stamped images, trimming away the stamped-on perforation border. Set aside.

3 Cut a second sheet of buff-colored paper to approximately 6" x 8.5" (15 cm x 22 cm), unevenly tear the edges, and sponge on brown ink for an aged appearance. In the center, lightly pencil in a grid with six 1.75" x 2 1/8" (4.5 cm x 5.3 cm) rectangles. Use a watercolor marker to color the center of the rubber faux postage stamp, and lightly stamp outside of the six rectangles.

Production Tips

- Perforating can be done not only with a rolling perforation wheel, but also with a professional stamp perforating machine. Another option is to perforate the paper using a sewing machine with a thick, unthreaded needle.

- Artistamps are meant to be shared with others, so keep the original sheet and have copies made to send to mail-art friends.

4 Using a perforating wheel, roll along the penciled-in grid lines all the way to the paper's edges. Use two-sided tape to adhere a cut-out stamp within each of the six rectangles in the grid. Mount the finished sheet of artistamps on cardstock backing.

Variation

Play with a variety of stamps and colors. Here, an ample border is randomly stamped with images related to the faux stamps' theme. As an alternative to making a sheet of identical artistamps, create a sheet in which the artistamps are each unique but share a similar theme and color scheme.

Deep Thermal Embossing

Few stamping techniques have more dramatic results than deep thermal embossing, also known as multi-layered embossing. The procedure is similar to encaustic
stamping, but embossing ink and powders are substituted for wax. Diane Lewis
has mastered the method of melting multiple layers of embossing powders to create a thick, glossy surface for stamping. A three-dimensional impression is made by
pressing an inked stamp deep into the smooth, heated surface—thus the name of the
technique. Artists and jewelry designers enhance and embellish the melted powder
by dropping in colored embossing powders, iridescent pigments, small beads, or
miniature seashells.

ARTIST: **Diane Lewis**

Getting Started

This technique requires special thick embossing powders designed specifically for deep thermal embossing. All consist of large, plastic crystals that melt into puddles when heated. Protect your art room by placing a large box lid upside-down on a flat surface. While embossing, place the cardboard square inside the lid, since crystals inevitably scatter when you begin heating the first layer of powder.

Materials

Assorted stamps

Cardboard

Cardstock

Decorative papers

Pigment or embossing ink pads
in black, terra cotta, paprika, copper

Interference pigments

Embossing powders (regular and thick)

Embossing tool

Two-sided tape (or other dry adhesive)

Wet adhesive

Embellishments: thread, beads, wax seal

1 Prepare a deeply etched, bold-lined stamp by saturating the rubber image with black pigment ink (dye ink will not work). Set aside. Cut out a 2.5" (6 cm) square of cardboard. Rub pigment ink pads directly onto the cardboard, using two or three similar colors such as terra cotta, paprika, and copper.

2 While the ink is still wet, dip the cardboard into thick embossing powder. Gently shake off the excess, and heat the surface with an embossing tool until the powder is completely melted. While the previous layer is still very hot, apply additional layers in the same manner until the surface is thick, glossy, and smooth. Three to four layers should be sufficient; however, some artists apply as many as 18. While heating the top layers, sprinkle a small amount of interference pigments in the wet powder.

Embossing Tips

- Thick embossing powder is now available in clear, bronze, gold, interference blue, black, and platinum. Apply a few layers of clear powder before adding colored embossing powders.

- To give the finished stamped image drama, use black, gold, or silver pigment ink on the stamp's surface.

- Sometimes the melted powder will crack after cooling and hardening, which makes an interesting effect that can be enhanced by rubbing dark pigment inks into the cracks. If you prefer a more perfect surface, reheat the cracks with an embossing tool to make them disappear.

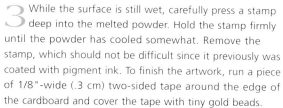

3 While the surface is still wet, carefully press a stamp deep into the melted powder. Hold the stamp firmly until the powder has cooled somewhat. Remove the stamp, which should not be difficult since it previously was coated with pigment ink. To finish the artwork, run a piece of 1/8"-wide (.3 cm) two-sided tape around the edge of the cardboard and cover the tape with tiny gold beads.

4 Prepare collage materials for the base of the composition. Cut out four layers of cardstock in analogous colors to complement the central image. Tear and cut pieces of decorative paper, and stamp or rub them with chalks or interference pigments. Emboss some of the pieces' torn edges using wet adhesive and embossing powders. Assemble the composition, layering the cardstock base and adhering pieces of decorative paper and the embossed cardboard. Embellish your artwork with beaded threads sealed with stamped wax.

Stamp Carving

Carving your own art stamps is a fun way to add images to your collection. Fashioning stamps from rubber erasers is similar to wood-block cutting, but it's much faster. The basic skills can be learned in just a few minutes. Once you have carved a few simple designs, you may want to expand your skills by carving large-scale images from soft printmaking blocks. For inspiration, turn to the Gallery of Artistic Stamping to see the remarkable, large-scale work created by award-winning artist Anne Bagby.

ARTIST: **Sharilyn Miller**

Materials

Rubber eraser, 1.5" x 3" (4 cm x 8 cm)

Source imagery

Paper

Nail-polish remover

Cotton balls

Linoleum-cutting tool

Stamping ink

Access to a photocopier

Getting Started

Purchase rubber erasers with the consistency of firm cheese, such as the high-quality, white erasers found in art-supply stores. For source material, trace the leaf shown here for your first project. In the future, select carving imagery from the copyright-free, black-and-white illustrations in clip-art books, typically available in bookstores and libraries. Or draw your own images by hand, starting with basic geometric shapes such as circles, squares, and stars.

1 Use a carbon-based photocopier to enlarge or reduce the image to a size that fits within the rubber eraser's parameters. Cut out the photocopied image, and place it face-down onto the back of the eraser.

2 Use nail-polish remover, which interacts with the carbon on the photocopy, to transfer the image to the eraser. Soak a cotton ball with remover, and rub the wet ball for a few seconds over the back of the photocopy. Rub in only one direction to avoid distorting the image. Lift a corner of the photocopy to see if the image has transferred to the eraser. If not, replace the corner and continue rubbing the photocopy with the polish-soaked cotton ball. Once the image has transferred, remove and discard the photocopy.

3 Carve out the white areas of the eraser with a linoleum-cutting tool with interchangeable blades. Starting with the finest blade, carefully trim around the image and carve out tiny detail lines and dots. Use wider blades to carve away larger portions of the eraser, taking care not to weaken the stamp by undercutting the image. When carving curved lines, it's easier to turn the eraser than the linoleum-cutter blade.

Carving Tips

- Most erasers are 3/8" to .5" (approximately 1 cm) thick, so they can be carved on the front and back. Some artists also carve tiny border images on the sides of erasers.

- Those with drawing skills may use a ball-point pen or permanent-ink laundry pen to draw an image directly onto the eraser, without going to the trouble of transferring a photocopied image. When drawing letters on the eraser, be sure to write them backwards.

- Once eraser carving has been mastered, try carving larger images from battleship linoleum or soft printmaking blocks available at art-supply stores. Many soft, durable materials can be carved and made into stamps: bottle corks, pencil erasers, soft wood.

4 Test the carved image by inking it well and stamping it on scrap paper. Some artists prefer a rough-cut look, reveling in the stray lines and jagged areas of the image. Others prefer clean lines for perfect repeat stamping. Continue carving away unwanted areas until the image is satisfactory.

5 Create a finished piece using the stamp's simple, graphic image in an artful design. This greeting card is fashioned from handmade paper with flower petals embedded in the pulp. The hand-carved leaf image is stamped in gold and embossed along the card's right edge, as well as stamped onto a separate piece of paper in magenta and turquoise, embossed with clear powder, cut out, and adhered to the cover.

Variation

Experiment making a range of hand-carved stamps, from fruit to decorative imagery. When creating letters or words, write them out normally, enlarge or reduce to an appropriate size, and lay the photocopy face-down on the eraser as described above. The letters will transfer backwards to the eraser, which will print a correct image once the letters are carved.

Stamping on Acetate

Ingenuity and craftsmanship are the keys to using finely detailed art stamps to their best advantage. For this unique project, Linda Yang-Wright uses acetate—an inexpensive art material—to transform her stamping into a fine art worthy of framing. Her method mimics that used by Hollywood artists who meticulously painted each cel of a cartoon in the days before computer-aided animation.

ARTIST: **Linda Yang-Wright**

Materials

Floral stamp

Clear vinyl acetate

Cardstock

Permanent black ink pad

Cel-vinyl acrylic paints and brushes,
or opaque paint markers

Two-sided tape

Getting Started

Art-supply stores are the best sources of clear acetate, but it also can be obtained from photography studios or graphic designers as well as architectural firms, which often discard acetate scraps. Cel-vinyl paints are not as easy to come by, but opaque markers can be found through mail-order craft suppliers. Or substitute gouache paint, an opaque watercolor.

1 Using permanent black ink, stamp a floral image onto acetate. When the ink is dry, flip over the acetate and begin coloring the back of the stamped image with cel-vinyl paint or opaque markers. Start with the finest details, such as the flower stamens and leaf veins. Take your time, since these details will show clearly in the finished piece. Allow each color to dry before proceeding with the next.

2 Continue adding layers of color, focusing on highlights and shadows. The colors may overlap as long as the colors applied first have dried.

3 Color in the largest areas last. The first layers of paint or marker will mask any colors applied over them, so don't worry about overlapping. Occasionally turn over the acetate to check on your progress. Eventually all areas of the flowers and leaves should be colored.

Acetate Stamping Tips

- Rubber stamps with very fine lines work well on acetate. Take care to hold the stamp firmly when pressing down, since acetate can be slippery.

- Images stamped on clear acetate can be easily reversed, giving artists more design options. To reverse a stamped image, do not turn over the acetate before beginning the coloring process. When the image is completely colored and dry, flip over the acetate and the stamped image will appear to be reversed.

4 Once you are satisfied and the coloring is dry, flip over the acetate and lay the design face up on a piece of gold metallic cardstock cut slightly larger than the design's border. Mount with two-sided tape.

5 Continue assembling the piece by adhering the stamped, mounted image to layered squares of black, green, and gold cardstock. Adhere the piece onto a frame of clear acetate which is bordered by a larger frame of green cardstock edged with gold.

Variation

Background and border papers, colors, and textures have enormous influence on any finished piece's appearance, but particularly so when the stamped material is acetate. Experiment with black, white, patterned, and collaged papers. Pastels and metallics render a soft, elegant look, while brighter colors make a bolder statement.

GALLERY OF
Artistic Stamping

2

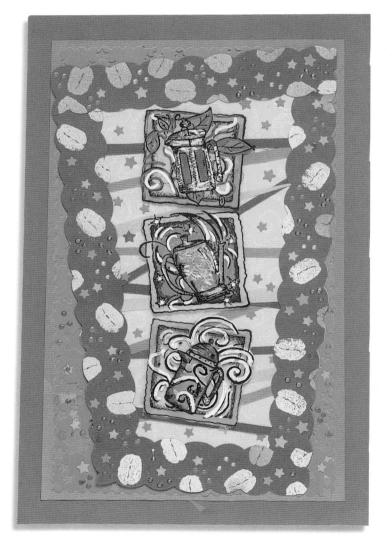

1

LINDA YANG-WRIGHT

1 *Bean Dream*
acetate, powder, fabric paint,
permanent ink

2 *Morning Glory*
acetate, permanent ink,
colored papers, fabric paint

3 *Hibiscus Frame*
acetate, opaque markers, cardstock

3

1

2

1 ANNE BAGBY
Spring Bulbs
acrylics and watercolors on canvas,
with hand-carved stamps used for
repeat imagery

2 ANNE BAGBY
Outward Bound
acrylics and watercolors on canvas,
hand-carved stamps

3 DIANE LEWIS
sponged, stamped cardstock with
deep thermal embossed centerpiece

3

1

1 JULIE VAN OOSTEN

faux postage and cancellation stamps, used
postage stamp, cardstock, mulberry paper

2 TRACY MOORE

series of faux postage stamps

3 MARTHA THURLOW

stamped velvet bags with string handles

2

3

MIXED MEDIA EFFECTS

Mixed media implies variety—and there is plenty to be had in this section. Stamp artists can make everything from handmade books to framed artwork using an eclectic assortment of materials.

Start with the eye-catching metallic effects of Lisa Renner's greeting cards, which incorporate unusual media such as wire and thin sheets of copper with cardstock stamped and treated with metallic embossing powders. If you love collage, Lynne Perrella's stamped notebook will spur your imagination. This designer takes art stamps to a new level by combining their beautiful imagery with decoupage, metallic paints, and found objects.

Two artists featured in this section combine stamping skills with their interest in making books by hand. Sherrill Kahn's easily constructed stamped booklets feature covers in which fabric paints, crimped paper, and beads are exquisite complements to art stamps of petroglyph figures. Julie van Oosten's miniature handmade books have hard covers and spines, and her technique of collage stamping renders a subtle background print perfect for bookbinding.

Finally, Zana Clark's passion for taking stamping beyond cards is evident in her large-format art. By combining stamp imagery with a torn-paper collage, you, too, can make framed artwork of your very own.

Metallic Accents

Marking a special occasion by stamping and coloring a personalized greeting is much more fun than buying a ready-made card, and the results will be treasured by the recipient. When the card incorporates shimmery metallic effects, the sense of value is heightened even further. Shiny copper and gold metallics against black cardstock are a striking combination in this project from stamp artist Lisa Renner. She combines unusual papers with her stamping and embossing techniques to make exquisite mixed-media collage cards worthy of framing.

ARTIST: **Lisa Renner**

Materials

Stamps: human figure, spiral, marble, papyrus

Cardstock

Lightweight cardboard

Card base

Thin copper sheet

Pigment inks in black, gold, bronze

Thick embossing powders in
black, metallic copper, metallic gold

Embossing tool

Embossing stylus

24-gauge copper wire

Beads and other embellishments

Two-sided tape

Getting Started

For this project, purchase a thin sheet of copper
and a piece of copper cardstock from your local
craft store. If copper-colored cardstock is not available, spray-paint ordinary paper or cardstock with
inexpensive automobile touch-up paint found at
hardware stores.

1 Cut out a 5" x 7.5" (13 cm x 19 cm) piece of copper cardstock and two pieces of black cardstock, one 6" x 8" (15 cm x 20 cm) and the other 2.5" x 5.5" (6 cm x 14 cm). Stamp the marble texture stamp on the copper cardstock and the papyrus stamp on the smaller black cardstock, and emboss using metallic copper embossing powder. On the large piece of black cardstock, stamp the spiral and marble texture stamps and emboss with metallic gold embossing powder.

2 Stamp the woman's figure in black ink in the center of the thin sheet of copper. Emboss with black powder, and heat set with an embossing tool until the ink puffs up. Once the copper sheet has cooled, indent it with a metal stylus, forming an outline around the stamped figure and small points on the surrounding copper surface.

Embellishing Tips

• In addition to incorporating metal beads and wire into your composition, consider including orphan earrings, broken bits of jewelry, watch parts, and computer circuit boards.

• Experiment with the number of metallic embellishments and their arrangement. Sometimes, less is more.

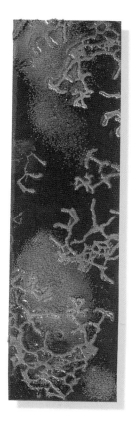

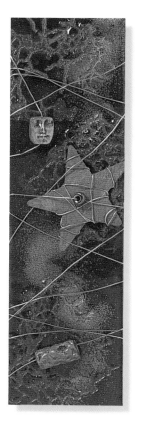

3 Prepare the narrow rectangle for the card's left side by cutting a 2" x 7" (5 cm x 18 cm) piece of lightweight cardboard. Follow the procedure described in the Deep Thermal Embossing chapter, applying thick embossing powders that are heated and re-heated until a hard layer of melted powder covers the surface. While the thick powder is still hot, press a pre-inked marble stamp into it to create a deep impression.

4 Allow the deep-embossed rectangle to cool. Meanwhile, string 24-gauge copper wire with a few beads. Wrap the copper wire around the rectangle, incorporating a metal star or other embellishments into the design. Assemble the composition and mount on a card base using two-sided tape.

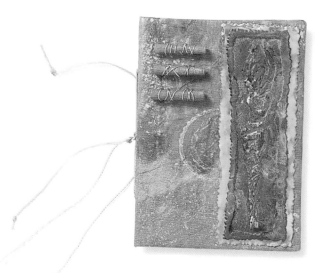

Variation

Try stamping the figure in a thin layer of clay instead of metal. Attach to a strip of copper and thin heavy cardstock layered with colored and embossed paper. To balance the composition, wrap rolls of colored paper with delicate copper wire.

Collage and Decoupage

As you gain confidence with rubber, ink, and paper, add collage elements to your artwork and use the collaged paper to make one-of-a-kind decoupaged items such as the journal featured in this chapter. Lynne Perrella first makes a collage of overlapping art-stamp images, adding torn strips of handmade paper to enhance the design. After reproducing her collage using a color photocopier, she adheres the copies to the cover of a composition book to make a delightful journal.

ARTIST: **Lynne Perrella**

Materials

Assorted stamps

Student's composition book, 7.5" x 9.75"
(19 cm x 24.5 cm)

Plain and handmade paper

Marbled or other decorative paper

Corrugated paper

Ink pads in black and assorted colors

Metallic acrylics

Metallic spray paint

Pastels

24" (61 cm) of 5/8" (1.5 cm) ribbon, for ties

12" (30 cm) of .25" (.5 cm) ribbon, for bookmark

Charm embellishments

Leather or suede scraps

Dry adhesive (two-sided tape or a glue stick)

Contact cement

Sponge

Craft knife and cutting mat

Getting Started

Since the collage you make in this project will be photocopied, the quality of paper you use is not important. Try stamping on plain, white bond paper or flattened, brown paper bags. At the copy shop, consider having the collage reproduced on acid-free paper. The cost will be a bit higher, but acid-free paper is the preferred archival material for long-lasting artwork.

1 Use art stamps, pastels, metallic acrylics, spray paints, and colorful inks to create a visual collage on paper slightly larger than the cover of a student's composition book. For added interest, layer irregular shapes of torn handmade paper between the stamped images. Take the finished design to your local copy shop and have two color photocopies made for the journal's front and back covers.

2 Use dry adhesive to adhere the color copies to the composition book's outside front and back covers. Use a sharp craft knife to precisely trim the edges. Cut a piece of corrugated paper to about .75" x 9.75" (2 cm x 24.5 cm), spritz it with metallic spray paint, and glue it to the front cover about .25" (.5 cm) from the spine. Cut the 5/8"-wide (1.5 cm) ribbon into two 12" (30 cm) strips for ties. Center a ribbon on the outside edge of both the front and back covers, and glue down an inch of each one.

3 Create a bookmark by gluing an inch of the .25"-wide (.5 cm) ribbon to the top of the inside back cover, placing the ribbon parallel to and roughly an inch from the spine. Cut two pieces of marbled paper to fit the inside front and back covers and adhere with dry adhesive.

Collage Tips

- If a collage composition seems bland, use pastel crayons to add colorful flourishes of free-hand squiggles.

- When reproducing the collage for your journal, make extra copies to have on hand for future projects such as decorative envelopes, wrapping paper, gift bags—whatever your imagination conjures up.

4 Tear a piece of handmade paper into an attractive shape, stamp randomly, and adhere it with dry adhesive to the center of the front cover. Affix a centerpiece to complement the overall design: a charm, piece of discarded jewelry, antique key, or, as shown here, a collage sandwiched between soldered pieces of glass.

5 To create four corner covers and two anchors for the ribbon ties, use a very sharp craft knife to cut thin scraps of leather or suede into the desired shape and size. Try stamping your leather scraps first with permanent ink. Affix the corners and anchors to the front and back covers with contact cement. Finish your journal by sponging metallic acrylics along the front cover's edges.

Variation

This collage adhered to a large envelope offers a glimpse into the art form's many opportunities for creativity. Add texture by combining stamped images with natural elements such as feathers and dried leaves, or personalize your collage by incorporating copies of family photographs, letters, and other mementos.

Stamped Booklets

At first glance, Sherrill Kahn's stamped booklets may seem complicated and time-consuming to make. But nothing could be further from the truth. Taken in steps, this project can be completed in less than an hour, making it perfect for children and beginning book artists. Once you've mastered the basic "petroglyph" booklet shown here, develop your own cover design using other creative shapes and embellishments.

ARTIST: **Sherrill Kahn**

Materials

Stamps: petroglyph figures, spiral

Heavy cardstock

Bond paper

Large sponge

Bottled acrylic paints in turquoise and blue

Metallic copper paint

Bone folder

Bottles with fine applicator tips

Brush for painting details

Dry adhesive

Glue stick

Paper towels

Water container

Craft knife and cutting mat

Access to a long-arm stapler

Getting Started

Car-wash and boat sponges work well for this project, since they are inexpensive, can be found in most hardware and grocery stores, and are good for painting because they never dry out. To prepare the sponge for stamping, cut it into 1.5" (4 cm) pieces, some in precise squares, others in ragged shapes.

One special booklet-making tool is needed: a long-armed stapler. Many print shops will allow customers who purchase products or services to use their staplers.

1 To create the booklet cover, cut two pieces of burgundy cardstock measuring 5" x 10" (13 cm x 25 cm). Fold one of the sheets in half, and use turquoise acrylic paint to stamp a petroglyph figure on the right front edge. Let the image dry.

2 Open the folded cardstock and use a craft knife to cut around the right-hand side of the stamped figure, leaving a 1/8" (.3 cm) border. Paint a metallic copper border along this right side of the stamped image. Fold and adhere the second sheet of cardstock to the inside with a glue stick. Once dry, unfold the cover and cut the edge as before, this time leaving a 1/8" (.3 cm) border around the metallic copper border. Using blue acrylics, stamp another petroglyph figure to the left of the main figure and a series of spiral stamps on the inside back cover. When the stamped acrylics are dry, sponge-paint the front and back cover. Stamp additional petroglyph figures on the front and back of the booklet.

3 Prepare the booklet's pages by cutting six pages of bond paper to approximately 5" x 8" (13 cm x 20 cm). Fold each page in half, separately, using a bone folder for a crisp fold. Insert the papers inside each other and then inside the booklet cover, aligning the folded edges with the inside "spine" of the book. Carefully unfold the booklet and place it face-down on a table. Using a long-arm stapler, staple two or three times along the fold.

Booklet-Making Tips

• To disguise the staples on the outside cover, paint over them lightly. To hide the inside of the staples, glue small, stamped pieces of paper over them. Allow the book to dry flat before folding again.

• If a long-armed stapler is unavailable, bind the booklet by poking four holes in the spine with a large embroidery needle. Then string embroidery floss, weaving thread, or book-binding thread through the holes and tie knots to hold the pages together.

4 Add finishing touches to the cover. Outline the middle figure with copper metallic paint in an applicator bottle with a fine-nozzle tip. Use short strokes of the paint for more control. With a fine brush, paint a turquoise checkerboard pattern around the right edge of the first stamped figure.

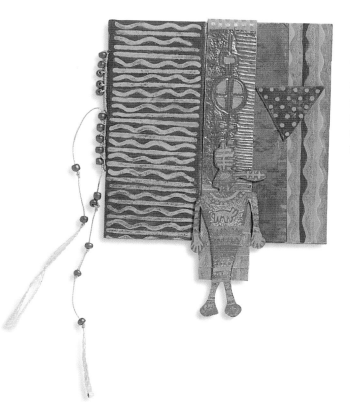

Variation

Make booklets using a variety of stamps and paint treatments. Add touches of whimsy by cutting out stamped figures and mounting them so they hang off the cover's edge. Use decorative thread and beads to embellish the booklet's spine.

Miniature Books

After mastering the technique for making a stamped, stapled booklet, the next logical step is creating a more complex small book with hard covers and a spine. The result is similar to a full-scale, bound book, except with the charm and allure of a miniature object. In this project, Julie van Oosten combines her passion for miniatures with her love of stamping. Because of the book's miniature size, its pages are glued rather than hand-stitched. The cover is embellished with art-stamped papers and ephemera for an old-time, nostalgic appearance.

ARTIST: **Julie van Oosten**

Materials

Assorted stamps

White bond paper

Cream-colored paper

Decorative paper

Heavy cardstock

Low-moisture archival adhesive,
such as bookbinder's glue

Small bottle with fine-tipped nozzle

Bone folder

Craft knife and cutting mat

Fine ribbon

Sponge

Archival waterproof ink pads in
 black, red, green

Embellishments

Gold wax

Getting Started

Prepare by pouring the glue into the small bottle
with a fine-tipped nozzle. This will make it much
easier to apply tiny amounts of glue.

When choosing papers and embellishments, look
for items with complementary colors. For instance,
if you intend to stamp your papers in green and red
ink, choose a bookmark ribbon and cover decorations with similar colors.

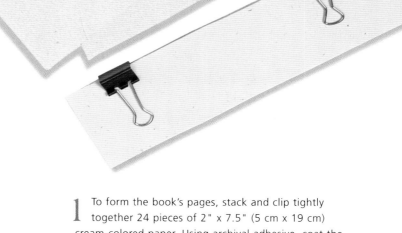

1 To form the book's pages, stack and clip tightly
together 24 pieces of 2" x 7.5" (5 cm x 19 cm)
cream-colored paper. Using archival adhesive, coat the
left-hand long edge of each sheet in the stack. Keeping
the sheets perfectly aligned, wipe off any excess adhesive,
and press the stack between heavy weights such as old
books or bricks wrapped in craft paper. Leave for at
least two hours or until dry.

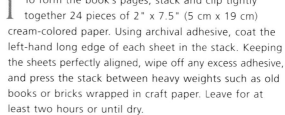

2 Make endpapers by cutting two 4" x 7.5" (10 cm x 19 cm) pieces of decorative paper and folding them in half lengthwise with the decorated side in. Glue down the back of one endpaper's right-hand folded side to the top of the stack of pages, and the back of the other endpaper's left-hand folded side to the bottom of the stack. Press firmly and allow to dry. Using a craft knife and mat, cut the stack of pages into three 2.5" (6 cm) sections. Set aside two of the small stacks of pages to use in future book projects.

3 Create collage-style paper for the book cover by stamping several images on white bond paper using black ink. Use a photocopier to reduce the paper to 75 percent, sponge on red and green waterproof inks, and set aside to dry.

Book-Making Tips

- When embellishing the cover, use decorative items such as charms and sealing wax or found objects such as feathers.

- Experiment with making books of various dimensions. The width of the spine is determined by the thickness of the book's inside pages and endpapers. The pages should be ever so slightly smaller than the covers; if necessary, when the pages are inserted in the book, trim them using a rotary cutter and cutting mat.

4 Cut two 1.75" x 2.5" (4.5 cm x 6 cm) pieces of heavy cardstock for the covers and one thin .25" x 2.5" (.5 cm x 6 cm) strip for the spine. Trim the cover paper to 3.75" x 5.75" (9.5 cm x 14.5 cm), and lay it face down. Position the spine and covers in the center of the cover paper, leaving a .25" (.5 cm) gap on either side of the spine, and adhere. Add support by gluing a 2" (5 cm) square piece of scrap paper onto the cardstock covers and center spine. Then press the paper flat, working a bone folder into all the crevices. Let dry.

5 Miter the corners of the cover paper by cutting them at an angle. With the inside of the cover facing you, fold the cover paper over the edges of the cardstock and adhere. Use a bone folder to smooth out any bubbles, and press the book cover open flat for half an hour while it dries.

6 Position and glue fine ribbon along the spine for a bookmark. Place the pages inside the cover of the book. Glue the outside endpapers to the inside book covers, and quickly remove any excess glue with a slightly damp sponge. Press the book under weights overnight. Embellish the front cover by adhering decorative items, and rub the pages' edges with gold wax to simulate gilding.

Large-Format Art

Stamp artist and designer Zana Clark's mission is to persuade stampers everywhere to go beyond greeting cards. To this end, Zana teaches her students to use stamps, handmade papers, and picture-frame mats to assemble large-format artwork that can be framed and proudly displayed. Substantive mixed media compositions such as the one featured here rely on one or two large, bold stamps that are used in repeat patterns and for the central image.

ARTIST: **Zana Clark**

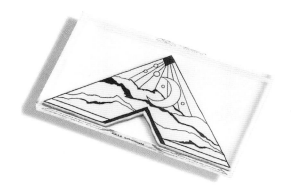

Getting Started

In addition to selecting an engaging stamp design worthy of repetition in your composition, make sure the papers used for the background collage complement the stamped images. Also choose an art mat that will set off the finished design to best advantage; neutral colors, such as white, black, taupe, gray, or beige, often work best.

Materials

Large art deco stamp

Black mat-board frame with gold inner mat, 16" x 20" (41 cm x 51 cm) with an 11" x 14" (28 cm x 36 cm) opening

Frame and protective glass, 16" x 20" (41 cm x 51 cm)

Mat board or other firm substrate, at least 12" x 15" (30 cm x 38 cm)

Cardstock

Handmade papers

Ink pads in assorted colors

Metallic gold embossing powder

Embossing tool

Chalks, pastels, colored pencils

Dry adhesive

Paper towels

Sharp scissors or craft knife and cutting mat

1 Stamp the mat several times with a large art deco image. Emboss the stamped areas with metallic gold embossing powder, and heat set with an embossing tool. Use chalks, pastels, and colored pencils to color in the stamped images.

2 Stamp the same image seven times on black cardstock. Emboss, color, and cut out the images. Set aside.

Composition Tips

• When designing your own composition, incorporate an odd rather than even number of stamped cutout images.

• Don't be afraid to overlap the foreground cutout images over the mat, since this can add a dynamic twist to your artwork.

3 Tear handmade papers into interesting shapes, and arrange them in an 11" x 14" (28 cm x 36 cm) collage on the mat board or other firm substrate. When the composition is aesthetically pleasing and works well with the decorated mat frame, adhere the papers to the substrate. Arrange the stamped cutout images in the foreground.

4 Mat the compostion as shown, and choose a frame that enhances your artwork. To protect the finished piece from sun damage, consider placing it behind glass with ultraviolet screening.

Variation

Achieve a completely different look with a pretty floral stamp, pastel color scheme, and mat board with a round opening.

GALLERY OF
Mixed Media Effects

1

2

1 **SHERRILL KAHN**
   metallic ink, card stock, fabric

2 **SHERRILL KAHN**
   metallic ink, card stock, fabric,
   braided thread, beads

3 **JULIE VAN OOSTEN**
   miniature stamps, dye inks,
   cardstock

4 **JULIE VAN OOSTEN**
   journal with old-style stamps
   on cardstock with
   polymer clay centerpiece

3

4

1

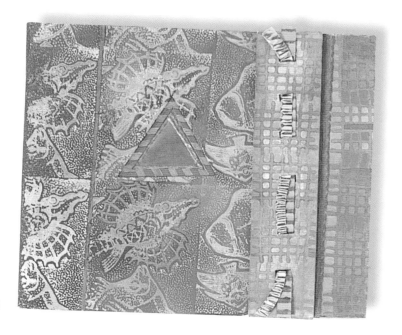

2

1 **LYNNE PERRELLA**
   overlapping stamp images, photo-
   transfer, pastels, found objects

2 **SHERRILL KAHN**
   metallic ink, cardstock, metal

3 **LISA RENNER**
   cardboard, paper, clay, ribbon

3

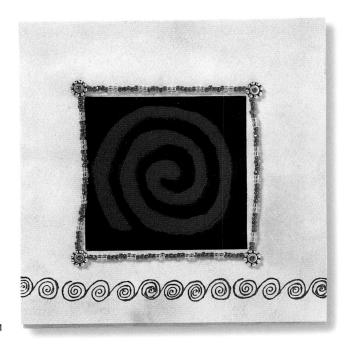

1

1 MARTHA THURLOW
stamped velvet, beads

2 SHERRILL KAHN
metallic ink, cardstock

3 LISA RENNER
clay, wire, beads, papyrus

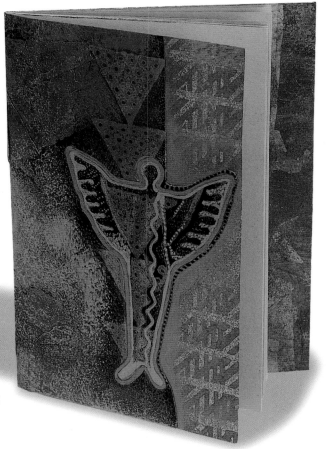

2

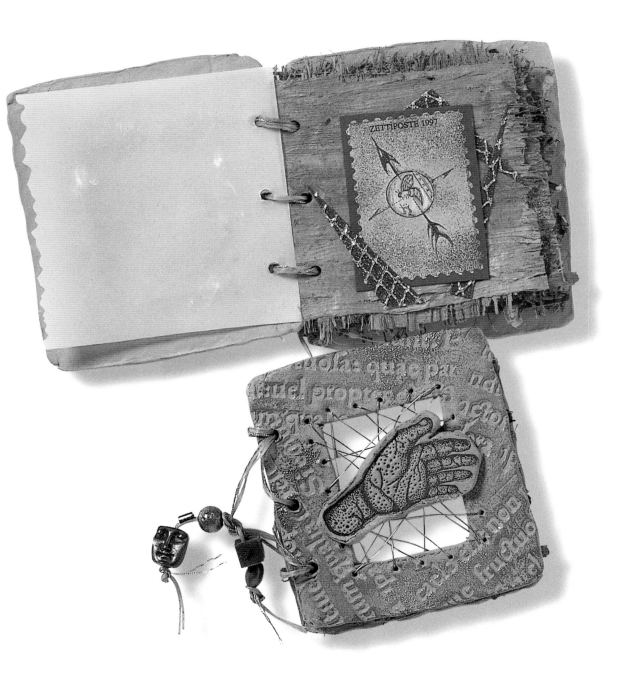

3

With One Stamp
CRANES

Large stamps with repeat patterns, such as this cranes stamp, are known as background stamps. They are used most often to print beautiful background images on cardstock or paper before stamping a larger central image. The cranes stamp pictured here was given to seven artists who were told to create "anything—the sky is the limit!"

Cranes stamped art from bottom left: *Seashell Frame* by Jill Post Fasken; *Framed Mirror* by Sandra Moertel; *Cherry Blossom Kimono* and *Silver Kimono* by Lea Everse; *Japanese Cranes* by MaryJo McGraw; *Collage Crane* and *Bookmark* by Jill Post Fasken; *Porcelain Box* by Michele DeMayo; *Crane Tiles* by Lynne Grant Mohr; and *Ribboned Book* by Sylvia Valle.

Framed Mirror
Sandy Moertel

Emboss the cranes stamp in silver on gold lightweight paper. Mold the paper to a framed mirror, and adhere it with glue.

Porcelain Box
Michele DeMayo

With green dye ink, stamp the lid of a round porcelain box with the background cranes stamp. Stamp the sides of the box with a grass stamp. Spray the porcelain box and lid with two light coats of acrylic sealer. Allow to dry overnight before rubbing chalk lightly on the sides of the lid; then spray again to seal.

Silver Kimono
Lea Everse

Using gold and silver powders, emboss the cranes background stamp on black paper. Run an embossing pen around the edges of the paper and emboss them with gold and silver. Adhere this piece to layers of cardstock in this order: black, gold, black. Mount this to specialty decorative paper, then to more black, gold, and black papers. On specialty decorative paper, emboss the kimono stamp with silver and gold powders, and cut it out. Adhere the kimono to the card with foam tape, and embellish it with a black tassel and a wax seal.

Seashell Frame
Jill Post Fasken

Emboss the cranes stamp in black on the shiny side of silver craft foil. Color in with transparent acrylics (customarily used on glass and found in the hobby section of craft stores), and allow to dry. Cut the foil to the size of a picture frame. Apply spray adhesive to the back of the foil, and mold it to the frame, wrapping it around and smoothing with your fingers. Spray with acrylic sealer. Stamp seashells on watercolor paper, heat set them with an embossing tool, watercolor the image, and cut it out. Shape curls in the paper with your fingers and mount it to the center of the frame with foam tape. Embellish the bottom-right corner of the frame with raffia, copper thread, and stones.

Beribboned Booklet
Sylvia Valle

Stamp and emboss the cranes background stamp in gold on black linen cardstock. Trim and fold it into a booklet. Insert a small pad of paper or sticky-notes inside. Emboss the central image in gold on black linen cardstock, trim it around the edges, and adhere it to shiny gold cardstock, then to the booklet. Adhere ribbon to the booklet, wrap, and tie.

With One Stamp
GRAPEVINES

The fruits of creativity come to the fore when the same set of rubber stamps is pressed into the hands of several different artists. Grapes, vines, and flowers are popular images with decorative artists, and the bold, flat designs lend themselves well to stamping in clay, on paper bags, and wood.

Grapevines stamp art, from left: *Goodie Bag* by Robin Dudley-Howes; *Notecard Holder* by Sherry Barncastle; *Golden Harvest* by Anna Leisa Ely; *Sheer Bow* and *Framed Artwork* by Jill Post Fasken; *Antique Wooden Book* by Lisa Renner; *Vintage Card* by Shelley Rymer; *Candy Cone Party Favor* by Robin Dudley-Howes; *Glorious* by Lea Everse; *Treasure Chest* by Lisa Renner; and *Napkin Ring With Napkin* by Robin Dudley-Howes.

Framed Artwork
Jill Post Fasken

Make molds using polymer clay with each stamp. Press Paperclay into baked molds. Gently pull out of mold and press into frame in desired pattern. Allow to dry completely. Fill in any cracks with spackle, and let dry. Paint with acrylic paints, glazes, and metallics. Seal with acrylic spray.

Goodie Bag
Robin Dudley-Howes

Stamp vines and grapes on a brown paper bag using green and purple ink. Antique with a tonal applicator stamp or a sponge. To make the fan, fold the top about halfway down in accordion style. Pinch the sides of the top fold together and staple. Fold over. Embellish with a jute bow.

Sheer Bow
Jill Post Fasken

Stamp vine and grapes on white,
wire-edged, sheer ribbon. Tie
into a bow with coordinating
colored ribbon.

Antique Wooden Book
Lisa Renner

The wood book is antiqued with products from Modern
Options. To prepare wood, brush primer onto the surface.
Brush on two coats of Blonde Bronze Metallic Surfacer.
Sponge on Instant Iron, leaving some of the metallic surface
showing. Brush on Instant Rust, and set aside. Brush Copper
Topper Metallic Surfacer on black cardstock. Lightly sponge
on Patina Green. Stamp grapevine. Heat set. Deckle the
edges and brush adhesive around them. Deep emboss with
bronze powder. Adhere to a thin sheet of copper with two-
sided tape. Mount assembly to a slightly larger piece of
black cardstock. Press image of grapes into polymer clay
and bake. Apply Rub n Buff Gold Leaf to surface. Glue to
top of book cover. Drill three holes at spine edge. Attach
together with gold rings. Embellish rings with polymer clay
triangles wrapped with copper wire. Note: For this project,
allow each application or coat to dry before applying the next.

Treasure Chest
Lisa Renner

This project uses faux finish products from Modern
Options. Prime a small wooden trunk with primer/sealer.
Brush on Copper Topper Metallic Surfacer. Let dry. Sponge
on Patina Green, and let dry. Lightly sponge on Burgundy
Tint, wiping off any excess. Dab on gold acrylic paint to
highlight selected areas. Spray surface with gold glitter
paint. Emboss grapevine leaves on purple cardstock with
copper metallic embossing powder. Cut out, and mount
with silicone glue. Add strands of angel-hair wire.

With One Stamp
KOOKABURRAS

The kookaburra chortles among the treetops in southern and eastern Australia, entertaining passers-by with its derisive laughter. Inhabitants of these areas awaken each morning to the mocking titters of this comical bird, which Australians often refer to as the "laughing jackass."

For years, this kookaburras stamp has been a bestseller. Stampers enjoy pressing the intricate image into polymer clay, cutting out its feathers from copper, or even embroidering the image with thread.

Kookaburras artwork, from top left:
Kookaburra Shaker Card by Lesley Bieniak;
Elegant Black Box by Stacey Apeitos;
Exchanging Information by Jill Smith;
Laughing Jackass by Phyllis Harrison;
Kookaburra Journal by Julie van Oosten;
In the Wild by Cathy Daulman; *Laughing*
by Ellen Eadie; *At Dusk* by Ann Grear;
Framed Kookaburras by Robyn Jaques;
and *Embroidered Kookaburras*
by Kate Mitchell.

Kookaburra sits in the ol' gum tree,
Merry merry king of the bush is he,
Laugh kookaburra, laugh,
How gay your life must be.

Kookaburra Shaker Card
Leslie Bieniak

Stamp kookaburras with black ink on white cardstock and heat set. Cut out the image, and color it with markers. On pale green cardstock, impress the flowering gum stamp randomly, using brown dye ink. On darker green cardstock, pencil in a frame, and bronze emboss the flowering gum image in top left corner. Repeat down the left side. Cut out the frame, carefully cutting around the images as shown. Mount the frame on a foam-core frame (slightly smaller to remain hidden). Adhere small gum nuts and leaves to the pale-green card, and mount the cutout kookaburras with foam tape. Inside the window area, sprinkle small gum nuts and leaves before covering the opening with acetate.

Framed Kookaburras
Robyn Jaques

Stamp kookaburras with black non-porous ink on thin sheets of craft metal, once on gold, three times on copper. Cut out the tree branch and leaves from the gold metal using sharp, pointed nail scissors. From one copper image, cut out the three foreground birds. From the second copper image, cut out the two background birds, and then cut into two pieces: the upper body with claws, and the tail with the piece of trunk attached (when assembling, the tail will tuck under the tree trunk). Using a foam mat under the metal, trace around the design lines with a fine-point stylus. Turn the piece face-down, and work the back with the larger end of the stylus to raise the features. Repeat with all pieces. Assemble with silicone caulking. From the third copper print, cut and shape one kookaburra and attach to a gum leaf. Write poem on leaf with black pen. Stamp background on green cardstock with black ink, using Australian stamp images. Color with pencils. Trace around design with a fine-point stylus. Assemble with picture frame.

Embroidered Kookaburras
Kate Mitchell

Stamp kookaburras on white cardstock. Cut into an oval shape, and color with watercolor pencils. Stamp leaves and gum nuts on separate cardstock, color, and cut out. Adhere both stamped cutouts on a green panel. Embroider gum nuts with pink floss. Adhere the finished piece to a folded rust card, adding gold corners.

At Dusk
Ann Grear

Bray rainbow colors of dye ink onto glossy cardstock, and set aside. Stamp and emboss kookaburras onto white cardstock, color with markers, and cut out. Adhere a green frame to the brayered piece, then adhere tree bark, leaves, and a yellow gum tree flower to the frame. Adhere cutout kookaburras as shown, and layer ensemble on a black card sprayed with gold spray-webbing.

Elegant Black Box
Stacey Apeitos

Stamp kookaburras with black ink into yellow polymer clay, trim the edges with a knife, and bake per package directions. When cool, accent with gold rub-ons. Trace the polymer clay shape onto the lid of a papier-mâché hatbox, then set aside. Glue string just outside the traced line, and allow to dry. Combine one part water with three parts white glue, and paint it onto the lid. Cover the wet lid with tissue paper, allowing it to wrinkle. Repeat this process with two or three sheets of tissue, and then decorate the box using the same technique. Allow both pieces to dry. With sandpaper, clean the tissue away from the rim edges of the box and lid. Paint both with black acrylics, and allow to dry. Use metallic rub-ons to accent, and seal with acrylic spray. Adhere polymer clay kookaburras to the lid, and add a bow.

With One Stamp
OPEN BOOK

Books open up worlds of inspiration, and this open book stamp provides visual proof of that. This deceptively simple Medieval-style book stamp can be used on canvas, cardstock, vellum, and a variety of papers to create everything from tote bags to gift boxes. Talented stamp artists seem to revel in the book's blank pages, using it to express their wishes, dreams, and innermost thoughts.

Open Book stamp art, from left: *Self* and *Venetian Book* by Carolyn Waitt; *Alphabet Book* by Maryse Carrier; *Journey* by Pat Pleacher; *Book Tote* by Frankie Fioretti; *Once Upon a Dream* by Barbara Close; *Manuscript* by Judi Riesch; *Potpourri Storybook Box* by Sandra Moertel; and *A Heart for Thee* by P. J. Dutton.

Manuscript
Judi Riesch

Stamp the book image on brown cardstock, once in black and again in sepia ink. Cut out. Stamp the book several times on vellum, and cut out the pages only, embossing the edges with an embossing pen and gold powder. Collage the pages with script imagery. Remove the cover from an old, discarded book, collage decorative papers onto it, and then adhere the black stamped book cover to the design. Cut the border off the sepia stamped book image, and adhere the border to the black-stamped image as shown. Assemble the stamped pages, and sew them into the spine of the book. Add a gold tassel and key charm.

Journey
Pat Pleacher

Stamp book image twice; stamp and write on one, and color in the other's details. Cut out the image with the writing and attach to the open book, using rolled paper or foam mounting tape to raise the pages. Stamp hands, color, cut out, and attach to book. Assemble the piece to black cardstock, and attach a green ribbon bookmark. Assemble on a background sheet decorated with stamps and photos, and then adhere on black cardstock.

Book Tote
Frankie Fioretti

Pre-wash and press a canvas tote bag. Mask off the center square with masking tape. Apply a thin wash of fabric paints with a foam brush, dry, and press smooth. Using darker colors, stamp fabric paint in positions shown. Mask the upper and lower books, and use tape to create outer borders. Apply thinned paint. Mask borders, and fill outer border with script background image. Stamp large words with lower-case alphabet. Fill book pages with stamped face and word images, and add key images. Press with a hot iron to heat set the paint.

Potpourri Storybook Box
Sandra Moertel

Stamp the book image four times with black ink on colored cardstock or on gift paper adhered to cardstock. Cut out the images. Sponge on wax shoe polish, dry, and buff. Glue the edges together as shown to form a box, and adhere gold cord along the top. Paint a half-pint cardboard berry basket with gold spray paint, dry, and insert inside the book box. Fill the basket with potpourri, and attach a burgundy bow and dried rosebud to the front.

Self
Carolyn Waitt

Stamp face using dye ink, and cut to the size of a miniature book page. Cut three more pieces of white cardstock the same size, inscribe a quote on one, and place that piece on top of the other two. Color the edges. Emboss book image in white and gold, cut out, and adhere to white mulberry paper with torn edges. Tie charm to a bookmark ribbon, and adhere to book as shown. Assemble piece on buff-colored cardstock.

paper stamping

The sheer variety of papers available is staggering. Everything from translucent vellum to sturdy matboard may be used in a wide variety of stamping projects. Examples of paper stamping in this section include everything from accordion-fold books and collage stamping to gift bags, tags, and mail art, paper art dolls, artistamps, mobiles, postcards, bookplates—and greeting cards, of course!

Many artists make their own papers in various weights and colors from recycled junk mail and dried herbs and flowers. Books and videos on this subject will get you started, but it is recommended that serious papercrafters take a weekend workshop for an introduction to this artform.

There are hundreds, if not thousands, of papers and cardstocks available through art and craft stores, rubber stamp stores, and via the Internet. Prices range from a few cents to $25 or more for a single sheet of high-quality decorative paper. When choosing materials for enduring art projects, look for acid- and lignin-free papers. For best results always use the highest-quality paper and cardstock that you can afford. Save money by purchasing paper in bulk from paper mills and stationers. Purchase whole reams of paper with a friend and split the cost. Buy rolls of expensive Japanese paper and cut it into small pieces to distribute among a group of artists who pool their resources. Many stamping clubs have sprung up for members to share paper, ink, rubber stamps, and craft tools.

Create simple books from an unlikely source: steno pads! Lined paper note pads

measuring 5" x 8" (13 cm x 20 cm) can be found at many stationery and office

supply stores. Make a pretty paper cover for them, and they become instant artists'

books. All you need are oversized sheets of colored cardstock, a few art stamps,

and pigment ink or acrylic paint for stamping.

steno pad covers

1 Using diagram provided (see "Templates," p. 297), measure 5" (13 cm) along the length of the piece and mark the spot with a pencil (point A on the diagram). Then measure inward by 4" (10 cm) and mark that spot (point B), and draw a line between A and B. Measure 4" (10 cm) inward at the bottom of the piece and mark that spot (point C). Draw a line between points B and C.

2 Use a sharp craft knife and a metal ruler to cut along the line between points A and B, then between points B and C. Discard the small cut out portion of cardstock. Use pigment ink or acrylics to stamp images on the cover.

3 Fold in the flap of cardstock as shown, creasing the fold with a bone folder (optional), and dab a little adhesive under one corner of the flap to hold it in place.

4 Measure 5" (13 cm) along the length of the cover and mark two spots on either edge, draw a line between them, and fold at the line as shown. Measure down .25" (.5 cm) from there and repeat with another fold. Place a steno pad on the inside of the cover as shown. Glue it in place. Fold the front cover over to hide the steno pad.

5 To make a front panel, stamp and emboss pieces of complementary cardstock, cut them to the desired size or shape, and glue them to the covers with adhesive.

MATERIALS

- Steno Pad Cover Template (see p. 297)
- Cardstock, cut into pieces measuring approximately 10.25" x 12" (25.5 cm x 30 cm)
- Metal ruler
- Pencil
- Craft knife
- Art stamps
- Pigment ink or acrylic paint
- Bone folder (optional)
- Adhesive
- Steno pad

tips

- *Any cardstock will do for this project, but choose high-quality papers with a smooth finish for best results. Children will enjoy making steno pad covers from construction paper for journals and customized school notebooks.*
- *Take your time making your first steno pad cover; once you've gained some basic bookmaking skills, it will become much easier.*
- *Precise measuring, drawing, and folding of creases with a bone folder will render the most professional look.*

artist: martha labardee, u.s.a.

A playful paper mobile can be made in less than an hour with thin matboard, pigment ink, and a few art stamps. Designed to hang indoors, it's a whimsical accompaniment to any home decor scheme. Try making your own paper mobile for the baby's room, game room, or kitchen area. Mobiles can be made in just about any size or shape. The same pattern can be used over and over again to make as many different mobiles as you desire, or the shapes can be altered as needed. The paper shapes the artist used have been diagrammed for your convenience.

artist: annie onderdonk, U.S.A.

paper mobile

MATERIALS

- Mobile pattern (see Templates, p. 292)
- Matboard
- Pencil
- Ruler
- Compass
- Craft knife
- Pigment inkpads
- Art stamps
- Matte acrylic spray
- Hole punch
- Needle-nose pliers
- Jump-rings
- Fishing line

1 Use the mobile pattern provided or design shapes on your own. Trace the pattern onto thin matboard using a pencil, ruler, and compass as needed, and cut the pieces out with a sharp craft knife.

2 Apply pigment ink to the cutout shapes directly from the pad. Stamp various images within the center of each mobile piece. When finished, seal the pieces with matte acrylic spray to keep the pigment ink from smudging.

3 Punch 1/8" (.5 cm) holes at the top and bottom of each mobile piece as shown. A larger punch may be made through the topmost piece. Use needle-nose pliers to open up the jump-rings. Slip the rings through the punched holes in the mobile pieces to attach. The mobile is now ready to hang suspended with invisible fishing line.

tips

- *The artist colored the borders of each shape with yellow ink, then applied a thin line of orange ink to the very edges to give each piece added dimension. The interior was smudged with turquoise pigment ink; special shadow background stamps or hand-carved stamps can be used to apply the color, but it is just as easy to apply the color directly from the inkpad.*
- *For the stamped images, the artist used dark teal-green ink that coordinates nicely with the yellow and orange and shows up well against the lighter turquoise background.*

Book lovers and collectors will enjoy making custom bookplates for their most cherished editions. And it's an easy task, once you master the art of stamp carving (please see the related chapter in the Creative Tools & Techniques section). The benefit to making your own carved stamp is that the same image may be used over and over, several times, to make multiple plates in minutes. Make your bookplates ahead of time and use them as needed. Children will enjoy making bookplates for their own textbooks and picture books; in this case, be sure to affix them with removable tape.

artist: agatha bell, U.S.A.

"ex libris"
bookplates

1 Transfer the pattern (see Templates, p. 293) to the linoleum block and carve out the design. Ink the block and print it on various light-weight papers.
2 Cut out the bookplates with decorative paper edgers and affix them with a glue stick to slightly larger pieces of handmade paper.
3 Apply archival double-stick tape to the back of each bookplate before affixing it to the flyleaf of your books.

MATERIALS
• Linoleum block
• Linoleum cutting tools
• Ink
• Assorted papers and paper edgers
• Glue stick
• Archival double-stick tape or removable tape
• Paper edgers

tips
• *Use different colored inks on the same printing.*
• *Stamp directly in your books instead of creating a separate bookplate.*
• *Using the same technique as described above, carve an address label and use it to stamp a return address on your personal correspondence.*

Make pretty postcards from colored cardstock and hand-carved stamps or commercial images! It's an easy way to recycle scraps of cardstock and practice printing hand-carved stamps. Or, if you prefer, decorate a matching envelope and stamp on folded cardstock to create one-of-a-kind greeting cards.

artist: linda milligan, U.S.A.

wild things
postcards

MATERIALS
- Hand-carved stamps
- Assorted cardstock scraps
- Ink

1 Create your own hand-carved stamps (please see Creative Tools & Techniques, p. 16), or use the Wild Things pattern in the Templates section (p. 294).

2 Cut leftover cardstock pieces down to postcard size: about 5.5" x 4.25" (14 cm x 10.5 cm).

3 Ink each hand-carved stamp and print it on the postcards.

tip
- *Create layered postcards like the ones shown by stamping on small paper scraps and affixing them to scrap cardstock.*

Light up your home with pretty votive candleholders custom-designed to fit your decor! It's easy—with paper, art stamps, and a glass candleholder. The glow of soft candlelight is enhanced by the stamped designs embossed and adhered to a simple glass votive. Because the stamped paper is adhered to the outside of the glass, it's perfectly safe to light a candle within. Place your votive candleholder in the guest bathroom, living room, kitchen, or dining area for a special touch of elegance. Your friends will be amazed when you tell them how easy it was to make it yourself.

artist: lisa glicksman, u.s.a.

votive candleholders

1 Use a plain piece of bond paper to wrap around the glass votive candleholder, and measure the height and circumference. Cut out the paper to the required size, and use it as a pattern.
2 Lay the paper pattern on a piece of decorative or handmade paper and lightly sketch the outline. For a ragged edge, dip a cotton swab in water and run it along the line you drew, and then tear the paper away.
3 Stamp and emboss the strip of decorative paper.
4 Brush acrylic gloss medium onto the back of the paper, and affix it to the glass by wrapping it around and gently pressing the paper against it to hold it in place. Once dry, apply an additional layer of acrylic gloss medium to the surface of the paper. Allow the candleholder to dry completely before lighting.

MATERIALS
• Bond paper
• Decorative paper
• Scissors
• Cotton swab
• Art stamps
• Embossing ink
• Embossing powder
• Embossing (heat) tool
• Acrylic gloss medium
• Votive glass candleholder

tips
• *Choose thin decorative or handmade papers that allow the light to shine through easily when the candle is lit. Test your papers first by holding them up to a light source; if the light shines through, they are appropriate for this project. Papers with inclusions such as flower petals or bits of straw or confetti make beautiful votive candleholders as well.*
• *As an option, use translucent paper to stamp and emboss various images, cut them out, and affix the cutouts to a glass votive candleholder with liquid adhesive or gloss medium. Seal the top with another layer of gloss medium.*
• *Try stamping with bleach onto lightweight paper to create an impression instead of using embossing ink and powder.*
• *Glue tiny beads or charms around the rim of the glass, or tie a ribbon or raffia around the bottom.*
• *Never leave a burning candle unattended.*

As stamping gains in popularity, more and more creative individuals are looking for ways to make their own original stamp tools. One of the more popular craft items on the market today is a dense foam material that can be heated with an embossing tool and then molded by placing it against firm-textured items such as leaves and plants, burlap, commercial rubber stamps, buttons, and beads. The foam cools in seconds, taking on the impression from the textured item. It's an easy way to make great stamping tools, one that kids seem to enjoy as much as adults. If you tire of the stamp you've made, simply reheat and press the foam against something else. Use plant cuttings to make the naturally beautiful stamps shown here.

heat and mold
stamping

artist: ann mason, U.S.A.

1 Heat the heat-activated moldable foam with an embossing tool for 30–45 seconds, taking care not to heat any one spot more than a few seconds at a time. Move the tool in a circular motion to cover the surface evenly, holding it about 2" (5 cm) away.

2 Quickly press the heated foam against the textured item. Hold it down firmly for a few seconds, then release the foam. You now have a stamp.

3 Apply inks or thin water-based paints to the stamp, and stamp as usual (see "Stamp Basics"). The resulting papers can be used for greeting cards or to bind books, as shown in these examples.

MATERIALS

• Textured items
• Heat-activated moldable foam
• Embossing (heat) tool
• Inks or paints
• Cardstock
• Bookmaking materials

tips

• *Choose an item to mold with firm texture such as a bunch of herbs, leaves, or even commercial rubber stamps.*
• *Making "natural" stamps with plant cuttings? For best results, select a plant that has texture but is not too thick. Try pyracantha, long-needled pine, and heavenly bamboo.*

These stamped whales are alive with motion; they seem to swim up from the ocean depths, buoyed by waves of watercolor. The secret lies in the application of watercolor brushstrokes. Applied loosely and allowed to spatter a bit, the washes of color simulate ocean waves. An easy afternoon project, children will enjoy making their own whale cards.

artist: ed giecek, U.S.A.

whale
greeting cards

1 Create your own hand-carved stamps (please see Creative Tools & Techniques, p. 16). Find the Whale Greeting Cards pattern in the Templates section (see p. 294). Fold white cardstock in half, or cut to the appropriate size for enclosure in an envelope.
2 Paint the front of the folded cardstock with the paint colors of your choice. Use an old toothbrush to spatter additional drops of paint in a random pattern. Allow the paint to dry completely before stamping.
3 Apply permanent or waterproof ink to a hand-carved stamp and print the images as shown. Paint and stamp matching envelopes to create custom stationery packets.

tips
- *Substitute pigment ink and embossing powder for permanent ink if desired.*
- *Try carving a host of sea creatures—sea turtles, fish, rays, sharks—to create greeting cards with an ocean theme.*

Artistamps—otherwise known as faux postage—are popular with rubber stamp artists who relish the challenge of working in miniature. Use tiny stamps, delicate applications of stamping ink, and acetate templates to make your own diminutive compositions. Once each "postage stamp" area is masked off, it's simply a matter of applying ink and rubber stamps. The artist's passion for faux postage led to the purchase of a rare, old-fashioned perforator, which explains how she was able to "perf" her postage sheets so perfectly. You can achieve near-perfect perfing yourself, by using a large sewing needle and a steady hand.

artistamps

artist: julie van oosten, AUSTRALIA

MATERIALS
- Acetate
- Ruler
- Sharp craft knife
- Plain white paper
- Low-tack tape
- Ink
- Art stamps
- Needle
- Sewing machine (optional)

1 Begin by creating an acetate stencil to mask areas on the paper where you will not be applying color—in other words, a stencil with small rectangular openings, each measuring about 1" x 1.25" (3 cm x 3.75 cm). Use a ruler and a very sharp craft knife.

2 Lay the stencil on a piece of plain white paper, tape it in place with low-tack tape, and begin to color the openings with soft applications of dye or pigment ink. Brush the ink directly onto the paper with the inkpad, going from light to dark. Some areas of each rectangle may be left white.

3 Stamp images in a collage fashion within the colored areas. Large numerals may be used to indicate a denomination. An imaginary country might be indicated with a title within the composition. Remove the stencil to reveal several rows of stamped miniatures.

4 Perforate between each stamped composition to create the illusion of real postage. You can do this by hand with a large sewing needle or by sewing the paper with a machine and a threadless needle. If perforating by hand, measure dots every $1/8$ or $1/16$ inch (.3 cm or .15 cm) in straight lines around each tiny composition.

tips
- *The secret to successful faux postage is patience. Take your time when creating the acetate stencil, designing and stamping a composition, and perforating each sheet by hand. The extra care will reap rewards later, when you amaze your friends with faux postage that looks just like the real thing.*
- *Many faux postage artists make color photocopies of their original work and perforate them before using the tiny stamps in their collage artwork. Trading sheets of artistamps is an enduring tradition among faux postage artists, and some sheets have become quite valuable.*

artist: judith bain dampier, CANADA

For a fun and easy craft suitable for both children and adults, make your own stamps with just a bit of foam insulation and a darning needle. The foam insulation used for this project is dense and comes in many colors; any other dense yet pliable material will work. But this project is best for simple line art, not detailed drawings. A wood-burning tool with a fine point may be substituted for the heated darning needle.

foam-stamped greeting cards

MATERIALS

- Dense foam insulation
- Craft knife
- Pencil or pen
- Darning needle
- Heat source
- Ink or paint
- Paper

1 Cut or break apart a piece of dense foam insulation, carving it to a smaller size with a craft knife. Use a pencil or pen to draw a simple line art design on the foam piece.

2 Carefully hold the darning needle and heat the pointed end with a candle flame or other heat source. Use the heated needle to incise the design into the foam.

3 You now have a stamp! Apply ink or paint to the stamp and experiment; if the design isn't quite clear enough, reheat the needle and dig it deeper into the foam.

tips

- The foam insulation the artist uses is dense and comes in many colors; it's readily available in North America. Any other dense yet pliable material will work. Note that simple line art is best for this project, not detailed drawings.
- A wood-burning tool with a fine point may be substituted for the heated darning needle.
- Handmade stamp pads and inks go hand in hand with these stamps. The recipe is simple: Mix a quarter cup of glycerin (found at major drugstores) with liquid food color and a few drops of water. Staple a few layers of felt to a foam meat tray and soak the foam with the ink. Store the handmade stamp pad in a plastic bag or an empty videocassette case.

Fanciful trading cards are fun and easy to make with cardstock and rubber stamps. Large numeral stencils, texture stamps, and sequin waste are used to create depth and interest in these rubber stamp collages. Trading cards are often swapped with fellow artists who share a common fascination with eclectic collectibles.

artist: olivia thomas, U.S.A.

trading
cards

1 Round the corners of rectangles. Stamp two or three large images on the cardstock with black ink. Lightly apply color to some of the stamped images with chalks or colored pencils. Note: Layering colors adds depth and texture.
2 Apply pigment ink to the background of each trading card with a sponge or by stroking the cardstock directly with pigment inkpads. Layering colors and incorporating stenciled images will create a collage effect.
3 Between layers of ink, use sequin waste, window screen material, large numeral stencils, and other items to stencil layered images. Use a fine-tip pen to sketch crosshatch patterns or handwrite snatches of poetry or love letters as a way of adding texture and mystery to the composition.

MATERIALS
- Cardstock cut into rectangles, each 3.5" x 5.5" (9 cm x 14 cm)
- Scissors
- Stamps
- Black ink
- Chalks
- Colored pencils
- Pigment ink
- Sponges
- Sequin waste
- Window screen
- Stencils
- Pens

tips
- *Mask some stamped images with artists' tape or liquid masking fluid, and apply color around them. When the masking material is removed, the stamped images will come forward in the composition.*
- *Stamp images with white pigment ink over a dark background to create ghostly impressions.*
- *For sturdier trading cards, stick the stamped layer of cardstock to another piece of cardstock the same size or slightly larger.*
- *Incorporate these cards into larger artwork compositions, trade with friends, or use them as playing cards.*

Collage stamping is a technique for incorporating several disparate images into a single composition in order to convey an idea or a theme. The artist chose five unrelated rubber stamps for this elegant greeting card, but she pulled together the composition with the skillful application of watercolor paints. When creating a stamped composition with watercolors, it's important to use permanent ink for stamping and to let it dry completely before applying the paint. Masking techniques are also very helpful when stamping a collage of images; you will find more information on this technique on page 8.

collage stamping

1 Tear a piece of 200-lb. watercolor paper into an irregular shape measuring approximately 2.5" x 3" (6 cm x 8 cm).

2 Choose five rubber stamps from your collection. Ink each with waterproof ink (any color; the artist chose black) and stamp the images randomly onto the watercolor paper. Allow the ink to dry completely before proceeding. To speed the process, heat-set the ink with an embossing (heat) tool.

3 Paint the stamped composition with top-quality watercolor paints for best results. Set it aside and allow the paint to dry completely. Use a gold metallic ink pen to enhance the torn edges of the watercolor paper.

4 Fold a piece of cardstock measuring 8.5" x 5.5" (22 cm x 14 cm) in half lengthwise. Cut or tear a piece of handmade paper to about 3.75" x 4.75" (10 cm x 13 cm) and affix it to the front of the folded card.

5 Affix the stamped and painted watercolor composition completed in step 3 to the center of the card as shown. Add dots of gold metallic in a random pattern, or spatter the card lightly with gold acrylic paint.

MATERIALS
- Watercolor paper
- Art stamps
- Waterproof ink
- Embossing (heat) tool
- Watercolors
- Paintbrush
- Gold metallic ink pen
- Cardstock
- Handmade paper
- Adhesive

tip
- *Embellishments such as raffia, buttons, beads, charms, and sealing wax may be added to the completed card.*

artist: susan brzozowski, U.S.A.

Pretty pastel gift bags with coordinating tissue papers and small tags are a welcome alternative to commercially printed gift wrap. By using only two to three complementary colors—such as light green and pale pink, shown here—the artist ensured a successful outcome. Stamp a plain white lunch sack or discarded bag from a department store, stuff it with pretty stamped tissue paper, attach coordinating handmade tags with a bit of ribbon, and this gift wrap alternative is almost as much fun to give as the gift it contains!

stamped gift
bags & tags

MATERIALS

- Decorative papers
- Plain paper gift bags
- Art stamps
- Dye ink
- Cardstock

- Decorative-edge scissors
- Dry adhesive
- Hole punch
- Ribbon
- Tissue paper

1 Stamp a plain white gift bag or lunch sack in a random pattern, and set it aside. Stamp one large image in a complementary color on a piece of white cardstock, cut it out with decorative-edge scissors, and set it aside.

2 Layer complementary decorative papers on the front of the bag and fasten them with a dry adhesive such as double-stick tape. Top the layers with the cardstock piece from step 1.

3 To make a small gift tag, stamp a piece of cardstock about 2" x 2.5" (5 cm x 6 cm) and trim it with decorative-edge scissors. Punch a hole in the corner, and attach the tag to the bag with ribbon or decorative fibers.

4 Stamp colored tissue paper in a random fashion, using colors that complement the matching gift bag and tag. Wrap a gift loosely in the tissue paper, and place it in the bag.

tips

- *Coordinate the ink colors with the colors in the printed papers; in this case, shades of pale green and pastel pink work nicely together.*
- *Leftover cardstock from this project can be easily stamped, folded, and made into greeting cards like the ones shown here. Using the same papers, ink colors, and rubber stamp images used on the gift bags and tissue papers guarantees that your greeting cards match.*

Stamping and decorating envelopes——otherwise known as mail art—has been a favorite pastime for artists throughout the world for many decades. Just about any stamp will do for this type of project, and it's quite common to find mail art envelopes embellished with hand-carved images, cancellation stamps, faux postage, and other decorative items. It's perfectly safe to drop your finished artwork into the mail. The grubby fingerprints, smudged ink, postal cancellations, and bent corners just add to the charm. For this reason, mail art is a terrific craft for children of all ages.

artist: jo mansell, AUSTRALIA

mail art

1 To create the background, apply colored inks or thin paints to a plain white envelope with a paintbrush, sponge, or other favorite art tool. Allow the envelope to dry before proceeding. Use black permanent ink to stamp the individual images in a collage style, as shown. It may be necessary to mask some images before stamping again around them; see "Stamp Basics" for more information on masking and stamping techniques.

2 As you stamp the envelope, be sure to leave an open area for the address, or use a large image, such as the scroll stamp shown here, to set off the address area. Use colored pencils, ink, paint, or other mixed-media art tools to enhance individual stamp designs.

3 Sponge a final application of ink around the edges of the envelope to frame the imagery within.

MATERIALS
• Envelope
• Ink or paint
• Painting tools
• Art stamps
• Black permanent ink
• Colored pencils
• Collage items (optional)

tips

• *Flat collage items such as faux postage and torn bits of newsprint or magazine pictures can also be affixed to the envelope with paste. Melted wax seals can also be used; have your postal carrier hand-cancel the envelope to protect the seal from damage.*

• *Take care when choosing postage for your mail art. It should complement the color scheme or overall design of the envelope. Some artists choose their postage first and design their envelopes around it.*

• *Many countries sponsor mail art competitions. Find out more from your local post office.*

Once you've mastered collage stamping, try making this easy, elegant accordion-fold book. Each paper panel incorporates a different, yet related, composition of torn watercolor papers stamped with permanent ink and painted with watercolors. This handmade book can be opened to show all six panels at once, or tied together in the back to display one spread at a time.

accordion-fold book

Making the Pages

1 Tear pieces of 200-lb. (91 kg) watercolor paper into irregular shapes, each measuring approximately 2.5" x 3" (6 cm x 8 cm).

2 Ink a rubber stamp with waterproof ink (any color; the artist chose black) and stamp several images randomly onto the watercolor paper. Allow the ink to dry completely before proceeding. To speed the process, heat-set the ink with an embossing (heat) tool.

3 Paint the stamped compositions with watercolors. Set them aside, allowing the paint to dry completely. Option: Use a gold metallic pen to enhance the torn edges of the paper.

4 Hand-letter, print, or stamp sayings onto torn watercolor papers and apply a light wash of watercolors to the surface. Allow the paint to dry completely.

5 Affix the stamped, printed, and painted watercolor compositions completed in steps 3–4 to handmade papers approximately 6" x 4.25" (16 cm x 10.5 cm). Add dots of gold metallic in a random pattern, or spatter the composition lightly with gold acrylic paint.

Making the Book

1 Measure and cut two pieces of bookboard to 6.25" x 4.5" (16 cm x 11 cm). Cover them with handmade paper, attaching the paper with acid-free wet adhesive and mitering the corners. Set the two book covers aside under heavy weights (such as bricks wrapped in clean fabric).

2 Cut or tear several pieces of handmade paper or sturdy cardstock to 2" x 4.25" (5 cm x 10 cm) and fold them in half lengthwise. To create accordion-fold pages measuring 6" x 4.25" (15 cm x 10 cm), attach the small pieces of paper behind each stamped and painted panel from step 5 (under "Making the Pages"), and then fold the pages accordion-style.

3 Glue the back of each end page to the inside of each completed cover from step 1, sandwiching a 20" (51 cm) piece of raffia or decorative yarn between them as shown to create a book closure— 8" (20 cm) trailing in front of the cover, 8" (20 cm) trailing behind.

4 To complete the book, add decorative beads to the raffia and tie them in place, decorate the front cover, and tie the book together.

MATERIALS

- Watercolor paper
- Adhesive
- Art stamps
- Waterproof ink
- Embossing (heat) tool
- Watercolors
- Gold metallic ink pen
- Handmade paper
- Bookboard
- Acid-free wet adhesive
- Raffia or thread
- Beads and other embellishments

tips

- *Each page in an accordion-fold book may be decorated differently, but using coordinating colors and stamp images helps tie a story together.*
- *Consider adding photographs or personal mementos to an accordion-fold book to create a quick and easy memory album.*
- *Use acid- and lignin-free papers and adhesives to increase the longevity of your artwork.*
- *If making an accordion-fold book seems too arduous, apply the collage-stamping principles under "Making the Pages" to a purchased book or journal.*

artist: marina lenzino, ITALY

Cardstock boxes with unique folds like this one present the stamp artist with a plethora of possibilities. The wedding box pictured here can be stamped with a variety of different images to create any number of gift boxes, from birthday surprises to holiday treats, gifts for anniversaries and other days special to you and your family. Simply color and stamp the panels, fold, and tie with decorative ribbon embellished with charms and beads. Specialty boxes with flower-petal folds are available through rubber stamp stores, some art and craft stores, and via mail-order.

wedding
gift box

artist: valerie menard, CANADA

1 Stamp and emboss a plain cardstock gift box with specialty folds (for a mail-order source, please see the Resources). Coat the inner petal folds with pigment ink and emboss with gold powder.

2 Fold up the box and tie together with ribbon. Add decorative beads and silk roses.

3 To make a small gift tag, stamp a piece of cardstock about 4" x 2.75" (10 cm x 7 cm), and fold it in half. Punch a hole in the corner, and attach the tag to the bag with ribbon.

MATERIALS
- Cardstock gift box
- Art stamps
- Pigment ink
- Embossing powder
- Embossing (heat) tool
- Ribbon
- Beads
- Silk roses

tips
- *Find out the bride's colors before stamping your gift box. Match the silk flowers to the type of flowers she'll be using in the wedding.*
- *For this type of project, the simplest stamping style is most effective.*
- *Small wedding gift boxes make nice party favors.*

For stamp artists, the appeal of shipping tags seems to be universal. The size (about 4.75" x 2.25" or 12 cm x 5.5 cm) and shape of manila cardstock tags, with reinforced hole protectors and dangling strings, are ideal for practicing stamp art compositions and color combinations. This project takes less than an hour to complete. After applying a background color in paint or ink, stamp a composition, add collage papers, beads, or charms, and finish with ribbon. The finished tags are pretty enough to display as is, but many artists mount them onto folded cardstock for instant greeting cards or add them to large assemblage projects or fine art on canvases.

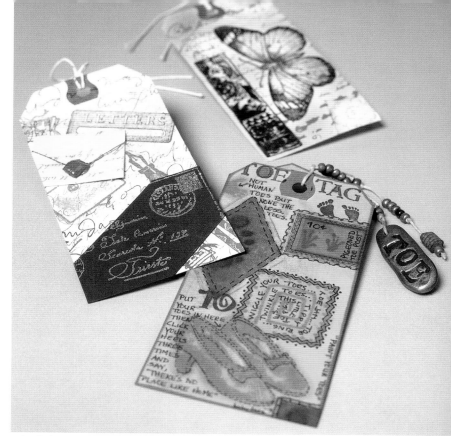

artists: barbara miller, USA; sandi najda-beck, USA; julia slebos, USA

tag art

1 Sponge dye or pigment ink onto a plain shipping tag to create a colorful background.
2 Stamp images onto the dyed tag in the arrangement of your choice.
3 Add collage items such as small decorative papers, artistamps, sealing wax, beads, or buttons. Add handwritten notes and doodles with permanent-ink pens.
4 Decorate the string by dyeing it or by adding decorative beads. Alternately, substitute the string with specialty yarns and fibers.

MATERIALS
- Shipping tags
- Sponge
- Dye ink
- Pigment ink
- Art stamps
- Collage items
- Pens

tips
- *Shipping tags are very inexpensive, usually sold in packs of 100 for $3 or $4 at stationery and office supply stores.*
- *Get a group of "tag artists" together and buy several packs of tags in different sizes, then divide the spoils between you.*
- *Try stamping and decorating several tags and stringing them together to create an artist's book. Or create a large accordion-fold book to display a decorated tag on each page.*

This beautiful paper clock will brighten any room in the house and can be made quite easily with your choice of art stamps and paper materials. A beautiful collage stamp was used for the face of this clock; you can mimic this effect with a selection of stamp imagery and masking techniques. The artist chose a soft celadon and lavender color scheme, but you can substitute different colors and images to suit your home decor. Bright complementary colors such as yellow and purple, orange and blue, or red and green are good choices, as are soft pastel shades.

paper clock

1 Cut a shape from matboard or foamcore to create a backing piece; the sample clock measures 6.75" x 7.5" (18 cm x 19 cm). Cut a piece of soft mulberry paper about 9" x 10" (23 cm x 25 cm), wrap it around the backing piece, and glue it in place. Set it aside to dry.

2 Trim a piece of plain white paper to 4.5" x 4.5" (11 cm x 11 cm) and, with permanent ink, stamp it with a variety of collage images, or use a single collage stamp similar to the one pictured. Let dry; then add color to the stamped image with light applications of pigment inkpads, pastels, colored pencils, or watercolors.

3 Apply glitter paint sparingly to highlight some areas, such as the dragonfly image the artist painted. Once dry (this may take several hours), layer the stamped piece to a piece of decorative paper 4.75" x 4.75" (12 cm x 12 cm), sticking them together with double-sided tape. Repeat with another layer of paper 5.75" x 5.75" (15 cm x 15 cm). Glue the entire ensemble to the backing piece from step 1.

4 Drill a hole carefully through the center of the piece for the clock shaft; the hole must be large enough to insert the clock mechanism. Follow the instructions for clock assembly included in the kit.

5 Affix stick-on clock numerals around the face of the clock as shown, insert a battery, and display your clock.

MATERIALS

- Scissors
- Matboard or foamcore
- Soft mulberry paper
- Adhesive
- Plain white paper
- Permanent ink
- Art stamps
- Pigment inkpads
- Glitter paint
- Decorative papers
- Double-sided tape
- Drill
- Clockmaking kit
- Stick-on numerals
- Battery

tips

- *The face of your clock can be stamped and decorated with any color scheme or stamp imagery. The key to success is using colors that contrast well so that the numerals (or images used in place of numerals) can easily be seen.*
- *Just about any large, flat object can be used as a base for a paper clock, but choose something that is both sturdy and easy to cut through. For this reason, matboard and foamcore are recommended.*
- *While square and circular clock shapes are traditional and certainly the easiest to work with, you are by no means limited to them. Try making a triangular-shaped clock or an abstract clock with an asymmetrical shape.*

In a hurry to wrap a gift? This fast and fancy Asian gift box is just the thing. Simply stamp and emboss a pleasing composition, highlight it with markers, cut, and paste the pieces on a plain cardboard box. The recipient will think you spent hours on a project that took just a few moments of your time.

Asian
gift box

artist: natalie petrarca, CANADA

1 Stamp Asian images onto cream cardstock with black pigment ink. Emboss with clear powder. Cut out the stamped images.

2 Lay the pieces onto black cardstock and use them as a template for cutting out graduated layers as shown. Glue the stamped pieces to the black cardstock cutouts.

3 Color in some stamped areas with a red marker. Add highlights to other areas with a white colored pencil.

4 Glue the layered cardstock pieces to the cardboard box as shown. Stamp and emboss additional images around the lid of the box if desired.

MATERIALS

- Cream cardstock
- Art stamps
- Black pigment ink
- Clear embossing powder
- Embossing (heat) tool
- Scissors
- Black cardstock
- Red marker
- White colored pencil
- Adhesive
- Plain cardboard box

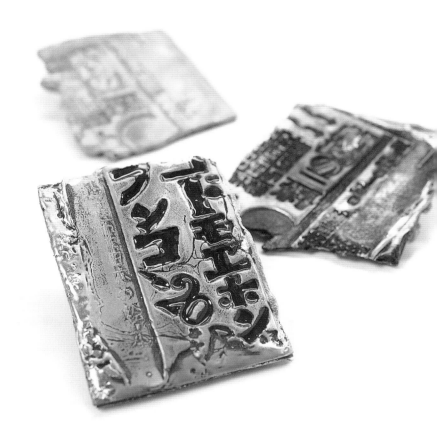

Make lovely pins that complement your wardrobe the easy way—with rubber stamps! These elegant brooches appear to have been made with gold and precious gems, but, in fact, they were created with thick embossing enamel and art stamps. A simple cardboard or matboard base forms the foundation of each brooch, which can be cut with a sharp craft knife into any shape or size.

artist: kathy martin, U.S.A.

elegant
brooches

1 Apply pigment or glycerin ink to an art stamp and set it aside.
2 Trim a piece of cardboard or matboard into a pleasing shape and apply pigment ink to it. Dip the piece into ultrathick embossing enamel, and immediately heat the powder with an embossing tool. As soon as the enamel is hot and melted, apply more powder and reheat it with the embossing tool. Repeat this process five or six times until the layer of melted powder is quite thick.
3 Press the prepared stamp (from step 1) into the hot, melted powder. As you press it, twist the stamp slightly and flatten it so the melted powder spreads over the sides of the matboard base, creating a textured outline. Remove the stamp and allow the tile to cool completely. Use jewelry adhesive to glue pin backs to each brooch.

MATERIALS
- Pigment or glycerin ink
- Art stamps
- Cardboard or matboard
- Craft knife
- Ultrathick embossing enamel
- Embossing (heat) tool
- Jewelry adhesive
- Pin backs
- Metallic rub-ons (optional)
- Acrylic paint (optional)

tips
- *Art stamps with thick lines and bold images are best for this technique; finely detailed stamps will not work as well.*
- *Option: After stamping, apply gold and silver metallic rub-ons to the surface of a brooch. Paint the depressed areas with acrylic paint. Apply a glossy varnish if desired.*

The creative use of a double cover makes these simple staple-bound books a surprise—and a treat for the eyes. Open one creative cardstock cover to reveal a second one nestled within! You can make your own hand-bound books with plain white paper and cardstock. Simply fold, stamp, and staple to make a book for doodling, stamping or journaling. This project is particularly well-suited for abstract stamping and for using repeat images in vertical rows. Embellish the stamped images with colored pencils or pastels, and add a raffia tie with beads or buttons to finish your book.

double-cover bound books

1 Cut two pieces of colored cardstock, one 8" x 8.5" (20 cm x 22 cm), the other 11" x 8.5" (28 cm x 22 cm). Fold each piece in half widthwise, pressing the fold down firmly with a bone folder or with the bowl of a spoon. Unfold; set aside.

2 Fold four pieces of plain or colored 11" x 8.5" (28 cm x 22 cm) paper in half widthwise. Press the fold down as described above. Then insert each paper into the fold of the others to create a folio; set aside. You may stamp and paint these papers or leave them blank, as desired.

3 Taking up the cardstock from step 1, stamp several repeat images in long columns with metallic ink. Overlap some stamp images, and sponge on additional colored inks or paints as desired. Collage items may be added, as well as beads and ribbon.

4 Insert the paper folio from step 2 into the fold of the largest piece of stamped cardstock; then fold this into the smaller piece of cardstock. This creates a layered double cover.

5 Open the book and staple the spine twice with a long-handled stapler. Scrap pieces of cardstock can be affixed to the spine to cover the staples, both inside and outside the book.

MATERIALS
- Cardstock
- Scissors
- Bone folder
- Paperstock
- Art stamps
- Sponge
- Metallic pigment ink
- Long-handled stapler

tips
- *For best results, choose high-quality cardstock and paper for this project. Poor-quality paper will either absorb too much ink or resist it entirely; it may tear easily and is generally difficult and disappointing to work with.*
- *A long-handled stapler is the only specialty item required for this project; most office supply and stationery stores carry them. Most photocopy shops make them available to their customers as well.*

artist: sherrill kahn, u.s.a

These exceptionally inventive and whimsical paper art dolls are a creative departure from the usual definition of the term. Although the dolls are not really designed for playtime, children will enjoy making their own with rubber stamps and inexpensive cardstock. The same pattern can be used over and over again to make as many different dolls as the imagination allows. Paper art dolls make fun gifts or party favors, and smaller versions can be affixed to layered cardstock for a special greeting card.

paper art dolls

1 Trace a Paper Art Doll pattern onto cardstock with a pencil (see Templates, p. 295). The pattern should include a torso, two arms, two legs, and a head and neck. Cut out the torso, arms, and legs, reserving the head-and-neck piece for later.
2 Use a makeup sponge to apply pigment or dye ink to the arms, legs, and torso, starting with the lightest colors first. Option: Apply the inked pad directly to the cardstock, but use a light touch.
3 Randomly stamp images with black permanent ink onto the colored doll parts. Placement of the stamp images is optional; a creative collage of stamped images can be successful.
4 Punch 1/8" (.5 cm) holes at the top of the torso near the shoulders, at the base of the neck, and in the hip area. Punch more holes at the top of each arm and leg. Set these pieces aside while you work on the doll's head and neck.
5 Lightly trace the head-and-neck pattern onto cardstock with a pencil, then choose a small- to medium-size rubber stamp to create hair—or perhaps a hat. The artist was creative in her use of nontraditional images for the hair on her dolls. Look closely: On each doll's head, you will find either a postal cancellation stamp, tiny pairs of scissors, or large coffee beans stamped in clusters. Once finished stamping, cut out the doll's head, neck, and hair as one piece. Apply ink to the doll's head and hair to simulate facial features and hairline. Draw or stamp eyes, nose, and mouth.
6 Assemble the doll pieces using tiny brads or eyelets that will allow for movement. Embellish with sheer ribbon for skirts, dangling charms for jewelry, jump-rings for earrings and bracelets, beaded wire for hair ornaments, or a piece of stamped accordion-folded cardstock to make a pleated skirt.

MATERIALS
- Paper doll pattern
- Cardstock
- Pencil
- Scissors
- Art stamps
- Makeup sponges
- Ink (dye or pigment)
- Black permanent ink
- Hole punch (1/8" or .5 cm)
- Tiny brads
- Embellishments: wire, buttons, beads, sheer ribbon, fibers, jump-rings

tips
- *For durable paper art dolls, be sure to use sturdy cardstock or manila file folders. Trace the doll pattern in any size, and cut out the pieces very precisely.*
- *To make a wide variety of fashion accessories for your dolls, use rubber stamp imagery on cardstock, or add ribbon, buttons, found objects, costume jewelry, beads, and charms.*

artist: naomi haikin, u.s.a

Sometimes a stamp image is so striking, it stands alone. Surrounded by a multicolored watercolor wash, this rockfish image hangs suspended over a seaweed bed of painted lace paper. A cleverly stamped frame sets off the composition nicely. By altering the stamp images and color schemes, you can make framed artwork that coordinates with your own home decor.

framed
watercolor painting

Watercolor Painting

1 Securely tape a piece of watercolor paper to a firm work surface. Tear off a piece of decorative lace paper (Japanese or Thai) and affix it to the center area of the watercolor paper using a paintbrush. Allow it to dry before proceeding.
2 Stamp the fish image in the center of the sheet (just above the lace paper) with permanent dye-based black ink. When it is dry, cover the fish image with art masking fluid to protect it from watercolor overlays. Allow it to dry completely.
3 Lightly mist the paper with water and drop paints into select areas, allowing them to flow naturally in a wet-into-wet technique. It's best to work from light to dark. Drop small amounts of isopropyl alcohol into the wet paint to create halo effects.
4 Once the surface is dry, remove the masking fluid with a rubber cement pick-up. Color inside the fish image with watercolor pencils, and use a black fine-line pen to go over the stamped image itself.
5 Using an old toothbrush, spatter white paint in some areas to suggest air bubbles.

Stamped Frame

1 Stamp overlapping sea-fan images in the upper left and lower right corners of the frame; emboss the images with gold powder. Stamp and emboss additional images of lily pads and fish as shown, using various colors of embossing powder.
2 Randomly sponge gold, lavender, and copper metallic paints onto the frame through a sheet of sequin waste, which acts as a stencil.
3 Spray the frame lightly with gold webbing spray.
4 Accent the fish and lily images with metallic gold leaf pens.
5 Lightly seal the frame surface with acrylic spray.

MATERIALS

- Masking tape
- Hot-press watercolor paper
- Decorative lace paper
- Adhesive
- Paintbrushes
- Art stamps
- Black permanent dye-based ink
- Art masking fluid
- Watercolors
- Isopropyl alcohol
- Rubber cement pick-up
- Watercolor pencils
- Black fine-line pen
- Toothbrush
- Bleed-proof white paint
- Wooden frame
- Gold embossing powder
- Embossing ink
- Embossing (heat) tool
- Sponges
- Metallic paints
- Sequin waste
- Gold webbing spray
- Gold leaf pens
- Acrylic spray

tips
- *Find art masking fluid, bleed-proof white paint, and other specialty art materials at art supply stores and in catalogs.*
- *Make sure the finished painting is bone dry before removing the masking tape and framing it. This will keep the paint from buckling.*

artist: leslie altman, U.S.A

Stamping on fabric to make handmade garments, art books, and home decor items is a fascinating, fast-growing field. Quilters, professional sewers, and interior decorators have discovered that rubber stamps are terrific tools for creating repeat patterns. The secret to a satisfactory outcome is to always use the highest-quality fabrics, dyes, and paints.

Canvas is usually stiff and sturdy—an excellent material for making tote bags, soft backpacks, floorcloths, window treatments, some upholstery projects, and stiff vests. Quality cotton and quilters' muslin with a tight weave are essential for good stamp impressions. Loosely woven fabrics tend to produce blurred images—use your stamped and painted cotton or muslin material to make soft art dolls, vests, jackets, quilts, and a variety of home decor accessories.

fabric stamping

Rayon often drapes better than cotton or muslin. It's the ideal fabric for stamped garments or home decor items that hang with soft folds. Make skirts, skorts, blouses, kimonos, wall hangings, window treatments, pillows, and similar items with plain white rayon stamped and painted with your personal touch. Silk is available in a variety of weights and textures. It may be dyed, painted, stenciled, and stamped with specially formulated fabric paints or dyes.

Velvet may be heat-embossed or stamped as usual with fabric paints. It's ideal for pillows, throws, soft jackets, vests, and upholstered items. When choosing velvet for heat-embossing, use silk, rayon, rayon-acetate, or any combination of these fibers. Rayon-acetate gives the most dramatic results, and the embossed images will be more long-lasting than on other fabrics. Avoid nylon, polyester, and any washable velvet.

Make garments from dark-colored muslin and cotton materials by stamping, stenciling, and painting with metallic fabric paints. They produce a soft glow when applied to dark fabrics that simply cannot be replicated on lighter colored materials. When stamping with ordinary fabric paint on dark fabrics, apply a layer of white fabric paint first, then stamp over it.

Stamped ribbon coordinates beautifully with gift wrap, but it's not limited to decorating gift boxes and bags. Consider making pretty stamped ribbons to embellish greeting cards, decorative boxes, artists' books, handmade journals, or home decor items. Starting with plain ribbon, dye or paint a soft-hued background. A light application of heat-set ink on your stamps will ensure success when working with small images. The stamped ribbon should be completely dry before it's used to embellish a gift or larger work of art. This project is very easy and can be completed in less than an hour, including drying time.

artist: denise ketterer, U.S.A

ribbon

MATERIALS

- Colored ribbon
- Water bottle
- Acrylic paint
- Paintbrushes
- Sponge
- Metallic paint
- Art stamps
- Crafter's ink
- Embossing (heat) tool

1 Spray a colored ribbon (orange, blue, and rose are shown here) with a water bottle to dilute the paint application.
2 Apply a wash of acrylic paint to the surface of the ribbon using either a big paintbrush or a sponge. Allow the paint to dry completely.
3 Rub metallic paint over the surface of the ribbon, and allow it to dry.
4 Stamp various images with crafter's ink in contrasting colors or metallics. Heat-set the impressions with an embossing (heat) tool, but take care not to scorch the ribbon.

tips

- *Fabric paint may be substituted for acrylics.*
- *To store ribbon and keep it from wrinkling, wrap it around a cardboard toilet paper roll. Tape the ends in place with a low-tack cellophane tape.*

Make your own fashion accessories from lengths of silk, dyes, and a large stamping block. Once heat-set, silk dyes are brilliant and permanent. Stamping dyed silk with a woodblock or hand-carved rubber eraser is much less time-consuming than layering applications of small art stamps— although that approach is perfectly acceptable as well. You can create intricate patterns by stamping images with different colors on top of one another, or by stamping and dyeing layers of complexity. There are many possible approaches to stamping a silk scarf; your choices of art stamps and dye colors add to the uniqueness of this project.

artist: paula grasdal, u.s.a

block-printed
silk scarf

1 Wash and dry the silk scarf. Stretch a piece of muslin onto a worktable. Then pin the washed and dried scarf to the surface. It should be taut once pinned.
2 If you choose to carve your own stamp, use the template provided (see Templates, p. 296).
3 Mix Procion dyes with a fixing agent according to the manufacturer's directions. Sponge and paint two similar colors onto the silk until it's saturated with dye. Keep scarf pinned while it dries completely. Mix darker color(s) of Procion dye, in the same color family as used previously, and combine with sodium alginate to thicken it. Roll into the thickened dye with a rubber brayer, then use the brayer to roll the dye onto an art stamp or large carved stamping block.
4 Beginning in the center of the dyed silk, apply the stamp to the surface. Lift stamp, apply more thickened dye, and stamp again until the entire surface is stamped.

MATERIALS
- White crepe de chine silk scarf
- Muslin
- Pins
- Art stamp or large stamping block
- Procion silk dyes
- Dye-fixing agent
- Sponges
- Sodium alginate
- Brayer

tips
- *Allow the silk to dry completely, heat-set, and then hand wash to remove excess dye. Some dyes may need to be heat-set with a steamer or by a professional.*
- *Place a layer of foam or carpet underlay beneath the muslin to ease the printing process.*
- *Experiment with background effects by mixing sodium alginate with the dyes before sponging and painting.*
- *Instead of carving a stamp, try making one by gluing cut pieces of cork or heavy felt to a wood block in an interesting manner.*

Fabric and paper roll-up beads are fun to make and easy enough for even young children to try, with adult supervision. All you need is a few scraps of fabric or painted paper, some fine-gauge wire, seed beads, and decorative fiber. By stamping the scraps with a highly textured rubber stamp image, you can make handmade beads customized to coordinate with any garment or jewelry item. Once you've made a collection of roll-up beads, string them on a simple necklace or use them to adorn a handmade book, stamped candles wrapped with raffia, or other stamping projects.

roll-up beads

1 Assemble a collection of torn paper or fabric strips approximately 1" x 5" (3 cm x 13 cm) on a stamping surface. Pour a puddle of acrylic paint with a strongly contrasting color onto a sheet of freezer paper, and dip a small sponge into it. Dab the sponge onto a rubber stamp, taking care to cover the entire stamp without applying too much paint.

2 Stamp the end of a strip, remove the stamp, and set the strip aside to air dry, which will take about 15 minutes at most. Heat-setting the fabric with an iron is optional.

3 Once you have stamped several strips of fabric or paper and allowed them to air dry, roll them on a dowel, a large knitting needle, a ballpoint pen, or a smooth chopstick. Roll the strip onto this implement partway, about 1" (3 cm). Then apply a generous amount of fabric glue or any thick, tacky glue to the back of the strip.

4 Continue to roll the strip and press down the edges with your fingers, applying more glue as needed. Once completely rolled, the bead can be removed and set on a nonstick surface such as freezer paper to dry for several hours or overnight.

5 The beads are lovely as is, but to enhance them, consider wrapping them with fine-gauge wire strung with seed beads and charms. Alternatively, wrap the beads with decorative yarn or fibers, securing them in place with glue. Use a small paintbrush to apply tiny amounts of metallic paint to the ends of each bead to coordinate with the wire or fiber. Allow the beads to dry completely before using them.

MATERIALS
- Fabric and/or paper
- Acrylic paint
- Freezer paper
- Sponge
- Art stamps
- Iron (optional)
- Rolling implement
- Fabric glue
- Paintbrushes
- Metallic paint
- Beads (optional)
- Yarn or fibers
- Wire

tips
- *This projects proves the stamp artist's axiom, "Never throw anything away." Leftover scraps of fabric from quilting and sewing projects, fabric you've dyed and painted with disappointing results, paintings and scraps of paper towel used to clean paint off your brushes—any of these materials may be used to make fabulous roll-up beads.*
- *The width of the paper or fabric strip determines the length of the bead, so consider tearing several strips in varying widths to increase your decorative options.*
- *Choose stamps with lots of texture. The actual image is not important because the fabric surface will be rolled up tightly. Small to medium-size stamps with intricate patterns work best.*
- *When finished stamping, carefully clean your stamps with a toothbrush and water. This is easiest when working with unmounted rubber stamps or hand-carved stamps.*

artist: sharilyn miller, u.s.a

This cheerful, whimsical napkin is easy and fun to make with scrap fabric. It makes a great practice piece before tackling larger items such as printed quilts or hand-stamped garments. Ordinary 100-percent cotton material is easy to obtain and works well for this project. Begin by ironing the fabric to create a smooth stamping surface. Dilute fabric paint or acrylics to a creamy consistency before sponge-dyeing the surface. Stamping with acrylics or fabric paint (full strength) over the painted background is a snap, and once the paint has dried, the napkins are easy to heat set with an ordinary iron.

artist: carolyn crowder, U.S.A

coffee
n a p k i n

MATERIALS
- Cotton material
- Pins
- Fabric paint
- Sea salt
- Sponges
- Muslin
- Iron
- Scissors
- Thread
- Needle

1 Use diluted fabric paint to sponge-dye the surface with interesting layers of color. To add starbursts, simply drop sea salt onto the damp surface and allow it to dry completely, then brush off.

2 Dip a sponge into fabric paint, and tap off any excess. Apply the painted sponge to the surface of a stamp, and then stamp the fabric. Repeat, using different colors as desired.

3 Once finished stamping, allow the fabric to dry completely. Heat-set the dye with an iron on the cotton setting, protecting the surface with a sheet of muslin or cotton between the painted fabric and the iron. Move the iron quickly over the surface to avoid scorching it. Once heat-set, the fabric may be safely laundered.

4 Trim the fabric to napkin size and sew the edges with a needle and thread or a sewing machine. Embroidery and beading techniques are optional.

tips
- *Smooth prewashed sturdy cotton fabric onto a worktable. If a taut surface is wanted, fit a piece of cardboard beneath the fabric and pin the fabric in place along the edges.*
- *Various colors of paint may be mixed and applied directly to the stamp for a marbled effect.*
- *Try using hand-carved stamps, real leaves, corks, vegetables, hand-carved potatoes, or kitchen implements instead of art stamps to make impressions on the fabric.*
- *Coordinate the colors of paint with your tableware, or make a batch of napkins for special occasions such as children's parties or even grown-up events.*

Customize a canvas tote with the stamps and paint colors of your choice! Perfect for college students on the go and seamstresses, quilters, and crafters, tote bags have never gone out of style. It's easy to make a fun and fashionable bag with metallic fabric paint and art stamps. Make a tote bag to celebrate a birthday, holiday, or other special occasion. Children will enjoy decorating their own tote bags with hand-carved stamps and bright paints. Try embossing the images for a shimmery effect. Any number of stamp combinations can be used on tote bags, and your paint choices are practically limitless.

artist: kathy meier, U.S.A

canvas
tote bag

1 To create a stamped border around the canvas tote bag, place the stamps (uninked) on the bag and determine how many stamped impressions are needed for the border design. Place masking tape around the perimeter of the planned design and use a pencil to mark the placement of each individual stamp.
2 Pour paint onto a freezer paper palette. Dip a sponge into the paint and apply it to the border stamp. Stamp where marked.
3 Use a different color paint to stamp a central design. Remove any masking tape. Allow all the paint to dry for 24 hours before heat-setting it by placing the bag in a commercial dryer for 45 minutes or by ironing it on the highest setting.

MATERIALS
• Tote bag
• Art stamps
• Masking tape
• Pen or pencil
• Fabric paint: green, metallic gold
• Freezer paper
• Sponges
• Iron or commercial dryer
• Embossing powder
• Embossing (heat) tool
• Small paintbrush

tips
• *Before the paint has dried, sprinkle it with embossing powder, allow it to sit for a few minutes, and then heat-set with an embossing (heat) tool. For best results, before embossing, remove any excess powder with a soft brush.*
• *Clean the stamps between each stamping impression for crisp images. Otherwise, dried paint may stick to the stamp and interfere with the images.*
• *If you choose not to emboss the images, use a small paintbrush to fill in paint details as needed because sometimes fabric will absorb paint from a stamped impression, and some areas may fade.*
• *Acrylic paint may be substituted for fabric paint. Add a bit of textile medium to the paint for optimum coverage.*

Create unique pillow beads with rubber stamps and tightly woven quilter's muslin.

Three simple steps—stamping, gluing, and stuffing—are all that is required. Appealing

to both adults and children, pillow beads can be used in various arts and crafts

projects. String them on a crocheted choker or add vintage beads, charms, and

pin backs to make decorative brooches. Dangle beads and charms, add clear

mosaic stones to enhance the imagery, or incorporate twisted wire into the design

of your beads.

pillow beads

1 Cut two pieces of fabric slightly larger than the stamp images you plan to use. The color of the fabric is not critical, as it will be stamped and painted on, but various effects can be achieved with different colors. White or cream-colored muslin can be stamped and painted with any pigment color, while black fabric is ideally suited to showing off metallic pigments.

2 Stamp one fabric piece with permanent ink. Remove the stamp and clean it right away (drop an unmounted stamp into a jar of water, or clean off a wood-mounted stamp with a moist cloth or baby wipe).

3 Allow the fabric to dry, then iron it to heat-set the ink. Paint the design with watered-down acrylics, using a paintbrush or fabric ink pens, and use a black permanent ink pen to add details.

4 Lay the two fabric pieces (from step 1) together, right sides out, and sandwich cotton balls between them while gluing the edges of the fabric together. Trim excess fabric and embellish each pillow bead with beads, decorative fibers, wire, charms, and painted designs.

5 Attach a pin back to a pillow bead to make a decorative brooch before using them.

MATERIALS
- Fabric
- Scissors
- Art stamps
- Permanent inkpad
- Water
- Iron
- Acrylics
- Fabric ink
- Permanent-ink pen
- Cotton balls
- Fabric glue
- Beads, charms, and fibers
- Pin backs
- Paintbrushes

tips
- *Embroider the pillow bead with floss.*
- *Finish the edges of each bead with paint, dip the painted edges into embossing powder, and heat-set immediately with an embossing tool.*
- *Instead of finishing the edges with paint, pull out the threads a bit to create a raveled edge.*
- *Substitute 200-count cotton sheeting material for quilters' muslin.*

artist: sandra mccall, U.S.A

Pillow bead necklaces are made with rubber stamps, paints, and cotton fabric. For this project, one prominent "pendant" bead (3" x 5" or 8 cm x 13 cm) is surrounded by stamped fabric pieces and smaller, accent pillow beads. Tiny roll-up beads dangle from the bottom, and the entire assemblage is sewn to a crocheted necklace band. Pillow bead necklaces are fun to make, but they are a bit more time-consuming than other fabric arts. It's best to create them in stages: Knit or crochet a necklace band, create several pillow beads, then assemble them on the band with beads and charms.

artist: sherrill kahn, U.S.A

pillow bead
necklace

MATERIALS

- Pillow beads
- Needle and thread
- Stuffing tool
- Cotton
- Fabric glue
- Acrylic paint
- Paintbrushes
- Seed beads
- Yarn

1 Create one large bead from the instructions in "Pillow Beads," but instead of gluing the edges of the bead together, hand-sew all the way around the perimeter of the design with strong thread and tiny stitches. Cut off the thread, then use a stuffing tool and tiny bits of cotton (smaller than a pea) to stuff the bead.

2 Paint the front of the bead, adding seed beads and charms as desired. Create two smaller stuffed beads, several fabric motifs, and small roll-up beads (see related material). Sew dangling roll-up beads with seed beads to the bottom edge of the large pillow bead. Use fabric glue to stick fabric motifs and more seed beads to the front of the large pillow bead until the composition is satisfactory.

3 Sew the pillow beads, roll-up beads, seed beads, and bits of stamped fabric to a crocheted necklace band as shown.

tips

- *Stamping with acrylic paint, permanent dye ink, or specially formulated fabric ink is optional. Heat-set the stamped image per manufacturer's instructions.*
- *Use a sewing machine if the pillow bead is a simple geometric shape, but if the stamped design is very intricate, it's much easier to sew it by hand.*
- *The pillow bead may be embroidered with floss before it is sewn and stuffed.*
- *Stuffing tools should be small, sturdy, and have a blunt pointed end. Try using a toothpick, a piece of sturdy wire, a knitting needle, or a straightened coat hanger. Take your time stuffing the bead to avoid creating lumps.*
- *The necklace band may be knitted, braided, woven, or knotted instead of crocheted.*

This cloth-covered diary is beautifully painted and embellished with a copper sheet that was first stamped and then blind-embossed. To blind emboss, a metal tool with a rounded tip called a stylus is used to press into the surface of the copper, creating a raised impression. The embossed design on this journal is successful because a large, impressive image was used, along with a freehand border drawn in an African-inspired pattern. Adding marbled papers and metallic beads to the cover is a quick and easy way to turn a store-bought journal into a personal diary.

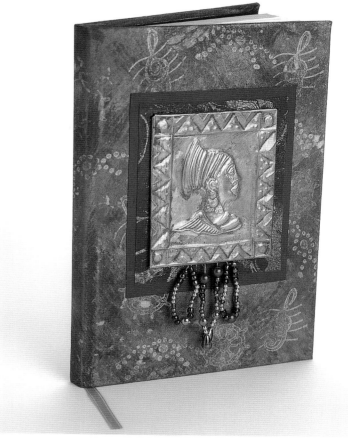

artist: lucy fitzgerald, AUSTRALIA

stamped & embossed diary

1 Use metallic pigment ink or acrylic paint to stamp images in a random fashion all over the book cover. Stamp both front and back covers, and use small stamps to decorate the spine. Set the book aside to dry.

2 Stamp a large, central image onto the copper metal sheet with permanent ink. Use an embossing stylus to impress the lines of the stamp design into the copper sheet, and add a freehand-drawn or stamped border. Turn under the edges of the copper sheet to measure approximately 3" x 3.5" (8 cm x 9 cm), and rub green acrylic paint into the crevices of the surface embossing to give the copper a patina look.

3 Cut decorative and/or marbled papers into rectangles approximately 3.75" x 4.25" (10 cm x 10.5 cm) and 4" x 4.75" (10 cm x 12 cm). Affix the papers in graduated layers to the center of the journal as shown. String three pieces of wire with beads and tie them into long loops. Attach the beaded wire to the decorative papers with jewelry adhesive.

4 Attach the embossed copper sheet to the journal cover using jewelry adhesive or caulking, and allow to dry.

MATERIALS

- Purchased book with a blank cover
- Metallic pigment ink or acrylic paint
- Art stamps
- Copper metal sheet, about 3.5" x 4" (9 cm x 10 cm)
- Green acrylic paint
- Permanent ink
- Embossing stylus
- Marbled papers
- Wire
- Beads
- Scissors
- Acrylics
- Jewelry adhesive or caulking

tips

- *When seeking diaries or blank journals to cover and decorate, look for books that can easily be stamped and embellished. Alternatively, make your own books from scratch—many books are available on this subject. When choosing a fabric-covered book, keep in mind that cloth with a tight weave provides the best stamping surface.*
- *The artist chose not to stamp the spine of this journal, but you easily can. Tiny alphabet stamps are a good choice for this area; you can even stamp a book "title" and author name, adding a date if space permits.*
- *Find copper metal sheets (sometimes called copper quilting metal) in art-supply and craft stores. The thin metal is specially made to be blind-embossed with a stylus.*

Chic and stylish, this topiary table setting makes a cheerful statement for springtime dining. Purchased woven placemats are custom-painted with small sponge stamps to add a decorative accent, while the colored napkins are easy to enhance with iron-on stamped muslin. Even the smallest, most detailed stamps can be utilized this way. The centerpiece for this table setting is the topiary placecards themselves. Made from Styrofoam and decorative dried moss inserted in small terra cotta pots, each placecard is a work of art and conversation piece in one.

stamped table setting

1 For the napkins, stamp an Eiffel Tower image onto white muslin with black fabric ink, and heat-set with a hot iron. Trim the fabric piece to the desired size; iron it to fusible webbing, then to a purchased napkin. Outline with a metallic gold pen suitable for fabric. Use a tied gingham ribbon as a napkin ring.

2 Prepare wood coasters for painting by cleaning and sanding them as necessary. Mask a rectangle in the center of the coaster and paint the top sage green. When completely dry, mask the green area, and paint the center rectangle with white acrylics. Allow to dry. Stamp the Eiffel Tower image in the center of the white rectangle with permanent black ink. Use small sponges to create a black and white checkered border around the rim of each coaster.

3 For the topiary placecard holders, paint small terra cotta pots in the same fashion as the coasters, stamping the rim with small sponge stamps, and seal with acrylic spray when dry. Fill the pots with Styrofoam and cover with moss; hot-glue in place. Attach moss to 3" (8 cm) Styrofoam balls with hot glue, then wrap with thin gingham ribbon as shown. Insert a straight twig or thin wooden dowel. Insert the bottom end of the twig or dowel in the moss-covered Styrofoam in the pot.

4 To make the placecards, stamp the Eiffel Tower image in black ink on white cardstock, trim, and affix to a piece of black cardstock. Trim and affix to a larger piece of white cardstock printed with a name, then edge the piece with a gold marker. Attach this to a final piece of black cardstock to create the layered place card.

5 Weave matching black and white gingham ribbon through the placemats, and glue it in place with hot glue or leave it loose as desired. Use small sponges to dab black and white paint to accent select areas of the placemat.

MATERIALS
- White muslin
- Black fabric ink
- Art stamps
- Scissors
- Iron
- Fusible webbing
- Napkins
- Metallic gold pen
- Gingham ribbon
- Wood coasters
- Sandpaper
- Masking tape
- Paintbrushes
- Acrylic paint
- Permanent black ink
- Small sponges
- Small terra cotta pots
- Acrylic spray sealant
- Dried moss
- 3" (8 cm) Styrofoam balls
- Hot glue and hot-glue gun
- Wooden dowels
- Cardstock
- Woven fabric placemats

tip
- *The artist used a computer to print the names of her luncheon guests, but you can substitute with hand lettering or stamping with an alphabet stamp set.*

artist: gaylynn stringham, u.s.a

Stamp and paint a cascading grapevine motif on your director's chairs to create a
stunning patio set. The resulting furniture will coordinate with your home or patio
decor easily and beautifully. Perfect for casual seating arrangements, a director's chair
can be folded and stored in a closet or under a bed when not in use. Using a
grapevine motif, create a realistic, dimensional effect by combining two or three paint
colors on each stamp impression. Add painted vines and leaf veins with a detail brush.
Be sure to take your chairs inside in inclement weather.

canvas director's chair

1 Lay out the canvas pieces. Squeeze light green ink and dark green ink on one small plastic plate. Spritz it lightly with water. Repeat with violet ink on the second plastic plate.
2 Use a soft sponge to apply paint to the rubber stamps. Stamp both pieces of canvas. Repeat stamping two or three more times before re-inking to create a soft, layered look.
3 To connect groupings of stamped images, add vines, stems, and tendrils with a fine detail brush, adding a bit of water to the ink if necessary to improve flow.
4 Heat-set the canvas in one of two ways: Apply heat from an embossing tool, moving the tool in circles to avoid scorching the fabric. Alternatively, set an iron on the hottest setting, lay the completed canvas pieces face-down on a paper bag, cover them with another paper bag, and iron the sandwiched fabric in a circular motion for about a minute.
5 Assemble the completed chair in a frame as shown.

MATERIALS
- Canvas director's chair with wood frame
- Bottled crafter's ink (violet, light green, and dark green)
- Two small plastic plates
- Squirt bottle
- Water
- Sponges
- Acrylics
- Art stamps
- Black foam brush
- Detail paintbrush
- Iron and brown paper bag as pressing cloth or an embossing (heat) tool

artist: babette cox, U.S.A

tips
- *Protect your work area with a dropcloth and have two large jars of water handy for rinsing paintbrushes and sponges.*
- *Practice stamping on scrap newsprint before commencing this project, as stamping with dense foam art stamps can be challenging at first.*
- *Note that dense foam block stamps have accent lines cut deeply into the foam. The dark green ink must be pushed down into these grooves with the tip of a black foam brush. Brush light green across the top. Accenting with a small amount of purple on the top of the leaf along with the lighter green is an option.*
- *The tendril accents require a bit of practice. Add a bit more water to the dark green ink. Load a detail brush with diluted ink and make a few swirls on a piece of scrap paper. When you feel comfortable, apply a few tendrils to the canvas. As a general rule, fewer tendrils and accents look better than too many.*

Natural leaves lend a realistic jungle appearance to this fabulous hand-stamped shower curtain. It's easy to achieve the look by placing real leaves in a random pattern on the curtain, then spraying it with several shades of green fabric paint. That's the secret to success: By using many shades of green instead of just one or two, the artist created a lovely layered look to the background imagery. Once the paint has dried, adding a metallic green border and pretty palm trees is a snap with rubber stamps. By stamping and painting your own shower curtain, you save money while decorating your bathroom with the colors and images of your choice.

artist: michelle newman, U.S.A

jungle
shower curtain

MATERIALS

- Large plastic dropcloth
- White or light-colored fabric shower curtain
- Leaves
- Fabric paint in several shades of green
- Spray bottles for each shade of green paint
- Sponges
- Metallic green paint
- Art stamps
- Iron or commercial dryer

1 Spread the dropcloth onto the floor to protect it from spilled paint. Lay the curtain on top of the dropcloth, smoothing out the folds.

2 Drop leaves onto the curtain in a random pattern.

3 Pour green paint into each spray bottle and add water (about 3 parts water to 1 part paint). Shake, then insert the spray nozzle in each bottle. Spray the shower curtain with the lightest shade of green paint, reposition the leaves, and then spray with a darker green. Continue rearranging leaves and spraying on paint until you run out of colors.

4 Once the paint has dried, discard the leaves. Sponge metallic green paint onto a border stamp (such as the Greek Key border shown here); stamp a border. Apply metallic green paint to a palm tree stamp and stamp that image over the remainder of the curtain.

tips

- *Allow the curtain to dry for 24 hours. Then iron the back or place the curtain in a commercial dryer for 45 minutes to heat-set the paints.*
- *Try using a different color scheme and stamp imagery to create custom looks for the guest bathroom.*
- *Make a shower curtain for the children's bathroom by using large puzzle pieces in place of leaves. Paint the curtain in bright colors to lighten an otherwise dim bathroom.*

Customize plain window treatments with the colors and images of your choice by printing them with large decorator stamps. By making your own curtains or shades, you can enhance the decor of your living room, den, bedroom, or home office. Try using hand-carved stamps, real leaves, corks, vegetables, hand-carved potatoes, or kitchen implements instead of commercial art stamps to make impressions on the fabric. Create fun-inspired curtains for your child's bedroom as well—kids can help decorate with potato stamps or even their own handprints.

artist: michelle newman, U.S.A

stamped curtain

1 Smooth a ready-made curtain onto a worktable. If a taut surface is wanted, fit a piece of cardboard beneath the fabric and pin it in place along the edges.
2 Pour acrylic paint onto a freezer paper palette, and dip a sponge into it. Tap off excess. Apply the painted sponge to the surface of a stamp, then stamp the fabric. Repeat, using different colors as desired.
3 Once finished stamping, allow the fabric to dry for 24 hours. Heat-set with an iron on the cotton setting, protecting the surface with a sheet of muslin or cotton between the painted fabric and the iron. As this is delicate fabric, move the iron quickly over the surface to avoid scorching it.
4 Hang the curtain as shown. Tie decorative silver cording with tassels at intervals.

MATERIALS
- Ready-made curtains of chiffon-type sheer fabric (polyester, cotton, organza)
- Acrylic paint: lavender, purple lilac, heather, metallic amethyst
- Freezer paper
- Sponges
- Art stamps
- Iron
- Silver cording with tassels

tips
- *When stamping, acrylic paints or inks may be substituted for fabric paints. Heat-set with an iron. If using acrylic paint, mix in a little textile medium for more even coverage.*
- *Paint colors may be mixed and applied directly to the stamp for a marbled effect.*
- *Coordinate the colors of paint and curtains with the room's decor. Creating curtains for the kids' rooms? Have them make painted handprints on the fabric (see the section on stamping with hands) with nontoxic washable paints or inks. Heat-set the fabric when dry.*

This lovely tablecloth with felt topper makes a beautiful fashion statement in the home, and it's easy to make with metallic paints and foam sponge stamps. To create the topper, large sponges cut into fun shapes are used to stamp the surface of a piece of felt. The tablecloth skirt is also made with felt and similarly stamped, then decorated with a pretty cord around the edges. Use your tablecloth and topper in the kitchen, living room, or bedroom. The paint colors and styles of stamps you choose will dictate the best place to display your handiwork.

tablecloth &
felt table topper

Topper

1 Pour the paint onto a Styrofoam plate. Dip the sponge stamps into the paint and stamp off excess.
2 Spread the felt on a flat padded surface. Stamp randomly on the felt surface; allow it to dry completely. Add paint strokes in a random fashion.
3 Sew decorative beaded fringe around the edge of the topper, or attach it securely with strong adhesive.

Tablecloth Skirt

1 Pour the paint onto a Styrofoam plate. Dip the sponge stamps into the paint and stamp off excess.
2 Spread the felt on a flat padded surface. Stamp a border about 1" (3 cm) from the edge, adding smaller stamped impressions for accents. Allow the paint to dry completely.
3 Sew metallic antique gold twisted cord around the perimeter of the skirt.
4 Arrange on a round table and add table topper.

MATERIALS

- Metallic paint: black, Inca gold, pure gold, antique gold, metallic aluminum
- Styrofoam plate
- Sponge stamps
- Felt: 36" x 36" (91 cm x 91 cm)
- Padded surface
- Flat paintbrush
- Beaded fringe
- Hand-sewing supplies or adhesive
- 2.5 yards (2.3 m) felt cut into a large circle
- 7 yards (6.4 m) metallic antique gold twisted cord

tips

- *Any acrylic-based paint may be substituted for metallic paint.*
- *For best results, practice stamping on scrap felt until you can stamp with the correct amount of pressure for adequate coverage without blurring the image. Once you have stamped the images, if some areas appear to be faded due to lack of colorant, use a flat paintbrush to apply extra paint as needed.*

artist: michelle newman, u.s.a

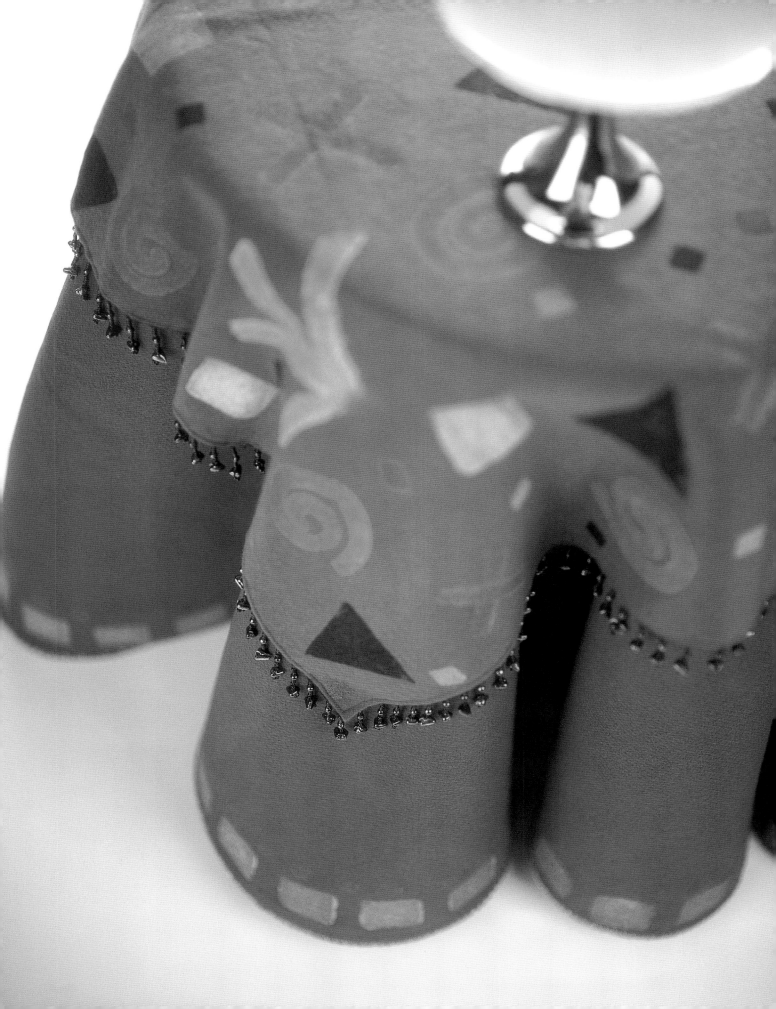

Botanical prints of natural leaves are ideal images for this lovely fabric wine bottle bag. The cool green and metallic paint colors lend a bright and cheerful air to these pieces, but they could just as easily reflect an autumn theme with the use of deep orange and earth-tone paints. Alternatively, try using deep green and burgundy paint on cream-colored fabrics for holiday table settings. By using natural leaves as stamps, you can create custom table decor that could never be duplicated by another artist. For best results, stamp with fresh green leaves featuring prominent veins. Use a new leaf each time you make a print to avoid smears from dried paint and to ensure a clear print.

canvas wine
bottle bag

artist: kathy meier, U.S.A

1 Gather fresh leaves with prominent veins. Clean and dry each leaf prior to stamping. To apply paint to the leaves, pour a small amount of paint onto a freezer paper palette (or other nonstick surface). Use a sponge to dab into the paint, then stamp off excess before applying it to the back of a leaf.

2 Lay the leaf paint-side down on the fabric gift bag in a pleasing arrangement, cover the leaf with clean paper, and roll a brayer over it firmly to transfer the paint to the fabric. Remove the paper and the leaf.

3 Repeat stamping as desired until the bag has been decorated to your satisfaction. Heat-set the paint by ironing the cloth on the highest setting.

MATERIALS
- Leaves
- Metallic paints: gold, russet, bronze, silver, pearl emerald green
- Freezer paper
- Sponge
- Cloth bag
- Clean paper
- Brayer
- Embossing (heat) tool

tips
- *When applying paint to leaves, try using two or three colors from the list provided (for example, pearl emerald green with russet and gold) to create a marbled appearance. Alternatively, apply light paint colors to the center of the leaf and darker colors to the outside edges.*
- *Immediately after removing the paper and leaf and before the paint has had a chance to dry, sprinkle the painted areas with embossing powder and heat-set with an embossing (heat) tool.*
- *As you gain confidence stamping small fabric pieces with leaves, consider making a large tablecloth with a leaf-stamped border, a holiday apron, or stamping on a blouse or skirt. Children enjoy stamping with leaves, too. Purchase inexpensive T-shirts for them to practice on.*

Here's a fun weekend project: Make a pretty stamped muslin pillow! All you need is a pillow form, muslin fabric, and paint. For best results, purchase quilters'-quality material and wash the fabric before stamping and painting it. Heat-set the paint with an iron; the pillow comes together quickly. You can share this easy project with your children, as the fabric and painting materials are relatively inexpensive and readily available. Brighten up any room in the house with your own hand-stamped pillows!

artist: lenna andrews foster, U.S.A

muslin pillow

1 Dip a sponge into fabric paint; tap off excess. Apply the painted sponge to the surface of a stamp, then stamp the fabric. Repeat, using different colors as desired.
2 Once finished stamping, allow the fabric to dry for 24 hours, then heat-set it with an iron on the cotton setting, protecting the surface with a sheet of muslin or cotton between the painted fabric and the iron. Move the iron quickly over the surface to avoid scorching it.
3 Trim the decorated muslin, if necessary. With right sides facing, sew three edges together with a sewing machine. Insert a pillow form and hand-stitch the remaining side with needle and thread.

MATERIALS
- Muslin material, enough to cover a pillow with seam allowance
- Sponges
- Fabric paint
- Art stamps
- Scissors
- Sewing machine
- Hand-sewing supplies

tips
- Smooth prewashed muslin fabric onto a worktable. If a taut surface is wanted, fit a piece of cardboard beneath the fabric and pin the fabric in place along the edges.
- Acrylic paints or inks may be substituted for fabric paints. Heat-set with an iron. If using acrylic paint, mix in a little textile medium for more even coverage.
- Various colors of paint may be mixed and applied directly to the stamp for a marbled effect.
- Try using hand-carved stamps, real leaves, corks, vegetables, hand-carved potatoes, or kitchen implements to make impressions on the fabric.
- Coordinate the colors of paint with your room decor. Make throw pillows in bright colors for children's rooms and holiday parties.
- Finish the pillow with embroidery and beading techniques if desired.

The striking design of this velvet-covered book belies the simplicity of the technique. An attractive accordion-fold book is beautifully bound with this luscious fabric. Folded paper, bookboard, velvet material, and rubber stamps are all you need to get started. The best results are achieved with bold, solid images—stamps designed with fine detail are easily lost in the plush velvet. Bold embossed images have great impact and hold up well to dry cleaning, too. For this reason, hand-carved stamps are terrific.

Embossed velvet can be used in a myriad of projects, from pillow covers to evening gowns. When choosing velvet, use silk, rayon, acetate-rayon, or any combination of these fibers. Rayon-acetate gives the most dramatic results, and the embossed images will be more permanent than with other fabrics. Avoid nylon, polyester, or any washable velvet.

stamped velvet book

1 Preheat the iron on the cotton setting. Lightly mist either side of the cut fabric. Place the stamp rubber-side up on an ironing board.

2 Lay the fabric nap-side down against the stamp, and hold it firmly in place with one hand. Press the heated iron against the fabric, taking care not to move it while you count to twenty. Then lift up the iron carefully, and peel away a corner of the velvet to examine the impression.

3 It may be necessary to press the fabric again for up to 10 seconds. A few trial runs with test fabric before attempting the actual project will make you an expert. Once the impression has been heat-set into the velvet, repeat the process until the entire piece of fabric has been embossed.

4 Cut out two pieces of velvet, approximately 6" x 7.5" (15 cm x 19 cm). Apply high-quality wet glue or double-stick tape to the backside of the velvet pieces. Lay the velvet down, adhesive-side up, and, centering the bookboard, lay it on the adhesive. Remove any wrinkles before cutting away the corners of the velvet.

5 Fold over the velvet. Repeat this process with the second bookboard and cut velvet material.

6 Draw a line horizontally across the middle of one of the bookboards, and apply dots of wet adhesive or double-stick tape to the line. Lay the ribbon along this line, centered. Set aside to dry.

7 For the accordion-fold pages, measure and cut a piece of sturdy paper or cardstock to 5.5" x 3.5" (14 cm x 9 cm). Fold the paper into eight panels. Using wet adhesive or double-stick tape, create an "X" on the back of each outer panel, and adhere the bookboards to them. Fold together the paper pages and tie the ribbon from back to front to hold the book together.

MATERIALS

- Template (see p. 297)
- Iron
- Water bottle with water
- Velvet
- Bold fabric stamps
- Paper
- Scissors
- Adhesive
- Bookboard
- Ribbon (approximately 1 yard or 1 meter)

tips

- *If the material is creased, steam out the wrinkles first. Then cut the material to a manageable size, about 2" (5 cm) bigger around than needed for the final project.*
- *Test heat-embossing with velvet scraps. The iron should be at the correct temperature before you proceed with the actual project.*
- *Look out for steam holes in the iron face—they will interfere with the embossed design. If you can find an iron with steam holes placed around the edges, so much the better. If not, a Teflon pressing cloth may be used to protect the velvet.*
- *If you used wet adhesive for this project, allow the book to dry for at least 24 hours.*

artist: mary o'neil, u.s.a

This beautiful velvet throw was heat-embossed with rubber stamps and sewn with a luscious satin liner and fringe. The bold stamps the artist used were designed specifically for this type of project; finely detailed stamps will not work as well because the intricate designs may be lost in the plush fabric. Try making a velvet throw with your own hand-carved stamps. This one can be made in about an hour.

artist: mary o'neil, u.s.a

velvet
embossed throw

MATERIALS

- 3 yards velvet (2.7 meters)
- Scissors
- Iron
- Water bottle with water
- Bold fabric stamps
- 3 yards satin (2.7 meters)
- Sewing machine
- 6 yards (5.5 meters) bullion fringe

1 Cut the 3-yard (2.7 meters) piece of velvet in half for two pieces of fabric 54" x 28" (137 cm x 71 cm). Preheat the iron on the cotton setting. Lightly mist one side of the cut fabric. Place a stamp rubber-side up on an ironing board.

2 Lay the fabric nap-side down against the stamp. Hold it firmly in place with one hand. Press the heated iron against the fabric, taking care not to move it while you count to twenty. Lift the iron carefully, then peel away a corner of the velvet to examine the impression. Reheat for up to 10 seconds if necessary. Repeat heat embossing until both pieces of fabric have been embossed.

3 Sew the two velvet pieces together to create one piece 54" (137 cm) square. Cut a lining of the same dimensions from satin fabric. Lay the lining and velvet fabric pieces right sides together and sew them in place, leaving a 6"–8" (15–20 cm) opening. Turn the fabric piece inside out and sew the opening closed. Attach 6" (15 cm) bullion fringe around the perimeter of the throw.

tips

- *If the material is creased, steam out the wrinkles first.*
- *Test heat-embossing with velvet scraps. The iron should be at the correct temperature before you proceed with the actual project.*
- *Look out for steam holes in the iron face—they will interfere with the embossed design. If you can find an iron with steam holes around the edges, so much the better. If not, a Teflon pressing cloth may be used to protect the velvet material.*

Velvet pillows can be expensive, but you can save money by making your own with good-quality velvet and the pillow pattern of your choice. First, choose velvet material in colors that complement your home decor. Select bold patterned stamps—avoid finely detailed stamps with intricate designs—and heat-emboss the fabric. Finally, construct the pillow according to the pattern directions. A diagram for making the ball pillow is included in the Templates section.

artist: mary o'neil, U.S.A

velvet embossed pillows

1 Lightly mist one side of the cut fabric. Place a stamp rubber-side up on an ironing board. Lay the fabric nap-side down against the stamp. Hold it firmly in place with one hand. Press the heated iron against the fabric, taking care not to move it while you count to twenty. Lift the iron carefully, then peel away a corner of the velvet to examine the impression. Repeat embossing for up to 10 seconds if necessary, and then emboss the entire piece of fabric.

2 For the ball pillow, enlarge the template design on a photocopier until the pattern is at least 12" (30 cm) long. Cut out the pattern and use it to create eight identical pieces of embossed fabric.

3 With right sides facing, sew two pieces of fabric together from point to point. Repeat with the remaining six pieces, leaving a 6" (15 cm) opening in the last panel. Turn the pillow inside out and stuff it with fiberfill until the ball is well rounded. Sew the opening closed by hand. Use a doll needle to sew a large button onto the center of the pillow or to attach a tassel.

MATERIALS
- Velvet
- Water bottle with water
- Bold fabric stamps
- Iron
- Template (see p. 298)
- Scissors
- Sewing machine
- Fiberfill
- Doll needle
- Hand-sewing materials
- Tassel
- Button

tips
- *If the material is creased, steam out the wrinkles first.*
- *Test heat-embossing with velvet scraps. The iron should be at the correct temperature before you proceed with the actual project.*
- *Look out for steam holes in the iron face—they will interfere with the embossed design. If you can find an iron with steam holes around the edges, so much the better. If not, a Teflon pressing cloth may be used to protect the velvet material.*
- *Any pillow pattern may be substituted for the ball pillow used in this project. Find patterns for pillows and other home decor items in fabric and craft stores.*

Although art dolls are often made of fabric, lace, buttons, and similar materials associated with ordinary dolls, the finished artwork seen here is truly exceptional. Stamped and painted fabric is sewn together, stuffed, and embellished with wooden numerals, window screen material, or other found items. They may be whimsical, but more often art dolls are serious forms of creative expression. While they make lovely decorations, their true purpose is found in the act of creation. Crafting an art doll is a very personal—sometimes spiritual—journey. As you make your own art dolls, incorporate personal mementos that have special significance for you.

fabric art dolls

1 Cut out two pieces of muslin fabric a little larger than the pattern provided in the Templates section (see p. 299). Prewashing is optional.
2 Pour acrylic paints onto a freezer paper palette and roll a brayer into them. Mixing two or three colors of paint will produce a marbled effect. Roll the brayer in the paint and apply it to the muslin fabric in quick, rough strokes, allowing some of the raw muslin to show through.
3 Let the fabric dry completely before stamping various images with acrylic paint, applying the paint to the stamps with a sponge. Make small dots by stamping with a pencil eraser.
4 To create the doll's face, stamp a face image with black fabric ink on scrap muslin. Allow the ink to dry, then color in the face with colored pencils and watercolor crayons. Cut it out in a circle and hand-stitch it to the doll's body, allowing the edges to ravel. Heat-set the fabric with an iron on the highest setting.
5 Begin stitching the two fabric pieces together, right sides facing; then turn the doll inside out and stuff it with cotton balls or fiberfill. Hand-stitch the last seam.
6 To attach legs, paint .25" (.5 cm) dowels with stripes of acrylic paint and cut them to size. Then insert a tiny eyehook into one end of each dowel. Sew the eyehooked dowels to the bottom edge of the stuffed doll.

variation

See materials list above.

Follow the same basic procedure described above to create this art doll (opposite, right), with the following exceptions:
1 Use a piece of plastic embroidery canvas as a stencil to sponge blue acrylics through; then overstamp this area with black paint.
2 Use ordinary window screen material as a stencil to sponge through silver acrylic paint. Accent with a silver gel pen.
3 Stamp the face onto paper, color it with colored pencils, cut it out, and then glue it into a small tin box. Glue this onto another piece of tin (from a can bottom or snuff container lid). Punch a few holes around the perimeter so the piece can be sewn to the doll's head.
4 Cut a small piece of stained window screen material and sew it to the surface of the doll, filling the screen material with buttons or other found items.

MATERIALS
- Muslin fabric with a tight weave
- Scissors
- Acrylics
- Freezer paper
- Brayer
- Sponge
- Art stamps
- Pencil eraser
- Fabric ink
- Colored pencils
- Watercolor crayons
- Iron
- Hand-sewing supplies
- Cotton balls or fiberfill
- .25" (.5 cm) dowels
- Eyehooks

tips
- *Write poems, dreams, goals, and wishes on scraps of paper and insert them into the doll.*
- *Before stuffing and sewing it, dangle charms or discarded costume jewelry from the doll, or sew beads or embroidery ribbon to the surface.*
- *Embellish the doll with a handmade wire necklace or beaded jewelry.*
- *In areas of dark painted fabric, overstamp background text stamps or similar imagery with white fabric paint.*

artist: olivia thomas, u.s.a.

Mariano Fortuny was a legendary designer who lived in Venice in the early twentieth century. His sumptuous velvets and silks printed with rich metallic pigments were highly sought after by the wealthy of Europe and North America. Unfortunately, when Fortuny died, his secret printing techniques went with him, but you can duplicate the look with modern-day metallic paints, art stamps, and fine velvet material. Your finished artwork will rival Fortuny's famous pillows at a fraction of the cost. Look for crushed velvet or velveteen; the types of velvet recommended for embossing will not work well with this technique.

Fortuny velvet pillows

1 Cut one piece of light blue velvet into a strip measuring about 18" x 6" (46 cm x 15 cm) for the middle panel, and two pieces of dark purple velvet into strips measuring about 18" x 3.25" (46 cm x 8.5 cm) for the two side panels. Trim another piece of velvet or comparable fabric that measures about 11" x 18.5" (28 cm x 47 cm) for the backing; set aside. Pin the three velvet strips to a padded surface with T-pins.

2 Pour metallic green paint onto a freezer paper palette. Dip a sponge into the paint, apply it to a leaf-shaped rubber stamp, and stamp across the two purple velvet panels, leaving about 1" (3 cm) between stamped images. Add large dots of purple paint with a round sponge or a rubber stamp.

3 Repeat the process with the light blue panel, printing a large pattern stamp in light purple paint. Allow all the panels to dry completely.

4 With right sides together, sew the three panels together lengthwise, leaving a .25" (.5 cm) seam allowance. To cover seams, apply strips of olive green trim with strong fabric glue or a sewing machine. Lay the front piece against the back piece (from step 1), right sides together, and sew almost all the way around, leaving a .25" (.5 cm) seam allowance.

5 Turn the pillow inside out and stuff it with fiberfill or a pillow form. Sew the opening closed by hand. Add decorative trim as desired.

MATERIALS
- Velvet: dark purple and light blue
- Scissors
- Padded surface
- T-pins
- Acrylic paints: metallic green, light purple, blue
- Freezer paper
- Sponge
- Art stamps
- Sewing machine or strong fabric glue
- Fiberfill or pillow form
- Hand-sewing supplies
- Trims

variation

- Another beautiful Fortuny pillow featured above has three middle panels and two outside panels. Stamp, paint, and sew the panels together before stuffing and trimming the pillow as described above.

tips
- *If the material is creased, steam out the wrinkles first.*
- *Test incorporating heat-embossed velvet panels with stamped velveteen panels. Consult the instructions for the stamp-embossed velvet book. Many quilting patterns can be used on this project; don't be afraid to experiment.*
- *Any pillow pattern may be substituted for the pillow used in this project. Find patterns for pillows and other home decor items in fabric and craft store pattern books.*

artist: michelle newman, u.s.a

home decor stamping

Handmade home decor items have never been more popular. The best thing about making your own decorative accessories is that each and every piece is custom-made to your specifications, using your color schemes and images that coordinate with existing furnishings. To purchase custom-made pillows, tiles, glass plates, and stemware would be much more costly than making them yourself—not to mention a lot less fun for you and your family.

The simplest projects include stamped light switch plates, star fruit coasters, candles, wooden keepsake boxes, and the floral mirror. As you gain experience and begin to master the basic painting and stamping skills required, try making kiln-fired tiles, a Japanese clock, stamping on walls, or painting pretty terra cotta pots.

As you complete each design, consider ways to vary the technique or apply your new skills to other home decor accessories. For example, the star fruit coasters are lovely examples of nature stamping with actual star fruit. Apply the same principle to stamping a child's bedroom walls or furniture as well as glass plates. Polymer clay can be used to form small decorative boxes, picture frames, and works of art for display in a bookcase. Wood boxes of all shapes and sizes can be painted, stamped, and embossed for a variety of purposes, from jewelry boxes to large furniture pieces. And you are by no means limited to these projects and ideas! When rubber stamps are combined with home decor projects, there are virtually no limitations to what you can do.

Complement any interior design scheme with stamped light-switch plates! A simple three-step process renders beautiful plates for decorating the kitchen, bath, living room, bedroom, or children's playroom. All you need is acrylic paint and a stamp. Start by painting a light application of acrylic-based paint onto inexpensive plastic light-switch plates. Allow the paint to dry, and consider applying a second coat in metallic colors. Once the surface is dry, apply more acrylic paint to your stamps and impress as many images as you desire. This technique works quite well with background stamps as well as small individual art stamps.

artist: sharilyn miller, U.S.A

light switch plates

MATERIALS
- Plastic light switch plates
- Paintbrush
- Acrylic paint
- Freezer paper
- Sponge
- Art stamps
- Acrylic sealer

1 Wipe the plate with a soft cloth, then apply one or two base coats of paint to the plate. Let dry for several hours between coats.
2 Pour two or three complementary paint colors onto a freezer paper palette (see Palette, p. 12). Dip a small square sponge into the paint and stamp off excess. Apply the painted sponge to an art stamp, tapping it on lightly, and coat the stamp evenly with paint.
3 Stamp the light switch plate, holding the stamp firmly in place without moving it. Remove the stamp carefully, apply more paint, and stamp again.

tips
- *You can find inexpensive plastic light switch plates at most hardware and home improvement stores.*
- *Once the switch plate has dried completely, apply several light coats of acrylic spray to seal it.*
- *Pigment ink may be substituted for acrylic paint when stamping, and the images may be embossed (see "Stamp Basics" for embossing techniques).*
- *Try using single stamp images, such as the bee or the seashells shown, as well as large background stamps. Both types work well for this project.*
- *If the paint smudges while stamping, clean it off immediately with a damp sponge. Repaint the surface if necessary, and stamp again. Too much paint on the stamp will cause the image to blur, and too little will leave a faint imprint.*

Nothing gives a room a more pleasant ambience than soft candlelight. Using rubber stamps, you can turn unadorned candles into elegant home decor items that complement your interior design. The process takes just a few minutes and it couldn't be easier: Heat and stamp—you're done! Be sure to purchase candles with flat sides as it can be difficult to stamp cylindrical candles without smudging the images.

artist: sharilyn miller, U.S.A

stamping on
candles

1 Apply pigment ink to an art stamp with bold images, and set it aside.
2 Lay a candle on its side on a pile of newsprint. Use the embossing (heat) tool to heat one side of the candle for 5–10 seconds. Take special care not to overheat and melt it.
3 When the candle surface is soft and pliable, press the inked rubber stamp into it firmly and allow it to set for 1–2 minutes. Gently pry it away from the candle; if it seems to be gripped by the candle wax, wait a few more seconds. When the candle surface has cooled sufficiently, the stamp should release easily, especially if you coated it first with pigment ink.
4 Repeat steps 1–3 until the entire candle has been stamped. Allow the candle to cool completely.

MATERIALS
• Pigment ink
• Art stamps
• Candles with flat sides
• Newsprint
• Embossing (heat) tool
• Metallic rub-ons (optional)
• Metallic acrylic paints (optional)
• Paintbrush (optional)

tips
• *Cover your work surface with newsprint to protect it from melted wax.*
• *Art stamps with thick lines and bold images are best for this technique; finely detailed stamps will not work well.*
• *When embellishing the candle with metallic rub-ons or paint, avoid getting color into the impressed areas of the stamped candle. The idea is to subtly highlight the stamped imagery by gently applying metallic color to the raised areas alone.*
• *Use metallic rub-ons or metallic acrylic paints to apply a sheen to the raised areas of the stamped candle. If using acrylics, dip a paintbrush into the paint and brush most of the paint onto a paper towel before applying it in a dry brush fashion.*

Charming paper placemats are just the thing for backyard parties or children's celebrations—and this is such a quick and easy project, you won't mind making dozens of placemats. Get the kids involved! They can use potato stamps or handprints as well as textured sponges and background stamps to create their own placemats. Stamp tissue papers with colorful acrylic paints, cut the tissue into strips, and weave them together. You can also use woven papers for collage elements in greeting cards or gift boxes.

artist: livia mcree, U.S.A

woven paper placemats

MATERIALS

- Colored tissue paper, nonbleeding
- Acrylics
- Freezer paper to use as palette
- Sponges
- Texture stamps
- Scissors
- Adhesive
- Removable tape
- White cardstock

1 Smooth a half sheet of tissue onto a washable work surface. Squeeze two or three colors of paint onto a freezer paper palette (see Palette, p. 14). Tap a sponge into the paint, and apply the sponge to a large background stamp.

2 Stamp the tissue paper in a random pattern. Repeat the process by stamping complementary colors of paint on another half sheet of colored tissue paper. Allow both papers to dry completely. Cut the stamped tissue paper into sixteen strips measuring 5/8" x 11" (1.5 cm x 28 cm) and ten strips measuring 7/8" x 10" (2 cm x 25 cm).

3 Lay the long tissue strips down side by side. Temporarily affix one end of each to the worktable with removable tape. Weave the short tissue papers through the long tissue papers, selecting colors at random.

4 Remove the resulting mat from the worktable and apply double-stick tape or a glue stick to the back. Place the mat on a large sheet of white cardstock. The cardstock creates a sturdy base while intensifying the colors of the painted tissue.

variation

- To make greeting cards, cut 2" (5 cm) squares from the stamped and woven paper placemats. Mount these squares directly to folded cardstock, leaving a 1/16" (1.5 mm) space between the blocks, or mount the squares to separate cardstock pieces before mounting them to folded cardstock.

tips

- *Combine paint colors and tissue colors at random.*
- *Choose color schemes that match your dinnerware, or purchase party plates in advance and create paper placemats to match them.*
- *Substitute textured sponges for background stamps. Because the papers will be cut into strips, any stamped image will do.*
- *Metallic paints are a nice accent for this project.*

Coordinate your home and garden decor with stamped and painted terra cotta pottery. Inexpensive pottery can be found at most hardware and home-improvement stores. Use leftover water-based paint from an indoor or outdoor wall painting project for base painting, and then add two or three colors of complementary paints to create a sponged- and painted-on design that matches your decor. A word to the wise: Unmounted stamps are highly recommended for this project, as they mold easily around the surface of a pot.

artist: sharilyn miller, U.S.A

terra cotta
pots

1 Clean the pottery with a scrub brush and water, and air dry. Seal the pottery inside and out with a pottery sealer, and allow to dry completely.

2 Apply one or two base coats of paint to the entire pot, inside and out, allowing the paint to dry for several hours between each coat. Pour two or three complementary paint colors onto a freezer paper palette. Dip a small square sponge into the two lightest colors and stamp off the excess paint. Apply the painted sponge to an art stamp, tapping it on lightly. Dip the sponge into a darker color, such as burgundy, and add small amounts to the stamp as an accent.

3 Hold the painted pot firmly with your left hand. With your right hand, apply the stamp to the pot; then use your left thumb to hold it in place while you press the stamp firmly against the rounded surface of the pot with your right hand. Repeat.

4 Dip the sponge into the paint and lightly stamp it around the lip of the pot. Allow it to dry, and seal with acrylic spray if desired.

MATERIALS
- Terra cotta pottery
- Pottery sealer
- Acrylic paint
- Paintbrush
- Freezer paper
- Sponge
- Art stamps
- Acrylic spray (optional)

tips
- *How do you know if a coat of paint has dried sufficiently? Touch the pottery gently with your fingertips; the paint may appear to be dry, but if the surface is cool to the touch, it's still wet.*
- *Although great care can be taken to seal the pot inside and out, protect it from moisture by using a plastic sleeve for flowers or plants.*

Making your own frames allows you to select the shape, size, and color that best suit your taste and design preferences. These air-dry frames can be made over the weekend, and they do not require firing in a kiln. Surprisingly strong and sturdy, clay picture frames are easy enough for children to make, under adult supervision. Prepare a work surface by draping it with a plastic cloth beforehand, and have plenty of water and scrub brushes available. When choosing stamps for this project, select either one large background stamp or a variety of smaller images that complement one another.

artist: carol heppner, U.S.A

clay picture frame

MATERIALS

- Rolling pin
- Air-dry clay
- Craft knife
- Art stamp
- Drying rack

- Watercolors
- Beige acrylic
- Paintbrushes
- Acrylic sealer
- Photo frame back

1 Roll out air-dry clay to 1/8" (.5 cm) thickness on a nonstick surface. Use craft knife to cut the clay into the desired frame shape; try classic rectangles and squares in various sizes, or abstract shapes. Stamp a design into the clay frame while it's still soft. Cut out a hole for the photo. Place the frame on a wire rack and allow it to dry for 24 hours.

2 Paint the dried frame with watercolors or acrylics; allow the paint to dry completely. Using a dry brush technique, paint beige acrylic over the raised areas of the clay. Let dry before applying a protective acrylic sealer.

3 Glue a photo frame backing to the frame, keeping the top of the photo backing unglued to allow insertion of a photo. Let dry. Insert a photograph. Enjoy!

tips

- *An inexpensive rolling pin for air-dry clay can be made with 1" (3 cm) PVC pipe cut to about 18" (46 cm) long. It's easily found at most hardware and home improvement stores. Place plastic caps on both ends, and the pipe provides handy storage for paintbrushes, craft knives, and other small tools.*
- *Instead of using beige acrylic to paint the raised areas of the frame, try complementary metallic paints or rub-ons.*
- *Add charms, buttons, ribbon, or other embellishments to the finished frame.*

Fruit and vegetable stamping provides a creative outlet for artists and crafters on a budget. The next time you go shopping for groceries, notice the shapes of fruits like apples, pears, peaches, and even star fruit. Imagine how the shape of the fruit can be used to stamp repeat patterns on home decor items such as these beautiful coasters. The possibilities are practically endless—all you need are water-based paint or ink and a surface to stamp on. Star fruit, in particular, lends itself to a variety of home decor items, even walls. When choosing such items to stamp with, look for firm, fleshy fruits and vegetables with low moisture. Fruits with soft flesh (bananas, strawberries) or high moisture content (oranges, grapes) may not yield the best results.

artist: livia mcree, u.s.a

star fruit
coasters

1 Prepare the saucers by sanding any rough areas and wiping them clean with a soft cloth.
2 Paint the saucers with acrylics and allow them to dry. Sand the surface lightly for a weathered effect.
3 Cut the star fruit in half for a larger stamp; cut off one of the ends for a smaller stamp. Remove the seeds from the fruit or leave them in for a different result.
4 Blend several paint colors for a marbleized effect and apply them to the star fruit stamp. Stamp a design in the center of each coaster. Allow to dry.

MATERIALS
- Terra cotta pot saucers: 4.25" (11 cm) for wine glasses, 5" (13 cm) for mugs
- Sandpaper
- Soft cloth
- Paintbrushes
- Acrylics
- Star fruit (carambola)
- Knife
- Polyurethane
- Toothpicks

tips
- *Apply polyurethane for a durable, practical finish.*
- *Use a toothpick to hold smaller pieces of fruit when stamping if you have trouble picking them up.*
- *Try other fruits or vegetables, such as okra, which yields a smaller star-shaped pattern.*

Simple wooden mirror frames can be picked up cheaply at yard sales, thrift stores, or flea markets. Paint and art stamps will transform your flea-market find into a treasured art piece. Use it to display a favorite family portrait, or have a mirror cut to size for it. This elegant project can be as simple or as complex as you desire, and it's so easy, children can make their own stamped and painted picture frames. The best stamps for this project are small- to medium-sized, with little or no detail. Look for images that look nice when stamped repeatedly together.

artist: lea everse, U.S.A

floral mirror

MATERIALS

- Picture frame
- Paintbrushes
- Black acrylic paint
- Sandpaper
- Gold acrylic paint
- Copper acrylic paint
- Sponge
- Art stamps
- Mirror or photograph

1 Sand and clean a picture frame. Paint it with flat black acrylic paint; two or three coats may be necessary. Sand the surface between coats for smoothness. Allow the paint to dry for 24 hours.

2 Apply gold and copper paint to an art stamp with a sponge. Immediately stamp the painted frame, reapply paint, and repeat stamping until the frame is complete.

3 Allow the paint to dry thoroughly before inserting a mirror or photograph for display.

tips

- *Bold stamps work best for this project. Finely detailed images may not stamp as well.*
- *Practice stamping on painted wood before attempting a final project. Too little paint will provide uneven coverage (which may or may not be desirable). Too much paint may blur the images.*
- *If you do make a mistake on a finished piece, immediately use a soft cloth to wipe away the wet paint and try again.*

Bring the outdoors in with this leaf-print lampshade,
which will add garden atmosphere to any room of your
home. Coat leaf stamps or actual leaves with an ordi-
nary household cleaner, such as dishwashing gel, and
apply to beautiful handmade paper. The bleaching action
of the gel creates patterns on the paper by subtracting its
ink. To restore some color to the subtracted shapes and
keep the leaf silhouettes, brush on permanent inks in
colors that complement the lampshade paper. Keep in
mind that handmade or natural papers aren't heat-
resistant, so it is important to coat the underside of the
paper with an adhesive layer of plastic, such as styrene,
before stamping.

artist: sandi obertin, U.S.A

leaf-print lamp shade

1 Coat leaf-shaped art stamps (or actual leaves) with a thin layer of dishwasher gel. Stamp images directly onto a sheet of dark green mulberry paper. Allow the images to dry thoroughly. Watch the bleaching action from the gel create impressions in the paper.

2 Apply permanent pigment inks in soft, muted colors to accent the stamped images with hints of color. Try violet, peony, turquoise, and teal.

3 Cut the paper to size (about .5" or 1 cm wider than the shade area) and mount it to a lamp shade frame with adhesive. To make finished edges, turn under .25" (.5 cm) of paper on both ends and glue them down.

MATERIALS
- Leaf-shaped art stamps
- Dishwasher gel
- Permanent pigment inks
- Mulberry paper
- Scissors
- Lamp shade frame
- Adhesive
- Lamp stand and electrical components
- Beads and other embellishments (optional)

tips
- *Allow the shade to dry thoroughly before assembling the electrical components. Add beads or other embellishments to the top of the shade for interest.*
- *Natural paper can be rendered more heat-resistant by coating the back with a thin layer of adhesive before stamping.*
- *Sources of illumination: Lamp shade kits can be obtained through art supply and craft retailers. Alternatively, find discarded lamps and shades at thrift shops and flea markets, dismantle them, and make new ones with beautifully stamped papers.*

Bold, singular images such as those shown here cry out for dramatic painting and stamping techniques. Starting with ceramic stone tiles, make a gorgeous home decor fashion statement with striking stamp imagery and paint specially formulated for ceramics and glass. Carefully taping off the borders is a quick and easy way to frame each composition. To keep the tiles from skidding, line the backs with felt.

artist: carol heppner, U.S.A

painted tiles

MATERIALS
- Ceramic tiles
- .75" (2 cm) low-tack masking tape
- Baby powder
- Black pigment ink
- Art stamps
- Embossing powder
- Embossing (heat) tool
- Glass/tile paints
- Acrylic sealer
- Glue
- Felt

1 Place masking tape around the edge of the tile to create a .75" (2 cm) border. Coat the taped-off central area with baby powder.

2 Apply pigment ink to the stamp, and stamp. Apply embossing powder; heat-set with an embossing tool (see "Stamp Basics").

3 Mix various glass/tile paints with gloss sealer to create a translucent coloring medium. Fingerpaint the paint onto the tile in a random fashion.

4 Immediately apply more sealer to even the surface of the paint. Remove the tape immediately afterward.

tips
- *Once the sealer has dried completely, glue a piece of felt to the back of the tile to create a nonskid surface.*
- *Some types of glass or ceramic paint can be cured in a home oven and then safely washed in a dishwasher. Other types air dry in about a week. Read product labels carefully, and follow the manufacturer's recommendations.*
- *Always use certified nontoxic paints and sealers for items that may come in contact with food.*

These finial bookends provide a creative and whimsical accent to anyone's home decor. Wooden finials are painted with a base coat of acrylics, then the surface is stamped with permanent black ink that won't smear. Adding a metal angle to the bottom of each finial with a couple of wood screws transforms them into serviceable bookends.

artist: carol heppner, U.S.A

finial bookends

1 Glue the finial onto the cap with wood glue. Allow it to dry for several hours or overnight.
2 Clean and lightly sand the finial if necessary. Coat the finial and cap with gesso; let dry between coats before painting it with acrylics in two or three complementary colors. Allow the paint to dry.
3 Stamp various images onto the finial with permanent black ink. Seal the piece with acrylic varnish.
4 Screw a metal angle to the bottom of each finial to create bookends; the angle will help keep the books straight on their shelves.

MATERIALS
- Post wooden finial and cap
- Wood glue
- Paintbrushes
- Gesso
- Acrylics
- Art stamps
- Permanent black ink
- Acrylic varnish
- Screws
- Screwdriver
- Metal angle
- Flat-bottomed glass marbles (optional)

tips
- Find wooden finials at hardware stores and yard sales.
- If you find it difficult to stamp directly onto the finial, stamp plain white tissue paper with permanent black ink, emboss the images if desired, and tear the paper into manageable pieces. Decoupage the tissue onto the painted finial with glue or decoupage medium and seal it with acrylic varnish. When the paper dries, it disappears, leaving the stamped images behind.
- Option: Glue glass marbles to the bottom of each bookend.

A pretty wood clock illustrates how easy it is to turn a small home decor item into something really special with paint and rubber stamps. Sealing the porous surface with bright acrylic paints prior to stamping it will keep pigment ink from soaking into the wood. After painting, emboss stamped images on the front of the clock to add personality and character. This project is suitable for any type of stamp, including hand-carved images. Since the images will not fill the surface area on each wood piece, the type of stamp imagery you choose is optional.

artist: ira ono, U.S.A

wood clock box

MATERIALS

- Wooden box with hole drilled for clock mechanism
- Soft brush or cloth
- Sandpaper
- Paintbrush
- Acrylic paints
- Sponge
- Stamps
- Pigment ink
- Embossing powders
- Embossing (heat) tool
- Clock parts

1 Sand the wooden box, and use a soft brush or cloth to remove any residual sawdust. Paint the entire box with one color of acrylic paint. Allow it to dry on a nonstick surface.

2 Use a sponge to apply just a touch of gold paint to the wood surface. Sponge on the paint sparingly and allow the background color to show through. Allow the paint to dry.

3 Stamp and emboss the tops of the painted wood box in a random pattern. Assemble the clock parts in the center of the wood box and insert a battery.

tips

- *When sponging on paint, take care not to allow it to run down the sides of the wood. If this does happen, however, allow the wood to dry and then touch up the sides with the background acrylic paint color.*
- *Metallic embossing powders make a nice accent for painted wood pieces.*

Transform everyday objects into beautifully stamped artwork! With a few rubber stamps, some tissue paper, and a glass vase, you can make a lovely objet d'art that you'd be proud to display in your home. Stamping round or cylindrical objects such as this vase or a drinking glass can be difficult to accomplish without smudging the images. This pretty tissue-paper collage vase illustrates an easier way: Simply stamp and emboss the paper, and then decoupage it to the vase. This technique ensures the perfect application of images to virtually any three-dimensional object.

artist: sandi obertin, U.S.A

tissue-paper
collage vase

1 Select a glass vase of any size, shape, or color. Wash and dry it thoroughly.
2 Choose an array of colored tissue paper in complementary hues, such as purple, magenta, bright blue, and green. Using pigment ink, stamp several leaf images (using actual leaves or commercial leaf stamps) onto one of the light-colored tissue papers, and emboss the images with gold powder.
3 Tear the tissue paper into pieces, carefully tearing around each embossed leaf image. Set aside, then tear the unstamped tissue papers into pieces no larger than 3" x 4" (8 cm x 10 cm).
4 Mix wet adhesive with an equal amount of water. Using a paintbrush, foam brush, or your fingers, apply the mixture to the unstamped tissue pieces, then apply the wet papers to the vase. Overlap them to create interesting color combinations. When the vase is completely covered with tissue paper, adhere the stamped and embossed tissue pieces in a random pattern on top. Allow the vase to dry for at least 24 hours.

MATERIALS
• Glass vase
• Tissue papers
• Pigment ink
• Leaf-shaped art stamps
• Embossing powder
• Embossing (heat) tool
• Adhesive
• Paintbrush or foam brush

tips
• *Protect your work area with a plastic dropcloth, as this technique can be quite messy.*
• *Find glass vases at garage sales, flea markets, and discount home decor shops.*
• *If using actual leaves in lieu of commercial rubber stamps, they must be soft and pliable.*
• *For a sleek tissue-paper surface, be very careful when applying the tissue to the vase and smooth out the wrinkles.*
• *Some artists prefer a textured surface; in this case, squeeze and wrinkle up the tissue paper while applying it to the vase.*
• *Wide-mouthed vases can be decoupaged with tissue paper on the inside for an interesting effect. In this case, reverse the process by adhering the stamped and embossed tissue pieces first, followed by the plain tissue pieces.*

Using the stamp images and colors of your choice, create beautiful glass tableware that matches your linens and silverware. From casual styles to more sophisticated looks, clear glass (or even sturdy plastic) plates are the obvious choice for the home decorator. This technique calls for some backward thinking. Instead of painting and stamping background images first and filling in the foreground images afterward, as in most artforms, the process is reversed. Stamp and paint foreground imagery first; then fill in with background stamping and painting afterward. That's because you paint the back of the plate but view it from the front, so images that were stamped and painted first will cover anything painted or stamped behind them.

The painted glass stemware complements the plates, adding the finishing touch to your table. A colorful lavender and yellow butterfly flits around a glass, painted in pretty stripes and a lovely rose in magenta and yellow adorns another. Because painting glass stemware can be tricky, it helps to use bold, dramatic stamp images like the ones the artist chose. Once the image is stamped in place, the painting is easy.

painted glass
plate & stemware

Painted Glass Plate

1 Stamp the flowers on the back of a clean, dry plate with permanent black ink. Allow the images to dry completely. Paint in the flowers with glass paint. Let dry.
2 Stamp the leaves with permanent black ink, allow them to dry, then paint them in as in step 1.
3 Paint the background area with the glass paints. Allow it to dry. Paint the back of the outer rim of the dish with a simple pattern. Allow it to dry completely before coating the entire back of the plate with glass sealer.

Painted Glass Stemware

1 Stamp the image onto the front of the glass with permanent black ink. Paint the image with glass paint. Allow it to dry.
2 Paint a simple pattern on the remainder of the glass, and let dry.
3 Seal the stemware with the glass sealer.

PAINTED GLASS PLATE MATERIALS
- Clear glass dish
- Art stamps
- Permanent black ink
- Glass paints
- Paintbrushes
- Glass sealer

PAINTED GLASS STEMWARE MATERIALS
- Clear glass stemware
- Art stamps
- Permanent black ink
- Glass paint
- Paintbrushes
- Glass sealer

painted glass plate tips

- *Glass can be slippery, so special care must be taken when stamping on it. Take your time, place the stamp precisely, and press down firmly without moving or rocking it. Hold the plate securely as you grasp the stamp in your other hand, and remove it with one quick motion to avoid blurring the image.*
- *Permanent ink may stain your stamps, so clean them immediately after stamping, before painting in the images.*
- *An alternative to stamping with permanent ink is to use pigment or embossing ink and emboss the images with powder (see "Stamp*
- *Pick up inexpensive glass stemware at yard sales and flea markets.*
- *If your first attempt at stamping on glass is unsuccessful, wipe off the ink with a damp towel right away. Repeat stamping until you are satisfied with the results.*

artist: carol heppner, U.S.A

Wall stamping is a great way to add color and design to your home. Look for large foam or rubber decorator stamps made specifically for interior design. Stamps with bold, silhouette-type imagery are best for stamping on walls; detailed images will not "read" as well. It's easiest to stamp on a fairly flat wall, but stamping on textured surfaces can also achieve interesting effects. Practice first by stamping the image(s) on scrap paper painted the same color as your walls. Cut the images out, affix them with masking tape, and design a pattern before stamping directly on the wall.

artist: grace taormina, U.S.A

wall stamping

MATERIALS

- Latex paints
- Painter's masking tape
- Foam brush
- Decorator stamps

1 Paint a two-toned wall with contrasting colors of latex paint, using painter's masking tape to create a crisp line. Allow the paint to dry completely before stamping.

2 Using a foam brush, apply two colors of paint to an ethnic stamp such as the one shown here. Use one color from the painted wall, and incorporate an additional color for added interest.

3 Stamp the images both vertically and horizontally to add variety to the border design.

tips

- *Stamping can be successfully completed on walls painted with latex paint in matte, satin, and gloss finishes. Semi-gloss and gloss finishes require a bit more care when stamping as inked stamps have the tendency to slide on a slick surface. Antiqued, glazed, ragged, marbled, and sponged walls provide wonderful backgrounds for stamped images.*
- *The best quality paint for wall stamping is 100-percent acrylic, but experiment with oil-based paints if you prefer.*

Create the look of a designer-decorated room with a striking leaf motif stamped in coordinating colors. Large rose leaves are further enhanced by white border wallpaper—and the wallpaper is as easy to stamp as it is to paste up. Create a reverse print by first painting the walls with a soft pastel shade such as lavender-blue. Stamp a leaf motif on the wall using a white or cream-colored paint, then stamp lavender-blue leaves on the white border wallpaper.

artist: grace taormina, u.s.a

leaf stamped
wallpaper & walls

1 Paint the wall with latex paint.
2 Apply white acrylic paint to a large foam stamp, and stamp the walls in a random pattern. Rotate the leaves and position them in a variety of angles.
3 On white border wallpaper, stamp the rose leaves with the same color paint used to paint the walls in step 1. Allow the paint to dry completely.

variations
- Sponge a sage green wall using two or three shades of green for a mottled look. Allow the wall paint to dry, then stamp a fern motif in yellow ochre and avocado green. To unify the design and tone down the colors, apply an antique glaze over the entire wall.
- Try applying two or three coordinating colors of paint to your decorator stamps before stamping on walls or border paper. The marbled effect is more natural than stark one-color stamping.
- Use a fine paintbrush to add whimsical flourishes to your stamped impressions. Practice first on scrap paper.

MATERIALS
- Lavender blue latex paint or color of your choice
- White acrylic paint
- Foam decorator stamp
- Wallpaper paste
- White border wallpaper
- Decorator stamps

tips
- *Use wallpaper paste to adhere the border paper to the wall as shown.*
- *When random stamping, try painting on just a portion of some stamps to create a more natural look, or overlap images to create dimension. To create trailing leaves, use chalk to lightly mark the direction of flow, and brush it off after stamping.*
- *Use border wallpaper to decorate the baby's room, bathroom, or children's play room.*
- *Also see "tips" section in "Wall Stamping."*

These beautiful placemat and napkin sets look like posh decorator items, but they're actually handmade. Use spray paint, acrylics, stencils, and art stamps to create original works of art for your table. Starting with plain canvas mats and cotton napkins, apply spray paint, then embellish the surface with stamped images that suit your decor style and color scheme. This is a great project for patio dining, themed parties, or holidays and other special occasions.

stamped & stenciled
table linens

Placemats

1 Cut sturdy sailcloth-type canvas to the appropriate size, rounding the corners or leaving them square, according to your preference. If making your own placemats, prepare the canvas with a coat of primer before painting. Ready-made canvas placemats are available from bed and bath linen suppliers.

2 Paint the placemats with copper and gold spray paint, and allow them to dry.

3 Paint long lines, squiggles, and other free-form designs with paintbrushes and acrylic paint. Pour out paint onto a freezer paper palette, and dip sponge into paint. Apply sponge to the stamp, and stamp images in a variety of colors, taking your cue from dinnerware and other home decor items you wish to match.

4 Place large stencils, sequin waste material, or doilies on the placemats and spray paint over them to create layered designs. Stamp over this pattern with different colors of acrylic paint.

5 When the paint has dried and you are satisfied with the design, add carefully drawn fine lines, squiggles, and dots with dimensional fabric paint.

Napkins

1 Stamp images onto cloth napkins as shown, using gold, violet, and olive green paint.

2 Once the paint has dried, heat-set the napkins with an iron on the cotton setting, or place them in a low-temperature dryer for 10 minutes.

3 Apply free-form accent designs with silver dimensional fabric paint. Do not heat-set dimensional paint, as it will stick to a hot iron. Allow it to air dry for at least 24 hours before laundering.

Specific Instructions: Fleur de Lis

First stamp squiggle designs onto plain white canvas with olive green, gold, and violet acrylics. Then position several doilies over the placemat, and lightly spray the surface with copper and gold spray paint. Allow to dry. Spray again with gold webbing spray. Then, add a fleur de lis stenciled design with violet paint, and stamp small flowers in olive green paint.

Specific Instructions: Free Spirit Squiggles

First paint the placemat with copper and gold spray paint. Then paint long vertical wavy lines, squiggles, and dots in silver acrylic. Stamp large squiggle images in olive geen and violet paint, then use silver paint to stamp large S shapes. Stencil a few circles (or stamp) in olive green and violet paint, then softly sponge on small dots through sequin waste. Stencil small flowers with green paint, and finish by applying free-form designs with silver dimensional fabric paint.

MATERIALS
- Canvas placemats, about 13.25" x 17.25" (33 cm x 44 cm)
- Gold and copper spray paint
- Paintbrushes
- Acrylic paint
- Freezer paper
- Art stamps
- Stencils (optional)
- Sequin waste
- Large plastic or paper doilies
- Silver dimensional fabric paint
- Cloth dinner napkins
- Iron or dryer
- Webbing spray paint
- Sponges
- Silver acrylic paint

tips
- *This project requires a lot of painting and messy spray paint applications. Set up a workstation outdoors or work in a well-ventilated area. Drape your worktable with a dropcloth to protect it from spills and overspray.*
- *The artist chose a stamp with a squiggle image that mirrored a silver napkin ring she intended to use. You can make your own matching napkin rings, or buy specialty rings and coordinate them with the stamps used on the placemats and napkins.*

artist: leslie altman, u.s.a

This Japanese clock is unusual, and so easy to make with your own art stamps. Start by cutting a piece of beige cardstock in a pleasing shape for the clock face. Back it with sturdy matboard, drill a hole for the clock mechanism, and you're ready to stamp a design on the front. The images tell the whole story—substitute Japanese imagery with designs that suit your decor for a custom-made look.

Japanese clock

MATERIALS

- Beige cardstock
- Scissors
- Black matboard
- Pencil
- Craft knife
- Adhesive
- Drill
- Art stamps
- Black pigment ink
- Clear embossing powder
- Embossing (heat) tool
- Red marker
- White colored pencil
- Clock kit

1 Design a clock face template and cut it from beige cardstock.
2 Lay the cut cardstock on black matboard and trace it with a pencil, leaving .25" (.75 cm) border. Cut this shape out with a sharp craft knife.
3 Glue the two together, and allow them to dry. Drill a hole carefully through both layers for the clock shaft; it must be large enough to insert the clock mechanism.
4 Stamp Japanese images onto the clock front with black pigment ink. Emboss with clear powder, then highlight the images with a red marker and a white colored pencil.
5 Insert the clock mechanism, following the instructions for assembly included in the kit.

tips

- *Use sturdy matboard, quality cardstock, and acid-free adhesives and papers to ensure the longevity of your clock.*
- *Try stamping with fruits or vegetables (as described in the Creative Tools & Techniques section) for a kitchen clock, or use cartoon characters for the baby's room.*

Seashells, small stones, antique photographs and cherished mementos—now you can store your most precious keepsakes in small wooden boxes that you paint and stamp yourself. This easy weekend project requires few materials and is fun for children to try as well. Start by painting a simple wood box in one flat color of acrylic paint. Add sponged-on paint in a contrasting color—allowing the base coat to show through—to create a softly mottled background. Once dry, the surface may be stamped and embossed with the images of your choice. Display your finished boxes proudly on a coffee table or bookcase.

artist: ira ono, U.S.A.

wooden keepsake
boxes

1 Sand the box lightly and use a soft brush or cloth to remove any residual sawdust from the wooden box. Paint the outside with one color of acrylic paint. Allow it to dry on a nonstick surface.
2 Use a sponge to apply just a touch of contrasting paint to the wood surface. Sponge on the paint sparingly, allowing the background color to show through. Allow the paint to dry.
3 Stamp and emboss the box surface in a random pattern with the images of your choice.

MATERIALS
- Wooden boxes with lids
- Sandpaper
- Clean cloth or brush
- Acrylic paints
- Paintbrush
- Sponge
- Stamps
- Pigment ink
- Embossing powders
- Embossing (heat) tool

tips
- *Try painting the box itself with one color, and then decorating the lid with sponged-on paint and embossed images.*
- *This project is suitable for any type of stamp, including handcarved images. Miniature coordinated stamp images work best when used together on small painted projects.*
- *Metallic embossing powders make a nice accent for painted wood pieces.*

For sheer versatility and fun, it's hard to beat these clay vessels. The artist stamped into air-dry clay and then wrapped it around cylinders to form lovely shapes. Just about any cylindrical object can be used for a mold—try glassware or a cardboard tube from a roll of paper towels. Use your wraparound vases to hold a sheaf of dried flowers, pencils, calligraphy pens, or anything you like! But take care—these vessels are for decorative use only; they're not intended for serving food or drink.

artist: carol heppner, U.S.A.

wraparound
clay vases

MATERIALS

- Air-dry clay
- Rolling pin
- Craft knife
- Art stamps
- Cylinder containers
- Plastic wrap
- Wire drying rack
- Paintbrushes
- Acrylics
- Acrylic spray sealer

1 Roll out air-dry clay to 1/8" (.5 cm) thickness (approximately). Cut the clay to the desired height and width for each vase. Stamp a design into the cut clay, pressing down firmly to make deep impressions. Quickly wrap the clay piece around a plastic-wrapped mold.

2 Roll a second piece of clay to 1/8" (.5 cm) thickness. Place the clay-wrapped cylinder on this piece, and cut out the bottom of the vase with a knife. Secure the bottom piece to the clay vase by smoothing the clay pieces together with your fingers. Allow the vase to dry on a wire rack for 12 hours.

3 Carefully remove the vase from the plastic-wrapped mold. Allow it to dry another 12 hours. Once dry, paint each vase with acrylics, and allow them to dry completely before sealing them with several light coats of acrylic spray.

tips

- *An inexpensive rolling pin for air-dry clay can be made with 1" (3 cm) PVC pipe cut to about 18" (46 cm) long. It's easily found at most hardware and home improvement stores. Place plastic caps on both ends, and the pipe provides handy storage for paintbrushes, craft knives, and other small tools.*
- *Prepare each cylindrical mold by wrapping it tightly with plastic wrap; this helps when you release the air-dry clay from the mold.*
- *For variations on this technique, try cutting out small holes from the clay or overlapping it as you wrap to create an interesting surface texture.*

This is a revolutionary way to use rubber stamps and hand-carved woodblocks: kiln-fired ceramic tiles. Ordinary stoneware clay is stamped, dried, and bisque-fired in a commercial kiln. The pieces are then glazed and fired again. The finished tiles can be used for home decor, displayed at art shows, or presented as gifts. To save money on kiln fees, the artist recommends enrolling in a ceramics class at your local college or university.

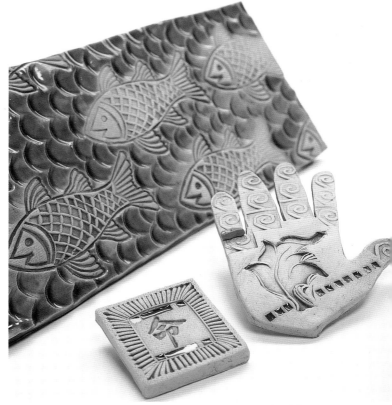

artist: gloria page, U.S.A.

kiln-fired tiles

1 Roll out a piece of wet buff-colored stoneware. Form it into the desired shapes, trimming as needed.
2 Stamp an impression into the damp clay, using commercial stamps, hand-carved rubber stamps, or carved wood blocks. Make any adjustments needed and trim excess clay from each piece with a craft knife.
3 Allow the clay pieces to air dry on sheets of drywall for 1 to 3 weeks, depending on local temperature and humidity. Once they are thoroughly dry, bisque-fire them.
4 Brush on a red oxide wash; then quickly remove most of it with a sponge, leaving behind a stained antique finish. Brush or pour on ceramic glaze as desired, applying about three coats to ensure an even coverage.
5 High-fire the pieces; allow them to cool naturally inside the kiln to avoid cracking.

MATERIALS
• Rolling pin
• Stoneware
• Clay sculpting tools
• Art stamps
• Craft knife
• Drywall
• Kiln, or access to one
• Red oxide wash
• Sponges
• Glaze

tip
• *To secure a hanger on the back of decorative tiles, use a heavy-duty epoxy paste (the artist recommends PC-7) from the hardware store and picture-hanging wire. Apply two globs of paste to the back of the tile, press the ends of the wire into each glob of paste, and allow it to dry overnight.*

Terra cotta clay is the perfect medium for quick and easy rubber stamping projects. Easy to form and manipulate, it takes great stamp impressions and air dries to a firm finish in just a few hours. This clay bowl is only an eighth of an inch thick, but it should withstand the rigors of most decorative uses. It is not meant for serving food, however, and should be cleaned carefully with a damp cloth, never washed or submerged in water. Find a medium-size kitchen bowl with an interesting shape to use as a mold, and protect your work area with a plastic dropcloth, as this technique can be messy.

burnished clay bowl

1 Using a rolling pin, roll out a ball of air-drying terra cotta clay to about 1/8" (.5 cm) thickness, in a rough circle about 15" (38 cm) in diameter. To add texture to the surface, roll the clay between two layers of pastry cloth or a textured washcloth.

2 Stamp a design in the center of the circle and a complementary design around the border.

3 Turn a kitchen bowl upside down on the work surface and cover it with plastic wrap. Drape the damp clay, stamped images down, over the plastic-covered bowl and gently press the clay against the plastic to form a shape. Allow the clay bowl to dry in this position for several hours or overnight.

4 When the bowl is completely dry, paint both sides with light green acrylic paint. Allow the paint to dry before applying bronze metallic paint to the surface with a dry brush technique.

5 Once the paint has dried, sand it on both sides to age the surface. Apply metallic rub-ons to the edge of the bowl, and gently burnish the entire surface with a soft cloth. Seal it with an acrylic varnish or spray as desired.

variations

• For a slightly different look, try making a clay bowl with white air-dry clay, paint it with a light cream base coat of acrylics, allow the paint to dry, then follow with teal green acrylics. Once the paint has completely dried, sand it lightly to expose the base coat, wipe off the surface with a soft cloth, and apply a spray varnish to seal it.

• Another project to try is a bronze plate with a blue patina. Create an air-dry clay plate with the above method, draping it over a small ceramic plate instead of a bowl. Paint the clay plate with green patina acrylics, allow the paint to dry, and then paint again with metallic bronze or copper paint. Allow it to dry, and apply transparent brown acrylic glaze randomly over the surface. Once dry, a light application of gold metallic rub-ons will add a lovely sheen to the plate. Buff the surface with a soft cloth and seal with an acrylic varnish or spray.

• A large platter is easy to make—just use more clay, roll it out flat, stamp it as described above, and use a large dish or platter as a mold. The first layer of paint is patina green; the second layer is copper. Sand the surface, apply metallic rub-ons as desired, and buff with a soft cloth. Seal the platter with an acrylic varnish or spray.

MATERIALS

• Rolling pin
• Terra cotta clay
• Pastry cloth
• Art stamps
• Bowl
• Plastic wrap
• Acrylics
• Sandpaper
• Metallic rub-ons
• Soft cloth
• Acrylic spray

tips

• *When stamping into clay, press down firmly to leave a lasting impression.*

• *Try making more bowls and vessels with this technique. Use garage-sale bowls and vases for molds.*

• *When cutting the bowl shape in step 1, it isn't necessary to trim the edges perfectly; leaving them uneven contributes to the artistic appeal of the final piece.*

• *Option: To seal the completed bowl, use water-based matte varnish.*

artist: pamela tarpy, u.s.a.

Creative stamping runs the gamut from shrink plastic to wood and paperclay, children's modeling compound, sea glass, polymer clay, and air-dry clays—even stone and slate material. It doesn't take a stamp artist long to realize that virtually any object or surface can be transformed with stamps and paint, dye, or ink.

Try working with Creative Paperclay® jewelry or making an abstract brooch from shrink plastic. Copper stamping is an exciting project that involves the use of liver of sulfur to create a rich patina on a copper surface. Once stamped and cured in the solution, the thin copper sheet may be used to decorate a card or make fabulous jewelry.

Children's modeling compound provides a surprising medium for stamped jewelry. Bits of sea glass are great for stamping, too. Make gorgeous brooches, pendants, and earrings by embossing stamped designs on the surface and adding jewelry findings. If leather is your material of choice, try making a lovely stamped journal or a treasure pouch necklace.

metal, wood, clay, and more

Wood is a popular medium for stamp artists. Everything from pegracks to recipe boxes can be made from this common material. The round wooden mini box is charmingly stamped and colored with pencils, while the wooden beads are made with a slightly more complex process of stamping and decoupage. An ordinary wooden serving tray can be decorated with paint and stamped designs to create a practical work of art.

Clays of all types—air-dry clays and polymers in particular—have long been a favorite with artists and crafters. Polymer clay can be used to make beautiful stamped jewelry pieces and even jewelry boxes. Air-dry clays are nontoxic and easy to work with. Children as well as adults will enjoy making their own jewelry and other items with clay.

Finally, try stamping on some really unusual materials—slate, for instance! The slate picture frame in this section was stamped with an ordinary sponge and then gilded with silver leaf to make a stunning decorative statement.

Make a pretty serving tray for parties on the patio!
Dragonflies and other garden motifs are easy to carve
into large rubber erasers; they're the perfect tools for
dressing up an ordinary wooden tray. If you prefer to
use commercial stamps, the large type designed for
home decor and wall stamping work well for this
project. Find them at craft stores, home improvement
centers, and garden shops.

artist: agatha bell, U.S.A

dragonfly tray

MATERIALS

- Wooden serving tray
- Sandpaper
- Soft cloth
- Foam paintbrush
- Acrylics
- Sponge
- Hand-carved stamp
  (or see step 2)
- Acrylic varnish

1 Lightly sand the wooden serving tray; remove any dust with a soft cloth. Paint the entire tray with acrylic paint and a foam paintbrush. Try painting the inside a different color from the outside of the tray for added interest.

2 Carve a stamp, as described in "Creative Tools & Techniques." Use the pattern provided in the Templates section (see p. 299).

3 Apply paint in a contrasting color to the hand-carved stamp and test-stamp it on a piece of paper. When satisfied with the effect, stamp the tray. Stamp within the four corners first, then add a stamped impression to the middle of the tray.

tips

- Once the paint is completely dry, apply two coats of matte or glossy varnish.
- This sturdy serving tool also functions as a decorative piece that can be hung on the wall. Simply affix a hanger to the back (the type that lays flat), and hang the tray on a nail when not in use.

Create your own buttons, beads, or pins, by forming and stamping patterns into children's modeling compound. The material is easy to manipulate and shape, and is the ideal medium for stamping primitive yet stylish patterns. Use simple stamp designs, such as fish, sun, star, and leaf patterns, to create stronger visual effects. Let the stamped modeling compound air-dry to rock hardness before painting with bright acrylic or metallic paints. Dry-brush the highlights of your design with metallic paint to enhance the texture of the stamped pattern.

artist: sharilyn miller, U.S.A

buttons & beads

1 Pinch off a piece of modeling compound and roll it into a smooth ball. Press the ball against a rubber art stamp or any firm surface with interesting texture. The material will be impressed with a reverse image. Mold and form it to create round beads, buttons, or other interesting embellishments. If making jewelry, use a toothpick to poke holes where you will need to add jump-rings later.

2 Allow the finished piece to dry on a nonstick surface. The drying time varies according to the climate you live in but, generally, expect it to take about a week. Once dry, the material can be painted with a variety of acrylic and metallic paints. Dry-brush the highlights with metallic paint.

3 Use jewelry adhesive to adhere pin backs or earring backs to finished jewelry pieces. Seed beads can be strung on thread and dangled from jump-rings inserted through holes.

MATERIALS
- Modeling compound
- Art stamps
- Toothpick
- Paintbrushes
- Acrylic paint
- Jewelry adhesive, pin backs, earring backs, jump-rings, seed beads (optional)

tips
- *To avoid modeling compound cracking as it dries, work the compound in your hands for several seconds before rolling it into a ball and impressing it with a stamp.*
- *If the compound sticks to the rubber stamp, remove it with a soft toothbrush and coat the stamp with clear embossing ink or cornstarch before stamping into the compound again.*

Scrabble fans will enjoy using discarded game pieces to make pretty stamped minimagnets. They're fun to display on the refrigerator, and children enjoy using their tiny stamps to make their own magnets. Look for game pieces at thrift stores, flea markets, and garage sales, or contact game manufacturers to obtain extra pieces. The stamping and coloring are easy enough for children to attempt (under adult supervision), and in no time at all you will have assembled a collection of magnets.

artist: lisa glicksman, U.S.A

stamped minimagnets

MATERIALS
- Magnetic backing
- Adhesive
- Wooden game pieces
- Art stamps
- Pigment ink
- Embossing powder
- Embossing (heat) tool
- Acrylics or colored pencils
- Acrylic craft varnish or sealer (optional)

1 Glue magnetic backing material to the back of a flat game piece.

2 Stamp an image on the front of the tile or game piece with pigment ink.

3 Emboss the image with embossing powder and a heat tool.

4 Color the tile with acrylics or colored pencils; seal with acrylic spray or varnish.

tips
- *For best results, stamp with dark ink and emboss with clear powder.*
- *Substitute other game pieces for Scrabble tiles. Try stamping and painting on puzzle pieces.*

Introduce a back-to-nature theme into your home with this slate frame. The natural texture and tone of the slate is complemented by simple triangular foil shapes. Simply embellish an unadorned frame with art stamps and silver crafting foil. It only takes a few minutes to customize a purchased frame and make it something special.

artist: livia mcree, u.s.a

gilded slate
frame

1 Cut foam sponges into triangle shapes that to fit along each side of the frame's opening, allowing about .25" (.5 cm) of extra space on either side.

2 Apply foiling glue to a pencil eraser and to the triangle sponges, and stamp around the opening of the frame as shown. On each side, stamp the triangle in the center with a dot on each side. Let the glue dry until it's clear, or follow manufacturer's instructions for application.

3 Apply crafting foil to the glued areas, smoothing it down with your fingers or an eraser to ensure even coverage. Brush off any excess foil with a stiff paintbrush.

MATERIALS

- Plain slate frame
- Foam sponge
- Foiling glue
- Pencil with unused eraser
- Silver crafting foil
- Paintbrush

tips

- *Apply acrylic craft varnish or sealer to foiled areas, if desired, to protect them from scuffing.*
- *Once the foil is removed, do not let the exposed backing touch any glued areas or it will pull off the glue along with adjacent foil.*
- *Use simple art stamps to apply glue to wood, metal, or glass frames. Ornate designs will not transfer well.*

Wood critters are simply designed and fun to paint and stamp. What really sets them apart from other woodcrafts is the application of rubber-stamped images that have been embossed with metallic powders. If you're handy with a scroll saw, it's easy to make your own designs with inexpensive wood. Otherwise, find interesting ready-made shapes at craft stores and hobby shops that specialize in woodcrafts. Option: Glue small magnets to the back of each wood piece to make refrigerator magnets.

artist: ira ono, U.S.A

hawaiian critters

MATERIALS

- Carved wood shapes, about 3/16" (.75 cm) thick
- Soft brush or cloth
- Sandpaper
- Paintbrush
- Acrylic paints
- Sponge
- Stamps
- Pigment ink
- Embossing powder
- Embossing (heat) tool
- Small magnets (optional)

1. Sand the wood critters and use a soft brush or cloth to remove any residual sawdust. Paint the critters on both sides and around the edges with one color of acrylic paint. Allow them to dry thoroughly on a nonstick surface.
2. Use a sponge to apply two or three complementary colored paints to the wood pieces. Sponge on the paint sparingly, and allow the background color to show through. Allow the paint to dry.
3. Stamp and emboss the tops of the painted wood pieces in a random pattern with pigment or embossing ink.

tips

- *When sponging on paint, take care not to allow it to run down the sides of the wood piece. If this does happen, however, allow the wood to dry, then touch up the sides with the background acrylic paint color used.*
- *This project is suitable for any type of stamp, including hand-carved images. Because the images will not fill the surface area on each wood piece, the type of stamp imagery you choose is optional.*
- *Metallic embossing powders make a nice accent for painted wood pieces.*

Custom-design your own beautiful luminaries with copper sheeting and the art stamps of your choice. It's a clever way to incorporate your favorite images and paint colors with a lovely yet practical home decor item. Purchase a glass candleholder at a thrift shop or yard sale. No matter if it's scratched or otherwise disfigured—the copper sheeting will cover any blemishes in the glass. Once the candle burns down, simply insert another one inside the glass holder, which should last for many years.

artist: lea everse, U.S.A

pierced metal
luminary

1 Measure and cut a paper template to fit snugly around the perimeter of the glass candleholder. Use the pattern provided in the Templates section (see p. 299). Mark the corners, and stamp images where they will appear on the sides of the luminary. Use the paper template to cut a piece of thin copper sheeting with metal shears.

2 Sponge the copper piece with metal craft paint, and allow it to dry.

3 Place the painted copper right-side up on a piece of foam or Styrofoam, lay the stamped paper template on top of it, and pierce through both layers with a large tapestry needle, using the stamped paper template as a guide.

4 Once finished, discard the paper template and wrap the painted, pierced copper sheeting around the glass candleholder. Apply a few dabs of crafter's cement or caulking to hold it in place. Embellish the candleholder with raffia strung with decorative beads.

MATERIALS
- Square glass candleholder
- Plain paper
- Scissors
- Art stamps
- Stamping ink
- Thin copper metal sheet
- Metal shears
- Metal craft paint
- Foam
- Tapestry needle
- Crafter's cement or caulking
- Raffia
- Decorative beads

tips
- *Copper metal sheets can be obtained at most craft stores, rubber stamping stores, and art supply stores.*
- *Use metal shears to avoid ruining your good scissors. Metal shears can be found at hardware stores and home-improvement centers.*
- *When wrapping the copper sheeting around the candleholder, mold and shape it around the corners and along the top and bottom edges with your fingers.*

Creative Paperclay® is a fabulous air-dry clay formed and manipulated in a variety of ways before it dries and hardens. White in color, Paperclay can be dyed and then painted with interference pigments that lend a pewter cast to the surface. Using metal objects, real leaves, rubber stamps, or any item with intriguing texture, impress images into the clay before allowing it to air dry. The pieces can be used to decorate art books or greeting cards, or affixed to jewelry findings to make pendants, earrings, and brooches. Feather-light Paperclay jewelry coordinates well with any wardrobe.

Paperclay jewelry

1 Don a pair of rubber gloves to protect your hands from dye and pigments. Pinch off a small piece of Paperclay and knead black dye-based ink into it. Add the dye a few drops at a time, and knead it until the clay is thoroughly black in color.

2 Roll out the clay on a piece of parchment to a thickness of 1/8" (.3 cm). Sprinkle silver interference pigments onto the surface and blend them into the clay, creating swirls and patterns with your fingers.

3 To create fascinating surface texture, fold the clay over and press an assortment of items into it: found items, rubber stamps, wire springs, sewing bobbins, jewelry parts, charms, computer circuitry, cookie cutters, beads, etc. Press and release, creating a pattern of black and silver on the surface.

4 Use a silver leafing pen to outline the edge of the piece. Allow the clay to dry for 24–48 hours, depending on the temperature and humidity in your area.

5 Glue jewelry findings to the back of the piece to create earrings, brooches, or a pendant. Brush on a protective layer of clear nail polish to seal the piece.

MATERIALS

- Disposable gloves
- Creative Paperclay
- Black dye-based ink
- Parchment paper
- Silver interference pigments
- Rolling pin
- Art stamps
- Jewelry findings
- Found objects with texture
- Silver leafing pen
- All-purpose clear glue
- Clear nail polish

tips
- *Freezer paper may be substituted for parchment paper when rolling out Paperclay.*
- *Add more interference pigments in the colors of your choice, and continue pressing objects into the clay.*
- *To make a nice presentation card for your Paperclay jewelry, cut a square out of folded white cardstock, spray the square with silver webbing spray, and twist it into a diamond shape. Glue the jewelry piece to it before inserting the diamond piece to the card.*

artist: leslie altman, u.s.a

These beautiful journals are proof that even a plain leather book can be turned into an elegant work of art full of creative expression—with the aid of rubber stamps and pearlescent paints. The hibiscus flowers seem to jump right off the cover of one sample, which was first stamped with permanent ink and then painted with pearlescent paints.

Looking for a faster route to success? Try stamping the cover with a strong contrasting permanent ink and heat-setting it with an embossing tool. In just minutes, you can make a personal gift for a friend—or even yourself!

artist: christine cox, u.s.a

leather journals

MATERIALS

- Newsprint
- Leather journal, tanned with vegetable dyes
- Art stamps
- Permanent ink
- Embossing (heat) tool
- Small paintbrush
- Pearlescent paints
- Rubber gloves
- Sponge
- Leather dye
- Leather sealer (optional)
- Cotton swabs

1 Stamp an image onto the leather cover with permanent ink and allow it to dry for at least 10 minutes. To speed the process, apply heat to the image area with an embossing tool, but take care not to overheat the leather.
2 To paint the image, mix pearlescent paints and apply them sparingly, working in layers from lighter to darker hues. Allow each layer to dry before applying more paint. Use a small brush for detailing.
3 Don a pair of rubber gloves before using a damp sponge to apply an even layer of dye to the entire book cover, avoiding the stamped image. The dye will completely cover the leather, so great care must be taken to avoid painting it over the stamped image.
4 Allow the journal to dry for several hours or overnight.

tips

- Purchase leather-bound journals tanned with vegetable dyes or make your own; kits are available at some craft stores.
- Cover your work surface with newsprint to protect it from dyes and paints.
- Use cotton swabs and other small tools to apply the leather dye to areas closely surrounding the stamped images.
- It isn't necessary to paint the journal after stamping. Simply stamped images—if carefully placed—can be quite dramatic and beautiful, making this craft a quick and easy one by anyone's standards.
- Apply a leather sealer to protect the finish and make the cover water-resistant.

This pretty wooden pegrack is easily painted and stamped with a variety of objects. The artist used an ingenious device: a handmade stamp made from a flat kitchen sponge wrapped in burlap. The surface texture of the burlap, when stretched tightly around the sponge, picks up paint and transfers an interesting pattern to just about any surface. Try this technique with other wood furniture and home decor items, hatboxes, or even the walls in your home.

artist: livia mcree, U.S.A

wooden pegrack

1 Sand the wooden rack as necessary; remove any dust with a soft cloth. Paint the entire pegrack with one color, using a foam paintbrush.

2 Make a burlap pattern stamp by wrapping a piece of burlap around the sponge cut to a comfortable size. Grasp the stamp by the ends of the burlap, making sure the fabric is taut against the sponge. Option: Glue, tape, or baste the ends of the burlap together to hold it in place.

3 Apply a second paint color to the burlap stamp and test—stamp it on a piece of paper. When satisfied with the effect, stamp the pegrack.

MATERIALS
- Wooden pegrack
- Sandpaper
- Soft cloth
- Foam paintbrush
- Acrylics
- Burlap material
- Flat kitchen sponge
- Acrylic varnish

tips
- *Once the paint is dry, apply two coats of varnish.*
- *To stamp around tiny areas—-such as the pegs—make ministamps with a small piece of sponge.*
- *Try this type of stamping with linen or other textured fabrics. Layer several colors and textures over one another.*

Never carry a cumbersome purse again—this handy treasure pouch necklace is just the right size for toting credit cards, identification, currency, and other small essentials. Best of all, the necklace serves a dual purpose: It's not only functional but decorative as well. The artist used commercial rubber stamps in combination with her own hand-carved images to decorate these leather purses. Use a large shipping tag or the diagram supplied for a pattern template.

treasure pouch necklace

1. Use a photocopier to enlarge or reduce the pattern template. Cut it out and tape it to a piece of sturdy leather with a smooth surface.
2. Cut out the purse with a sharp craft knife. To finish the cut edges, color them with a black permanent marker or a laundry pen. Use a ballpoint pen to lightly mark where the holes will be punched along both sides of the purse (refer to the diagram). Punch out the holes with a 1/8" (.3 cm) hole punch.
3. Apply heat-set inks to the leather directly from the inkpad. Begin with the lightest colors and overlap with strokes of darker, contrasting colors. Once finished with the background shading, stamp various images in a collage fashion as shown in the samples. Heat-set the inks with an embossing (heat) tool, taking care not to overheat any one area.
4. Mix interference pigments with gum arabic and water. Spatter them lightly over the leather piece. When it is dry, seal the leather with a light coat of acrylic spray. Allow to dry for several hours or overnight.
5. Bend the purse as indicated in the diagram to create a bottom edge and a top flap. Align the holes along both edges and insert wire through them to bind the edges together. Then press the folded purse under weights for several hours.

MATERIALS

- Pattern template (see "Templates" section, p. 297)
- Smooth leather
- Sharp craft knife
- Permanent marker
- Ballpoint pen
- Hole punch
- Heat-set ink
- Art stamps
- Embossing (heat) tool
- Interference pigments
- Gum arabic
- Water
- Acrylic spray
- Wire
- Fibers
- Adhesive
- Coin
- Beads and charms

tips

- *Use a very sharp craft knife to avoid injury and a self-healing cutting mat to protect your work surface while cutting out the purse.*
- *Choose sturdy leather at least 1/16" (.25 cm) thick for a strong purse, but don't use leather that is too thick or you may have trouble bending it. To ease the bending of stiff leather, score it lightly on the backside with a bone folder.*
- *To create a decorative necklace, string four or five long (30" or 76 cm) fibers together and tie them in knots at 4–6" (10–15 cm) intervals. Tie both ends to the wire holding the purse together. To create a decorative embellishment, punch a hole through the center of the top flap and glue an Oriental coin over the top, string decorative fibers through the hole, and tie them in place. Add beads, shells, and charms as desired.*

artist: doris arndt, u.s.a

Sea glass may be an unusual base for a stamping project, but once you get used to the idea, you'll find many applications for it. Bits of sea glass can be sanded, drilled, stamped, and embossed to create charms and pendants for necklaces, brooches, and earrings. This project requires small stamps, a drill, and embossing powder—that's it. You can make a set of jewelry in about an hour. The artist chose a seashell stamp motif to carry through the ocean theme. Your choice of stamps is limited only by the size of the sea glass. Collage stamps, which are composed of many different bits of images, can be used to stamp sea glass and other small items. Try coloring your jewelry pieces with markers or chalks before sealing with a light application of acrylic spray.

artist: kristina ernst, U.S.A

sea glass
jewelry

MATERIALS

- Sea glass pieces
- Sandpaper
- Art stamps
- Pigment ink
- Embossing powder
- Embossing (heat) tool
- Colorant (optional)
- Acrylic spray
- Drill
- Jewelry findings
- Silver earring hooks
- Silver chain

1 Prepare the sea glass by washing it carefully and lightly sanding it to remove any rough edges. Using pigment ink, stamp the prepared sea glass with the images of your choice. Apply embossing powder and emboss with a heat tool.
2 Option: Color the images with colored pencils, acrylics, markers, iridescent pigments, or the colorant of your choice.
3 Seal the piece with a light application of acrylic spray.

tips
- *Drill a hole at the top of each sea glass piece. Insert wire jewelry findings for earrings and pendants; string the largest pendant from a silver chain.*
- *When coloring sea glass, use a light touch. Try colored pencils or pastels for a light application, watercolors or acrylics for more even and opaque coverage.*
- *Find sea glass at pet shops and aquarium stores. Medium- and large-size pieces work best for brooches and pendants, while smaller pieces are best for earrings.*

This round wooden box makes a lovely home decor item and can be used to hold postage stamps, polished stones, seashells, or other small treasures. It's easy to transform an ordinary wooden box into a keepsake item with rubber stamps and coloring media. Choose stamp images that reflect your favorite themes, as the artist did. After stamping the box with pigment ink, coloring options include acrylics, colored pencils, watercolors, chalks, and markers. Sealing the finished box with acrylic spray or painted varnish completes the project and protects the surface from water damage.

artist: olivia thomas, U.S.A

round wooden
mini box

1 Clean and sand a wooden box.
2 Stamp various images onto the box lid and around the sides using black or dark brown pigment ink. Heat-set the ink by applying an embossing (heat) tool to it, taking care not to heat any one area for too long.
3 Color the stamped images with the coloring medium of your choice. Spritz the box with a small amount of acrylic paint. Allow the box to dry completely.

MATERIALS
• Round wooden box
• Sandpaper
• Art stamps
• Pigment ink
• Embossing (heat) tool
• Chalks, markers, acrylics, watercolors, or colored pencils
• Acrylic sealant

tips
• *This technique can be applied to many wooden objects besides boxes: finials, bookstands, picture frames, light switch plates, and small unfinished furniture items.*
• *Seal the box with two or three light coats of matte acrylic spray or painted varnish.*

These jewelry pieces look like they were formed from beaten metal, but they are actually made with air-dry clay. Stamped impressions depicting ancient motifs lend an antique air to the necklaces and brooches pictured here. The secret is in the application of metallic paint and patina solutions (please see the Resources section for information about these products). Paint the pieces first with metallic acrylic paint, then with metalicized copper paint. Spray on a blue patina solution, and allow the pieces to oxodize. The most difficult part of this project? Waiting for the clay to dry.

antiqued clay jewelry

1 Using a rolling pin, roll out a small amount of air-dry clay to about 1/8" (.5 cm) thickness, in a rough oval shape. To add texture to the surface, roll the clay between two layers of pastry cloth or a textured washcloth.

2 Impress several rubber stamp images into the bottom half of the oval, turn it over, and make stamp impressions on the opposite end and side of the oval. Fold the clay over to form a half-circle, leaving space for a chain or cord to pass through at the top. Use a ballpoint pen or a toothpick to poke three holes at the bottom of the pendant for the jump-rings.

3 On a separate piece of rolled-out clay, stamp a small leaf image three times, cut out, and poke holes near the top of each leaf. Allow all the clay pieces to air dry thoroughly; drying times will vary according to local temperature and humidity.

4 Sand the dried clay pieces with fine-grade sandpaper and wipe them clean with a soft cloth. Paint each piece with copper or metallic acrylic paint, then paint with metalized copper paint and spray on a blue patina solution. Allow the pieces to oxidize to the desired effect. Apply a light coat of metallic rub-ons in autumn gold to the surface of each piece.

5 Attach the three leaves to the bottom of the pendant with copper jump-rings. Add a beaded chain to form the necklace.

MATERIALS

- Rolling pin
- Air-dry clay
- Pastry cloth
- Art stamps
- Craft knife
- Sandpaper
- Soft cloth
- Paintbrushes
- Metallic acrylic paint
- Metalized copper paint
- Plastic wrap
- Blue patina solution
- Metallic rub-ons
- Copper jump-rings
- Copper chain
- Beads

tips

- *Protect your work area with a plastic dropcloth, as this technique can be messy.*
- *When stamping into clay, press down firmly to leave a lasting impression.*
- *Option: To seal the completed jewelry, use acrylic spray or water-based matte varnish.*
- *To make brooches instead of pendants, simply use the central piece as a brooch, poke holes in the soft clay so you can add beaded dangles on jump-rings, and attach a pin back to the back of the dry, painted piece.*

artist: pamela tarpy, u.s.a

Present home-preserved peaches with special packaging: your own hand-stamped label! Rubber stamps and sticker paper make custom labels easy. The next time you're canning preserves at home, try making a beautiful label to complement the container. A stamp with an image that hints at the contents is perfectly appropriate. Add a bit of raffia, and you've preserved an artful presentation. Use the same stamps and inks to decorate recipe cards and a box to hold them.

artist: sherri helzer, U.S.A

stamped kitchen
labels & recipe set

MATERIALS

- Sticker paper
- Sponge
- Dye or permanent inkpads
- Art stamps
- Canned preserves
- Fibers, ribbon, or raffia
- Wooden box
- Sandpaper
- Chalks
- Interference pigments
- Matte acrylic spray
- File cards
- Embellishments

1 Beginning with sticker paper about 2.5" (6 cm) square, sponge on a textured background in soft, muted colors (like the peach and yellow the artist used). Stamp the sticker paper with an image such as the peaches stamp used by the artist, using terra cotta ink. Overstamp the first image with a label stamp in dark brown or black. Apply the sticker to a jar of preserves. Wrap the top with raffia, ribbon, or decorative fibers.

2 To make the recipe box, sand a wooden box and stain it lightly with peach and beige chalks. Stamp the box with brown ink and dust it with gold interference pigments. Over-stamp this background with dark brown ink, and dust the box again with bronze interference pigments. Seal the box with acrylic spray.

3 To make the recipe cards, stamp background imagery with light-colored ink. Handwrite or computer-generate "A Favorite Recipe" at the top of each card in permanent ink, and handwrite your favorite recipe. Wrap the cards with raffia, ribbon, or fibers and tie them together with buttons, beads, or other embellishments. Enclose the cards within the wooden box.

tips
- *When overlapping stamped images, stamp the background images first using lighter colors. Darker colors (like dark brown or black) will show up well against the light stamping.*
- *Concerned about smudges? Use permanent ink instead of dye or pigment ink.*

Large wooden beads commonly used by macramé artists can be stamped and used as decorative drapery pulls or necklaces with the aid of tissue paper. Because these beads are too small to stamp on directly, first stamp onto tissue paper then decoupage the paper onto the surface of the bead. Coloring and glazing techniques finish each design, which can then be incorporated into a variety of art projects.

wooden beads

1. Paint wooden beads with white acrylic paint and set them aside to dry.
2. Use permanent black ink to stamp several small images onto tissue paper. Cut out the images close to the edges. Glue them carefully to the surface of each painted bead, overlapping some images for effect and taking care to smooth any wrinkles.
3. When the decoupaged beads have dried completely, color them with markers, colored pencils, or sponged-on dye ink.
4. Seal each bead with two to three light coats of acrylic spray.

MATERIALS

- Large wooden beads
- Acrylic paint
- Permanent black ink
- Art stamps
- Tissue paper
- Acrylic spray
- Glue
- Markers, colored pencils, or dye ink
- Acrylic sealant

tips

- *A final coat of acrylic sealant adds a crystal lacquer finish to the beads.*
- *For necklaces, string the decorated wooden beads with purchased beads, charms, and chains.*
- *For drapery pulls, cut several pieces of decorative fiber to the same length, double them, and push the doubled-over end through the bead. Run a braided piece of fiber through the doubled end to create a pull. Push the bead up as far as it will go to hold it in place.*
- *If beads don't capture your fancy, remember that many other small wood items—finials, bookstands, picture frames, for example—can be decorated in the same manner.*

Small wood pieces can be stamped and assembled to make an intriguing front for a handmade book, like the example here. Lightweight, inexpensive, and easy to find at craft stores and hobby shops, wood pieces cut in numerous shapes and sizes provide an interesting departure from the usual stamping surface. Once stamped and painted or collaged, the pieces can be used for jewelry projects or incorporated into large assemblage artwork. Try making a pretty brooch or pendant, or create a three-dimensional sculpture. When it comes to stamping on wood, you are only limited by your imagination.

stamped miniature book

1 Prepare the small wood pieces by sanding them lightly and buffing them to a smooth finish, then apply a thin coat of acrylic paint or matte medium to the wood surface to prevent the pigment ink from soaking into it.

2 Using permanent ink or crafter's stamping ink, stamp the prepared wood pieces with the images of your choice. Allow the ink to dry; then color in the images with a light application of pigment ink or acrylic paint. Set them aside.

3 Cut two pieces of bookboard or heavy cardboard to approximately 2.75" x 3" (7 cm x 8 cm). Cover the bookboards with handmade papers, gluing the paper in place with archival adhesive. Use silicon glue to attach the wood pieces to the cover, adding collage items, beads, and charms as desired.

4 Construct pages approximately 2.5" x 2.75" (6 cm x 7 cm) from one piece of paper 16.5" x 2.5" (42 cm x 6 cm). Fold the paper five times to create an accordion-fold book. Stamp each page in the book and rub the top of the stamped images with pigment inks.

5 Affix the outside pages of the accordion-fold book to the insides of both bookboards from step 3. Allow the book to dry completely. Add a bead and yarn to create a book closure.

MATERIALS

- Collage items
- Small wood pieces
- Sandpaper
- Paintbrushes
- Acrylic paint or matte medium
- Permanent ink
- Art stamps
- Pigment ink
- Bookboard
- Handmade papers
- Archival adhesive
- Silicon glue
- Bead
- Decorative yarn

tips

- *Choose collage elements such as handmade papers, fibers, beads, and charms in advance. Once items that fit a particular theme are chosen, it's much easier to assemble the book.*
- *Pigment ink can be used to lightly brush on color, enhancing the surface texture of handmade paper. It can also be used to color the wood pieces, to age the inside papers of a book, or to color strings or fibers used as book closures.*
- *Jewelry adhesive may be substituted for silicon glue.*
- *An assemblage of stamped wood pieces can be used to make a collage brooch or other decorative items.*

artist: carolyn wait, u.s.a

Make a beautiful keepsake treasure box from a discarded cardboard jewelry case. By cleverly stamping the same image four times in the center of the lid, create the look of Mexican tiles for a fraction of the cost. The air-dry clay is easy to form and stamp into, and it dries to a firm finish in a short time. To enhance the metallic appearance of your jewelry box, apply metallic paints and rub-ons, burnishing the surface with a soft cloth.

sunflower box

1. Using a rolling pin, roll out a ball of air-drying terra cotta clay to about 1/8" (.5 cm) thickness, in a square about 5" x 5" (13 cm x 13 cm). To add texture to the surface, roll the clay between two layers of pastry cloth or a textured washcloth.

2. Stamp a design in the center of the clay. Repeat four times, as the artist did, to create "tiles." While the clay is still wet, drape it over the outside lid of a cardboard jewelry case, forming the sides with your fingers until the lid is completely covered with clay. Spritz with water as necessary. Allow the clay to air dry on the box lid.

3. While the clay is drying, paint the bottom of the jewelry case with bronze acrylics, inside and out. Randomly paint metallic copper paint over the surface, and immediately spritz the surface with patina blue paint. Layer various colors of transparent acrylic paint, spattering it on for a decorative affect.

4. Apply the same type of painterly effect to the clay lid once it has dried completely. Green and purple paints can be applied first, followed by metallic bronze or copper. Once the paint has dried, sand it on both sides to age the surface. Apply metallic rub-ons to the surface, and buff with a soft cloth.

5. Paint four decorative wooden dowel caps with copper acrylics. Once dry, layer brown and purple transparent paints over the dowel caps, and then wrap the dowels with copper wire. Glue the wooden dowels to the bottom of the box.

MATERIALS

- Rolling pin
- Air-dry terra cotta clay
- Pastry cloth
- Art stamps
- Cardboard jewelry box, 3" x 3" x 3" (8 cm x 8 cm x 8 cm)
- Spray bottle with water
- Paintbrushes
- Acrylics
- Metallic copper paint
- Patina blue paint
- Transparent paints
- Sandpaper
- Metallic rub-ons
- Soft cloth
- Decorative wood dowel caps
- 20-gauge copper wire
- Adhesive

tips
- *When stamping into clay, press down firmly to leave a lasting impression.*
- *Option: To seal the completed box, use water-based matte varnish.*

artist: pamela tarpy, u.s.a

Bits of sea glass form the unlikely basis for these abstract art brooches. By stamping on shrink plastic, the images can be shrunk down to about a quarter of their original size—just right for jewelry. Once the images have been stamped, colored, and cut out, shrinking the plastic is easy with an embossing tool.

sea glass brooches

1 Prepare the shrink plastic by lightly sanding both sides with sandpaper. Using a circular motion, sand the entire piece carefully to ensure even coverage of pigment.

2 Using permanent ink, stamp the prepared shrink plastic with the images of your choice. Allow the ink to dry, then color in the images with a light application of chalks or dry pastels.

3 Cut out the stamped images and apply heat to them with an embossing tool. After a few seconds, the plastic will shrink. Wait until the plastic stops shrinking, and then quickly shut off the embossing tool and press the shrink plastic down with a smooth object such as cardboard. This will ensure the plastic cools with a smooth, flat finish.

4 Glue the shrink plastic pieces to the sea glass with silicon glue.

5 Attach beads or charms to the brooch as desired, or wrap the sea glass with wire as shown.

6 Once the brooch has dried completely, affix a pin back and allow the glue to dry.

MATERIALS
- Shrink plastic
- Sandpaper
- Sea glass pieces
- Permanent ink
- Art stamps
- Chalks
- Scissors
- Embossing (heat) tool
- Cardboard or other smooth object
- Silicon glue
- Wire
- Pin backs

artist: linda milligan, u.s.a

tips
- *Find sea glass at pet shops and aquarium stores. Medium- and large-size pieces work best for brooches. Wash the sea glass carefully. It should be smooth, but use sandpaper to remove any rough edges.*
- *When coloring shrink plastic, use a light touch, keeping in mind that the hues will greatly intensify once the plastic is shrunk. Colored pencils may be substituted for chalks or pastels.*
- *Jewelry adhesive may be substituted for silicon glue.*
- *Large pieces of shrink plastic may be heated and shrunk in a toaster oven at about 275–325°F (135–165°C) in lieu of an embossing tool.*

What a lovely gift this would make—polymer clay jewelry in its own decorative box! The artist cleverly used the same stamp images and paint colors to create jewelry pieces and a treasure box to hold them. Mixed copper and gold polymer clays form the metallic foundation for these pieces, which are then stamped, cut into geometric shapes, and painted with metallic acrylics in violet, gold, copper, and olive-green. The process is quite simple; a fun project for making holiday gifts or birthday presents for the special people in your life.

jewels in a box

Jewelry

1 Polymer clay must be conditioned before use by molding and shaping it by hand. Once the clay has warmed and softened, run it through a hand-crank pasta machine up to twenty times, which actually strengthens the clay by changing its molecular structure.

2 Prepare and condition copper and gold polymer clays. Mix copper with gold clay, and pinch off four small pieces, one piece about twice as large as the other three.

3 Roll each piece of polymer clay into a ball. Roll out the largest ball flat, choose an art stamp with an abstract image, and press it down firmly into the clay. Cut out a pear shape. Set it aside.

4 Create a leaf and stem with scrap clay, and press them down firmly on the pear. Repeat the process with the remaining polymer clay, rolling out each to flatten it and then stamping abstract images into the surface. Cut out small circles, triangles, and other pleasing shapes to create earrings and brooches.

5 Bake the clay in a toaster oven as directed; each brand of polymer clay requires a different temperature and baking time. Keep an eye on the clay as it bakes. (If it gives off a strong odor or turns brown, the oven is too hot, or the clay may have been baking too long; remove the pieces immediately.) Allow the baked pieces to cool for several minutes before proceeding.

6 Paint each piece with metallic acrylics in violet, gold, copper, and olive green, and allow them to air dry. Seal the pieces with acrylic spray (matte or glossy). Attach pin backs or other jewelry findings on the back with jewelry adhesive. Allow the adhesive to air dry for 24 hours before wearing the jewelry.

Jewelry Box

1 Prepare and condition the polymer clay as in step 1 under Jewelry Technique.

2 Roll out enough clay (about 3/8" or 1 cm thick) to cover the top and sides of a small papier-mâché box and lid.

3 Stamp the entire sheet of clay with abstract images.

4 Cut a strip of stamped clay and cover the sides of the lid, sticking it in place with white glue. Cut a strip of clay large enough to cover the top of the lid, and stick it in place with glue.

5 Bake the lid per package directions, as in step 5 under Jewelry Technique.

6 Place the polymer clay lid onto the papier-mâché box. Prepare a strip of stamped clay to wrap around the box, glue it in place with white glue, and bake the box, following steps 1–5 above.

MATERIALS

- Copper and gold polymer clay
- Pasta machine
- Art stamps
- Craft knife
- Toaster oven
- Paintbrushes
- Metallic acrylics
- Acrylic spray
- White glue
- Jewelry adhesive
- Jewelry findings
- Small papier-mâché box

tips

- *When choosing art stamps for use with polymer clay, look for deeply etched, bold designs. Highly detailed stamps will not result in satisfactory impressions.*

Note: Pasta machines, toaster ovens, and other kitchen items used with polymer clay should never be used afterward to prepare food because residue from the clay is toxic to ingest. Buy such items inexpensively at yard sales and reserve them for craft use.

artist: debbie shipley, U.S.A

Fossils are fascinating works of nature's art; their intriguing patterns and designs have inspired artists for many years. Now stamp artists can make fossil-like jewelry pieces using patterned art stamps and white polymer clay. Once stamped and baked, the pieces are allowed to cool and then coated with brown antiquing medium. As the medium dries, it penetrates the tiny cracks and grooves. Sanding the dried polymer clay removes most of the brown pigment from the surface, but leaves enough to simulate the look of an aged bone or fossil. Strung together with small purchased bone beads, it's difficult to tell the real thing from the imposter.

faux fossil

necklace

1 Prepare and condition white polymer clay as described under "tips" below, and then pinch off five pieces, one piece about twice as large as the other four. Irregularly sized beads are more interesting than perfectly sized ones.

2 Roll each piece of polymer clay into a ball. Choose an art stamp with a seashell impression, and press it down firmly on the largest ball, flattening the clay. Use a round toothpick to run a hole through the clay near the top, lengthwise. Set it aside.

3 Repeat the process with the remaining polymer clay, rolling each ball into a long tube before sandwiching it between two rubber stamps to create impressions on both sides. To create four-sided beads, turn the polymer clay over and smash the unstamped sides. Then use a round toothpick to poke a hole lengthwise through each bead.

4 Transfer the clay beads to a toaster oven and bake as directed; each brand of polymer clay requires a different temperature and baking time. Keep an eye on the clay as it bakes. (If it gives off a strong odor or turns brown, the oven is too hot or the clay may have been baking too long; remove the pieces immediately.) Allow the baked beads to cool for several minutes before proceeding.
Note: Pasta machines, toaster ovens, and other kitchen items used with polymer clay should never be used afterward to prepare food because residue from the clay is toxic to ingest. Buy such items inexpensively at yard sales and reserve them for craft use.

5 Paint a thick coat of brown antiquing medium on each bead and allow it to dry. Rub off excess paint with a soft cloth or damp sponge. Use a fine-grade sandpaper to roughen the top layers of each bead, removing the antiquing medium from the surface while allowing it to stain the impressed grooves to simulate old ivory.

6 Allow the beads to dry completely. Seal with acrylic spray, and string with real bone beads and spacer beads.

MATERIALS

- White polymer clay
- Pasta machine
- Art stamps
- Round toothpicks
- Toaster oven
- Paintbrushes
- Antiquing medium
- Sponge or soft cloth
- Fine sandpaper
- Acrylic spray
- Bone beads
- Spacer beads
- Cord

tips

- *Polymer clay must be conditioned before use by molding and shaping it by hand. Once the clay has warmed and softened, run it through a hand-crank pasta machine up to twenty times, which actually strengthens the clay by changing its molecular structure.*
- *When choosing art stamps for use with polymer clay, look for deeply etched, bold designs. Highly detailed stamps will not result in satisfactory impressions.*
- *To impress both sides of the polymer clay at once, sandwich it between two stamps and press them firmly together. The clay will flatten between the two stamps and receive impressions on both sides.*
- *Dark brown acrylic paint may be substituted for antiquing medium in step 5.*

Stamping on copper is a very easy technique that yields spectacular results in minutes. Fashion a stunning treasure box or sensational greeting cards by the simple application of liver of sulfur to thin copper sheets. The method requires good ventilation, but the results are worth the inconvenience. Copper metal sheets can be found at most craft and art supply stores. Liver of sulfur, a specialty item, is available at bead stores that carry jewelry-making supplies, at rubber stamp stores, or in jewelry craft catalogs. When cutting copper sheets, preserve your good scissors by using metal shears found at most hardware stores.

copper-stamped
treasure box & card

Copper Stamping

1 Fill a small plastic tub with about an inch of cold water.
2 Cut out a piece of thin copper metal sheet, and wipe it clean with a cotton ball dipped in alcohol.
3 Use the felt piece to make a "stamp pad" with petroleum jelly instead of ink. Lay the felt on a plastic plate, and rub a smooth, thin layer of the petroleum jelly onto it. Stamp into it with a rubber stamp, and then stamp the copper piece. Remove the stamp quickly, taking care not to smear the image. If it smears, wipe the copper clean with an alcohol swab, and try again.
4 Submerge the stamped copper piece into the plastic tub of cold water. Pour about 3 tablespoons of liver of sulfur over the copper piece. The petroleum jelly creates a "resist" or barrier that the liver of sulfur will not penetrate. Observe how the unstamped areas turn black. The longer you wait, the more mottled and blackened the copper surface will become.
5 Use tweezers to remove the copper piece from the liver of sulfur solution. Rinse it under clear running water. Set it on a paper towel to dry, and dab off excess water with a paper towel. Once dry, wipe off any remaining petroleum jelly and "scaling," a chemical residue from the reaction of the copper with the liver of sulfur.

Treasure Box

1 Create small stamped copper pieces using the process outlined in "Copper Stamping."
2 Cover a papier-mâché box with decorative paper. Adhere the papers to the box with strong adhesive and let dry.
3 Trim the stamped copper pieces, and blind emboss them by rubbing the stylus tip against the stamped copper sheet to create raised areas within the image.
4 Adhere the copper pieces to the treasure box. Thin copper sheets will bend easily and cleave to most objects with strong adhesive.
5 Punch holes into the box to string it on a cord, adding decorative beads for embellishment.

Greeting Card

1 Create stamped copper pieces using the process outlined.
2 Trim the copper pieces to size. Try making one large central image or several cutout pieces to assemble in a collage.
3 Assemble cards by affixing with adhesive graduated layers of decorative paper to a piece of folded cardstock. Try paste-painted paper, discarded giftwrap, or papers previously stamped with pigment ink. Attach the copper pieces last to create points of interest.

tips

• *Papiér-mâché boxes are available in many sizes and shapes from craft retailers.*
• *Sand the copper prior to stamping to create more or less patina.*
• *After treating the copper with liver of sulfur, burn it with a candle flame for more mottled effect.*
• *Changing the ratio of liver of sulfur to water will make a difference in the appearance of the copper, as will the length of time the copper remains submerged in the sulfur bath. For deep black lines, mix 1 tablespoon liver of sulfur with 1 cup water, pour it into a plastic tub, and immerse the copper sheet.*

MATERIALS

• Shallow tub of water
• Copper metal sheet
• Metal shears
• Rubbing alcohol
• Cotton ball
• Small piece of felt
• Petroleum jelly
• Plastic plate
• Art stamps
• Liver of sulfur
• Tweezers
• Paper towel
• Stamped copper pieces
• Decorative papers
• Cardstock
• Adhesive

TREASURE BOX MATERIALS

• Stamped copper pieces
• Small papier-mâché treasure box
• Decorative paper
• Adhesive
• Embossing tool
• Stylus
• Decorative bead
• Cord with tassel
• Hole punch, awl, or drill

artist: sandra mccall, u.s.a

A bold, abstract design is easy to achieve with art stamps and shrink plastic. This creative brooch was first stamped, cut out, then shrunk under an embossing (heat) tool. Stamping images onto shrink plastic allows the artist to miniaturize the composition and turn it into a spectacular piece of costume jewelry. Once the plastic has cooled, it can be colored with paints, dyes, inks, colored pencils, or pastels. Small pieces can be adhered together or attached to one another via jump-rings to create a tiny assemblage jewelry piece. Matching earrings or necklace pendants can be made in the same manner.

abstract
brooch

1 Using pigment ink or crafter's stamping ink, stamp the prepared shrink plastic with the images of your choice. Allow the ink to dry. Cut out an abstract shape, roughly rectangular, from the stamped shrink plastic. Punch seven holes along the bottom edge of the piece.

2 On a separate piece of shrink plastic, stamp three triangles and cut them out. Do the same with eight identical petroglyph images. Cut them out carefully, and punch holes in their heads so that jump-rings can pass through.

3 Shrink all the plastic pieces using an embossing (heat) tool or a toaster oven set to 275–325°F (135–165°). After a few seconds, the plastic will shrink down, as will the punched-out holes. Wait until the plastic stops shrinking, then quickly shut off the embossing tool and press the shrink plastic down with a smooth object such as cardboard. This will ensure the plastic cools with a smooth, flat finish.

4 Paint the stamped and shrunken pieces with acrylics; a tiny paintbrush may be needed. Metallic acrylic paints are especially effective. Allow the paint to dry completely before proceeding.

5 Use silicon glue to adhere the shrink plastic pieces together as shown. Use needle-nose pliers to open the jump-rings and pass them through the tiny holes in the main piece of the brooch and through the heads of the petroglyph images. Stick one of the petroglyph images directly to the main piece as shown. Affix a pin back and allow it to dry.

MATERIALS
- Shrink plastic
- Sandpaper
- Art stamps
- Pigment ink
- Scissors
- Hole punch
- Embossing (heat) tool
- Cardboard or other smooth object
- Acrylics
- Tiny paintbrush
- Silicon glue
- Needle-nose pliers
- Jump-rings
- Pin back

tips
- *Prepare the shrink plastic by lightly sanding both sides with sandpaper. Use a circular motion; sand the entire piece carefully to ensure an even coverage of pigment.*
- *Jewelry adhesive may be substituted for silicon glue.*
- *Large pieces of shrink plastic may be heated and shrunk in a toaster oven at about 275–325°F (135–165°C) in lieu of an embossing tool.*
- *Tiny seed beads may be added as an embellishment.*

artist: sherrill kahn, u.s.a

Sierra &
Stephanie

FRAME

back

ground

stamping for scrapbooks

As an art form develops over time, it seems to become more and more sophisticated and refined. The artists who work within a particular medium become more adept at designing and at using their tools. Choices become more numerous as the availability of materials begins to grow. More artists are attracted to the medium, and they bring other skills and methods with them, so the range of supplies and techniques increases even more.

This has happened with rubber stamping. More people are creating within this discipline, and more companies are producing better and better designs and products for us to use. This has also happened with scrapbooks and memory products. As more people are attracted to preserving and beautifully presenting their family photographs, more companies are making more diverse and refined scrapbooking products.

These two areas are now on the verge of a merge. Stampers want new ways to use their stock of stamps and accessories, and scrapbook enthusiasts want new ideas for building their libraries of memory pages.

If you're a stamper who has yet to try scrapbooking, you will find lots of help and inspiration in this section to get started. If, on the other hand, you're a scrapbooker who is searching for new ideas for artistic albums, you'll see how stamps can be used to meet that need.

The key to creativity is experimentation. I believe that each of us is creative, that it is built into our systems to be so. We have a need to create in order to fulfill the purpose that each of us carries throughout life. To go along with that belief, I think the most joy and happiness comes with the surprises that occur when we try something new.

So leaf through, start anywhere, and try the techniques, mix and match, or make your pages as close to the artists' methods as possible—it really doesn't matter. Just start and, most of all, enjoy the creative process.

—Betty Auth

To Make the Page at Left

The background is created in two steps. First, stamp a sheet of pale, neutral cardstock with a large home decor fern stamp, randomly covering the page with two or three colors and leaving a faint impression. Use the medium lacy leaf stamp over the top of the fern layer, filling in some of the blank areas. Finally, stamp the small leaf multiple times on white cardstock with a heavier coat of the same colors. When dry, add letters to each stamping. Outline the letters with black pen and cut out the leaves. Place the words on the page, add a couple of blank leaf cutouts, and stamp a border along one edge of the page to balance the design.

Backgrounds

Combined with photographs or artwork, backgrounds are the most elemental part of a scrapbook page. They set the mood for the entire page, and act as a key to communicate the look and feel of all the elements and embellishments that will be added. In some cases, the background can stand alone, the only additions being the mechanics necessary for mounting or identifying the photographs.

A variety of coordinating backgrounds may be stacked and layered to increase depth and interest on a page. Stamping and embossing the entire background with dozens of small, patterned stampings is also effective.

Forever Yours: Double Wedding Pages

ARTIST: VICKI SCHREINER

To construct these coordinating wedding pages, stamp the roses and words with gold ink on white cardstock, then color the images with art pencils. Cut out the motifs and set aside. Make the frames on the left page by cutting squares, ovals, and rectangles, about ½" (1 cm) larger all around than the photos, from moss green cardstock. Trim the edges of the cardstock with paper edgers and adhere the photos, centered on top of the shapes. Make the large photo frame on the right page by cutting two corner triangles from the lace place mat and fitting them together to form a rectangle. Cut another smaller rectangle of handmade paper and center it on top of the lace one. Center the photograph on top of the handmade paper and add ribbon trim along each edge.

Place the framed photos on the striped pages, leaving room for ribbon garlands at the top of each page. Glue ribbon across the tops of the pages and add embellishments to the ribbon and to the frames.

MATERIALS

- **Stamps**
  Forever Yours
  Small rose engraving
  Romantic rose garland
  Romantic rose corner
- **Ink and Inkpads**
  Metallic gold ink
- **Papers**
  White cardstock
  Moss green cardstock
  White lace paper place mat
  Handmade paper
- **Miscellaneous**
  Art pencils
  Moss green acrylic paint, clear glaze base
  Removable tape
  Sponge
  Victorian paper edgers
  Ribbon

Step 1

Here is an easy and effective way to make a striped background. First, measure and lightly mark the top and bottom edge of the cardstock where the stripes will go. Place the cardstock on a large cardboard work surface, and lay the stripes with removable tape, extending them over the edge of the paper onto the cardboard. Sponge a thinned layer of paint and glaze base over the entire page, including the tape. Dip the sponge in the paint mixture and blot lightly on folded paper towels before applying to the page so the paint won't seep under the edges of the tape.

Step 2

Allow the paint to dry and carefully remove the tape to reveal the striped background. Repeat this background striping on as many pages as you need at one time so the colors on facing pages will match.

Step 3

Randomly stamp over the stripes with the rose stamp and gold ink, retaining a light and airy appearance. Ink the stamp and blot lightly on a folded paper towel to remove some of the ink. Experiment on a separate sheet of cardstock until you achieve the look you want, then re ink and stamp over the striped background.

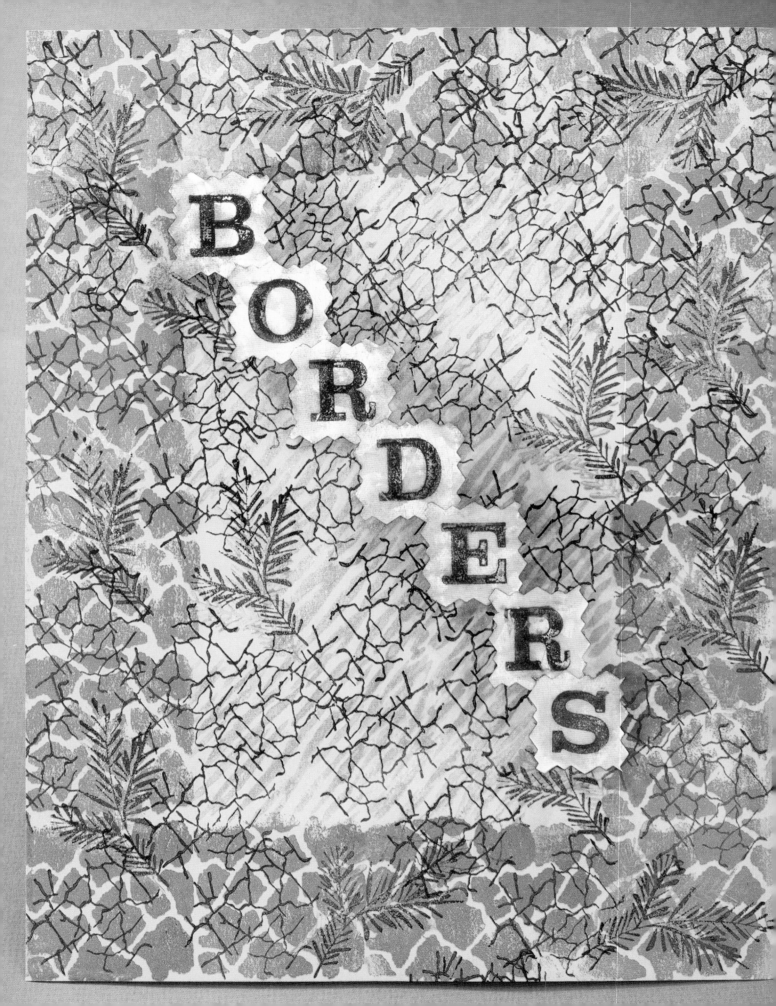

To Make the Page at Left

Choose a bright turquoise cardstock and stamp the border all around with a giraffe stamp and bronze or gold metallic ink. Using the same ink, fill the center of the page with repetitions of a tiger stamp. With black pigment ink, cover the entire surface with the largest pattern on a crackle cube stamp. Randomly stamp a black leaf image over the page to fill in empty spaces. Stamp letters on gold foil with black embossing ink and dry with a heat tool. Cut out the individual letters with paper edgers and glue in place. This treatment could be used to add color and depth to any page.

STAMPING TRICK

To make a straight, clean inside edge on a border around an entire 8 1/2" × 11" (22 cm × 28 cm) page, cut out a rectangle of copy paper or cardstock 2" (5 cm) smaller all around, which would be 4 1/2" × 7" (11 cm × 18 cm). Center this mask on the page with temporary adhesive, then stamp the border. Remove the mask to reveal a border with a sharp, clean edge.

Borders

There is a very fine line between what is considered a border and what is considered a frame, and sometimes it's impossible to separate the two. When referring to a border, we usually think of a design that goes around all the edges of the page. Although a border may frame a page, the term "frame" is most often used for a design that surrounds an individual element on the page.

A border gives a scrapbook page a more finished look and increases the beauty and elegance of photographs and other elements that it surrounds.

For the page shown at left, a wide, even border was stamped on the page before any other elements were added. You could also place photos first and add a border that overlaps some of them and ties the elements together. A border may be repeated stampings of the same image, or it may include several different images. Try different stamps in different, coordinating colors, and try several different stamps in the same color.

Stamp a pale background cardstock with slightly darker neutral color ink and fill in the open areas with watercolor pencils that match the photographs and other images on the page. Artful borders can also be used all around a page to enhance photos or other artwork.

Today is Friday: Simple Stamped Border

This is a wonderful and simple way to display a child's school papers. The page is clear and direct, enhances the subject, and is very easy to duplicate. If you have a good photo of the child as well as a school assignment, you have the basic elements for creating this treasure.

ARTIST: pj DUTTON

QUICK TRICK

Tie page elements together by framing them all with the same thin border in black or a color. Angle some of the elements on the page instead of lining everything up in straight rows.

MATERIALS

- **Stamps**
  Block letters
  Block numbers
- **Ink and Inkpads**
  Black pigment
- **Paper**
  Black cardstock
  Red cardstock
- **Miscellaneous**
  Black photo corners

To Make the Page

Cut a piece of black cardstock about a ¼" (5 mm) larger on all sides than the photo and mount the photo to it. Repeat for the school paper, rounding the corners of the cardstock. Trim ¼" (5 mm) off the edges of the red cardstock, round the corners, and stamp the border around the sheet. Mount the red cardstock to a sheet of black. Move the items around until you are satisfied with the arrangement, then glue the school paper to the background and mount the photo with black photo corners.

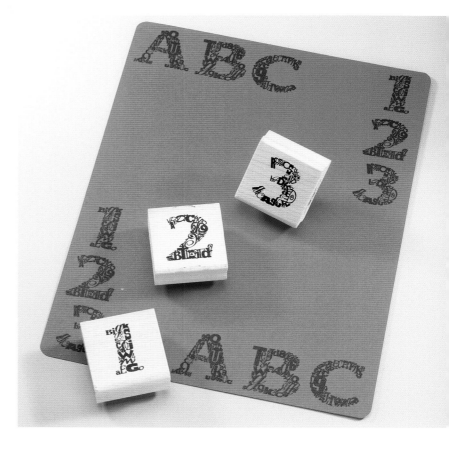

To Make the Page at Left

Ink a solid block frame stamp with a sponge, leaving the center of the stamp free of ink. Randomly stamp with several colors over the entire page, cleaning the stamp between colors. Use a smaller frame stamp to fill in some of the blank areas, then stamp the small frame several times on some coordinating parchment stock and emboss in gold. After the embossing has set, add colored pencil in the center of each stamped frame for contrast. Next, stamp the letters with pigment ink inside each frame. Cut out the framed letters and apply to the background with paper glue. Finally, trim the edges of the background paper with paper edgers and glue the entire layout to a sheet of contrasting cardstock. This method can be used successfully with photographs or artwork by simply changing the number of frames and using different letters.

Frames

Creating just the right frame to complement treasured artwork and photographs can be both rewarding and enjoyable. Frames can add just the right mood to a photograph or piece of art, and they can focus attention on the area of a page you wish to highlight. They can be subtle decorations or pronounced design elements. A frame can be created as a separate element that is added to the page, giving it dimension and texture. This chapter contains a variety of ideas for creating unique frames for scrapbook pages.

Simple frames may be stamped around a photograph to contrast or coordinate with the background paper. To create this look, stamp the background first, then trim the photograph and glue it on top of the stamped frame to preserve a clean edge.

Flower Babies: Accents as Frames

You can embellish a frame by adding one or more paper appliqués. Here, single and multiple images are stamped on a separate sheet of paper, then cut out and glued partially over the edge of the photographs and the background. The pink and fuchsia flowers surrounding the sweet faces enhance these adorable baby photos.

This method allows the freedom to experiment with colors and shapes before committing to a particular design. You can stamp many flowers, hearts, stars and other shapes on white paper, cut them out, then sprinkle them on the pages of your scrapbook, only gluing down the ones you like.

ARTIST: SANDRA McCALL

MATERIALS

- **Stamps**
  Small flowers
  Large oak leaf, leaf spray and fern
- **Ink and ink pads**
  Small petal shaped and Cat's Eye pigment ink pads
  Magenta to green dye inks
- **Papers**
  One sheet plum cardstock
  Two sheets white cardstock
  One or two sheets pale yellow paper
  Two or three sheets white copy paper
- **Miscellaneous**
  Scissors
  Household bleach
  Paper towels
  Large nylon paint brush or brayer

QUICK TRICK

When making copies of your photographs, print several different sizes, including some as small as postage stamps, so you can arrange them in a variety of ways before affixing them to the page. Repeating the same image in several sizes can be used to focus the eye where you want it to go for maximum impact.

Getting Started

Step 1
Protect your work surface and wear old clothing since you'll be using bleach. Start with a sheet of light colored cardstock. You could also try a matte copier paper or art paper.

Step 2
Press the small pigment ink pads directly on the paper, alternating and turning them as you work to swirl the colors all over the page. Rub the colors into the paper with paper towels.

Step 3
Paint or brayer dark magenta to green dye ink over the surface, covering the pigment ink.

Step 4
Pour the bleach into several layers of folded paper towels in a dish and pat the stamps on the bleach as you would use an ink pad. Stamp off most of the dye ink, revealing the leaf patterns in pigment ink underneath. The bleach will lighten as it dries, and you can speed the process with a hair dryer or heat tool. Rinse stamps immediately in cool running water and dry them.

Making the Flowers

Stamp the flower images on white cardstock using dye ink, and cut them out leaving small white margins around them so they will stand out from the page.

Finishing the Page

Up to seven layers of paper are used in some areas of this precious scrapbook page. Layer successively smaller sheets of plum, yellow, and faux batik papers. Mount the photographs in various sizes on white cardstock and cut them out with a narrow white margin. Place the photographs on the background and sprinkle flowers around the page to tie it all together. Make the labels from pale yellow cardstock.

To Make the Page at Left

Stamp the background with a large flower block and then a smaller leaf stamp using multicolored ink. With paper edgers, trim about 1/2" (1 cm) from all four sides of the page and save the trimmed pieces. Mount the entire page on a sheet of contrasting cardstock. To make a perfectly square corner, stamp and emboss a flourish on the lower right corner of an uncut vellum sheet. Use paper edgers to trim it into a rounded fan shape. With a glue stick and a narrow line of glue, adhere only the straight edges of the vellum to the edges of the background. Vellum wrinkles easily when liquid glue is applied, so a glue stick is a good choice. Glue a thin strip of the reserved background piece over the glue line on the vellum corner to hide any wrinkles. Cut another piece of vellum into a fan shape, stamp the word on it, trim the upper curve with paper edgers, then tuck it into the corner pocket.

STAMPING TRICK

Sort through your stash of leftover and experimental stamped paper to find the colors and patterns that work with the page you are constructing. Cut two perfect squares about 1" – 2" (3 cm – 5 cm) across then cut them into triangles to make four matching corners.

ARTIST: BETTY AUTH

Corners

Corners for scrapbooks originated as a handy way to hold photos on a page. Our grandmothers only saw them in black, with gummy backs that had to be moistened. Today's corners still act as photo anchors, but their looks have expanded to include pure decoration and fanciful creativity. Almost any stamp with a fairly solid shape can be turned into a corner, and there are examples for you to discover throughout this book.

Garden Beauties: Folded Origami Corners

ARTIST: SUSAN JAWORSKI STRANC

These gorgeous pages incorporate origami folding into the construction of the corners. The artist is an avid gardener, and has made dramatic pages to enclose some of her most stunning blooms. Why not make art scrapbooks to display photos of your own favorite hobbies? Change the papers and colors to suit a number of themes from model airplanes to butterfly collections.

To practice origami, begin with a 4" × 4" (10 cm × 10 cm) or a 6" × 6" (15 cm × 15 cm) square of paper. Once you have perfected the technique, move down to a 2" × 2" (5 cm × 5 cm) square for the actual corners.

STAMPING TRICK

Origami papers are often very shiny, but the metallics are dazzling when they are stamped and embossed. Use a large, open stamped image so the folding won't interfere with the details in the embossing and cause it to crack.

Folding the Corners

Fold a square as you read the steps, always looking one or two steps ahead. Dashed lines indicate folds.

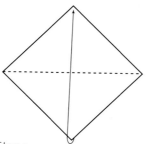

Step 1
Lay a square of origami paper diagonally on the work surface, right side down, and fold the lower point up to form a triangle.

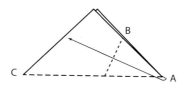

Step 2
With the folded edge at the bottom, fold point A to the center of the left side of the triangle, making the top of the folded corner parallel to the base of the triangle.

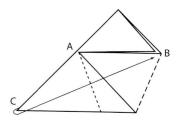

Step 3
Fold point C to point B.

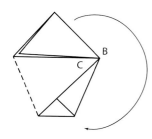

Step 4
Rotate the piece 180 degrees.

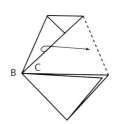

Step 5
Unfold the right corner.

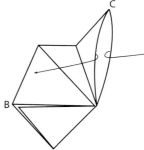

Step 6
Slip your finger inside the corner to open it.

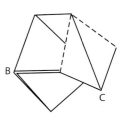

Step 7
Flatten the corner, aligning the front and back creases. Unfold the left corner and repeat steps 6 and 7.

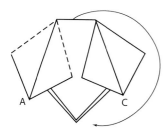

Step 8
Rotate the piece 180 degrees and turn it over.

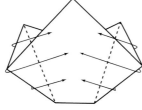

Step 9
Fold both corners in toward the center, following the original crease lines.

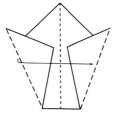

Step 10
Fold the piece in half from left to right.

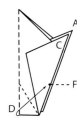

Step 11
To make creases in the base, fold the bottom of the piece up, matching point D to point F.

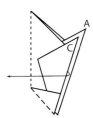

Step 12
Unfold the base and open the piece back to the way it was in Step 10.

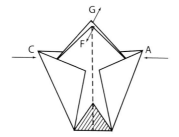

Step 13
Insert a finger into the center of the piece to open it.

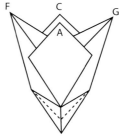

Step 14
Make a half turn from left to right and push the triangular base section up inside the piece.

Step 15
The finished piece, ready to accept the corner of your artwork or photo.

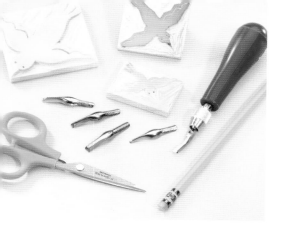

To Make the Page at Left

Make cutout shapes that act like die cuts by carving three sizes of simple bird shapes from stamp carving blocks. Lightly draw the designs onto the carving block with a lead pencil or draw them on paper, cut them out, and trace around the paper shapes onto the block. Keeping the design minimal, carve around the bird and add just a few details. For the background, choose bright blue cardstock and a purple, pink, and green rainbow inkpad. Using the purple range of the pad, stamp the smallest birds heading toward the upper left corner of the paper. Use the green and pink color range to stamp the medium birds heading toward the upper right corner. Stamp the largest birds with opaque white, some heading left and some right. Use all the colors to stamp two large birds on dark blue cardstock and cut them out. Stamp letters on yellow cardstock and cut them out, then make a yellow banner and decorate the folds with sepia chalk. Glue the letters to the banner, the banner to the background, and the two large birds as if they're holding the corners of the banner. Trim the background with paper edgers and mount on yellow cardstock.

Die Cuts

Traditional die cuts for scrapbooking are machine-cut paper shapes available at arts and crafts or scrapbooking stores. They come in a variety of colors and themes, and may be purchased singly or in packets. There are many ways to combine cutout shapes with stamps, and you will see them scattered throughout this book. For a quick and simple addition, decorate purchased shapes with stamps to match your other artwork, as shown on page 287. To add interest and dimension to a scrapbook page, stamp an image and then cut it out completely or partially to create your own faux die cut shape.

STAMPING TRICK

Add personal flair to your pages by carving your own stamps. It's sometimes difficult to find the exact image you want for a given situation, so express your sentiments by making the stamps yourself. See the Basics section, page 8, for instructions.

Fall Foliage: Decorated Die Cuts

To use different cutout shapes on the same page without having them clash, tie the theme and the elements together by stamping on the cutouts and also on the background paper. Then use art pencils to blend all the pieces together.

ARTIST: VICKI SCHREINER

QUICK TRICK

Colors can be used to pull together various elements on a
scrapbook page. If the pieces of a layout seem to clash, try
using art or oil pencils and touches of the same colors over
the entire page to help coordinate them.

MATERIALS

- **Stamps**
  Tiny cluster of ivy
  Fall leaf
- **Ink and Inkpads**
  Khaki, bamboo, and bronze pigment inkpads
- **Paper**
  Dark olive cardstock
  Barn wood, plaid, and white papers
- **Miscellaneous**
  Fall leaf and acorn die cuts
  Oil color pencils
  White plastic eraser (to erase the oil color pencils if needed)

Getting Started

These acorns and leaves are part of a seasonal packet
containing a variety of colors and shapes. While they are pleasing, and the basic colors are appropriate for the fall scrapbook
theme on page 50, they need some additional embellishment
to blend with the page.

Making the Border

Stamp the fall leaf around the edge of the barn wood paper, turning the stamp for each impression, and color softly with oil pencils.

Making the Frames

Use a craft knife to cut along the lines of the plaid paper to
make frames for each photo, lightly glue them around the photos, then mount the framed photos on slightly larger pieces of
dark olive cardstock. Glue the photo assemblages to the background page and scatter the acorn and leaf cutouts over the
page, letting some overlap the edges of the frames.

Stamp the red leaves with the leaf
stamp and bamboo ink. Stamp the
lower part of the acorns with the
tiny ivy pattern and bronze ink. Let
dry and use oil pencils to lightly
color the leaves on the acorn, covering the rest of the shape with a
white paper mask to protect from
smudges as you work. Add pencil
shading to the bodies of the
acorns to emphasize the caps.

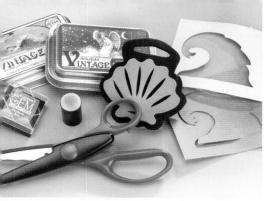

To Create the Page at Left

Start with a sheet of white cardstock, a shell home decor stamp, some wave cutouts, and a variety of blue, turquoise, and sea foam green pigment inks. You'll also need a sponge dauber, white pigment ink, and some paper edgers in a wave pattern. Stamp the shells over the white cardstock, varying the colors of ink. With the wave edgers, trim the stamped page to 6" × 9 " (15 cm × 23 cm), saving the strips. With light blue ink, stamp four shells on a second sheet of white cardstock and cut them out. Arrange three of the shells in a banner, glue lightly together, and stamp the letters on them. Embellish the waves with white pigment ink and a dauber sponge. Assemble the page, layering the 6" × 9" (15 cm × 23 cm) stamped paper slightly left of center on a sheet of blue card-stock. Trim some of the reserved strips and align them vertically and horizon-tally near the top and right edges of the blue cardstock. Daub some color on the fourth shell and glue it over the strips at the upper right. Glue the waves in place, then daub a bit of dark blue ink on the curl of each wave, along the base of the word banner, and around the base of the upper right shell.

Stickers

The aisles of craft and scrapbooking stores are filled with wonderful stickers to use on your pages, and occasionally these purchased stickers are just what you need. But sometimes you want stickers that are special, and will highlight your photos in a particular way. When this is the case, make your own stickers with stamps. If you have a laminating machine with sticker-making capabilities, you can run your stampings through it to create stickers. If you don't have a machine, you can usually take your stamped images to a scrapbooking store and have them turned into stickers.

QUICK TRICK

To create a foamy, frothy appearance on the tops of the waves, use a dauber and white pigment ink before you push the shapes out of the background, and lightly daub the white ink along the tops of the waves. When they are pushed out, the lines will be crisp and the foam will fade in toward the body of the waves.

Buddy and Friends: Repeating Borders

ARTIST: SANDRA McCALL

The border along the bottom of these pages is made up of several small versions of the cat photo shown elsewhere. The cat has been cut out and applied over the top of a checkerboard strip. This is a very effective treatment because it harmonizes with the other elements, adds depth, and emphasizes the importance of the precious cat.

Notice how the narrow checkerboard carries across from one page to the other, tying them together and repeating the colors and patterns.

MATERIALS

- **Stamps**
  Two or three small flowers
  Background swirls
  Checkerboard border
  Saying with heart flowers
- **Ink and Inkpads**
  White, yellow, and black pigment pads
  Rainbow dye inkpad
  Blue and magenta dye inks
- **Papers**
  Two sheets of black cardstock
  Monoprinted or handmade paper for middle ground
  Two sheets of 20# all-purpose copy paper
- **Miscellaneous**
  Variety of markers
  Deckle paper edgers
  White or silver gel pen

Getting Started

Before beginning to assemble this page, make several color copies of the photographs. Vary the sizes of the photos, and use deckle paper edgers to trim some of them. You will need about ten stamp-sized copies of one photo for the lower border. Choose a small version of one of the photographs used elsewhere on the page.

Making the Background

Use white pigment ink to stamp the swirl pattern over the two sheets of black cardstock for the background. Make two sheets of monoprint paper or select two coordinating sheets of handmade paper. Make the checkerboard strips by stamping several rows of checks on white copy paper. Rub some yellow pigment ink over the checkers, then spot-color them with markers to coordinate with the monoprint paper. Stamp fifteen to eighteen flowers on copy paper with dye inks and cut them out.

Lay the two black background sheets next to one another on the work surface. Trim two pieces of monoprint or handmade paper to cover about two-thirds of each page and mount them similarly on each black page. Mount a strip of checkerboard across the bottoms of the pages, ½" (1 cm) up from the bottom, and make sure they are even. Cut out eight or more small photos and place them on top of the checkerboard strip, spacing evenly on each page.

STAMPING TRICK

When stamping, save all your scraps and small bits to use later. The bright flowers seen on these two pages are also used in a very different context with the babies on page 36. When you find an image you like, stamp extras and use them throughout your scrapbook pages.

Adding the Photos

Mount the remaining photos on the two pages, over the background and the middle ground. Use the largest photos or the featured photos on the left page, and the smaller ones on the right. Cut more strips of checkerboard and make frames and lines from the left page to the right page, continuing them at an angle across the two pages to tie the composition together. Cut out the small flowers and scatter them over the pages along with the stamped saying. Write some labels on black cardstock and cut them out to make the title blocks, then mount them on the pages.

Paper Mobile

(PAGE 148)

(Reduce or enlarge pattern as needed.)

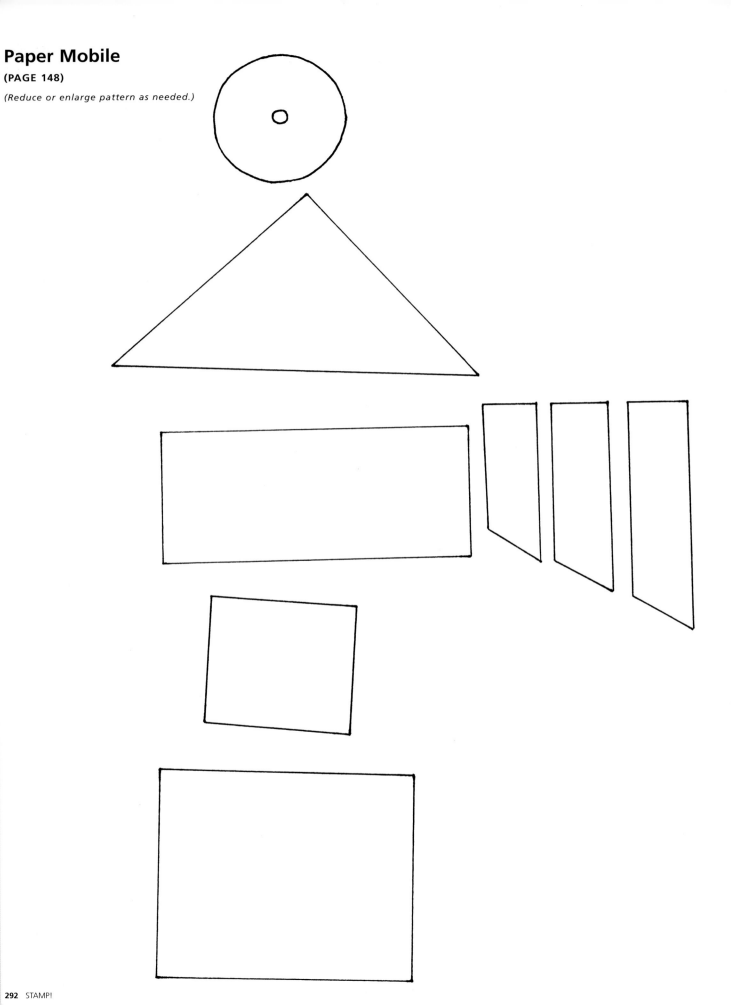

"Ex Libris" Bookplates

(PAGE 149)

(Reduce or enlarge pattern as needed.)

Wild Things Postcards

(PAGE 150)

(Reduce or enlarge pattern as needed.)

Whale Greeting Cards

(PAGE 153)

(Reduce or enlarge pattern as needed.)

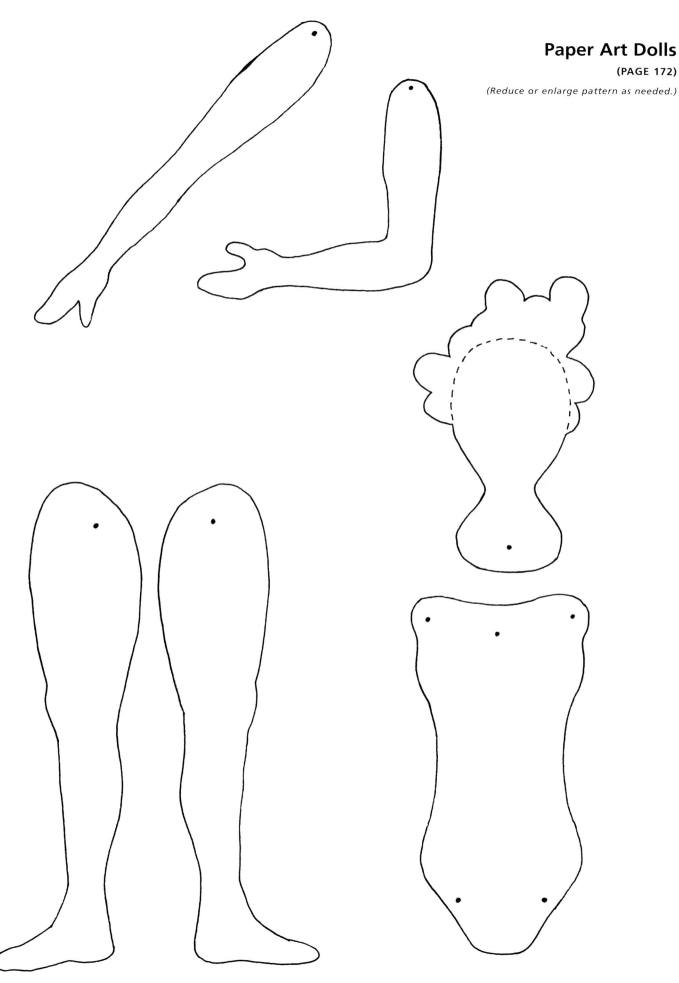

Block-Printed Silk Scarf

(PAGE 179)

(Reduce or enlarge pattern as needed.)

Steno Pad Covers

(PAGE 146)

(Reduce or enlarge pattern as needed.)

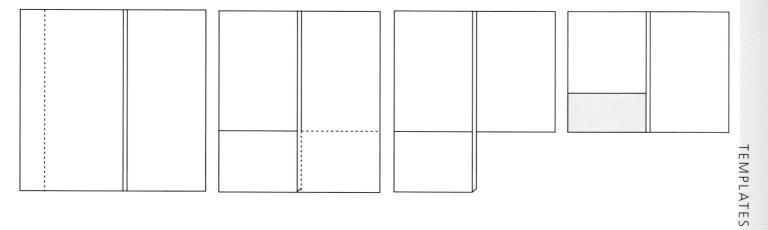

Treasure Pouch Necklace

(PAGE 244)

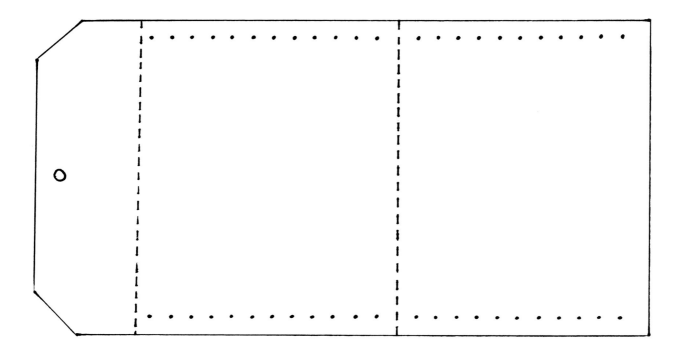

Velvet Embossed Pillow

(PAGE 201)

(Reduce or enlarge pattern as needed.)

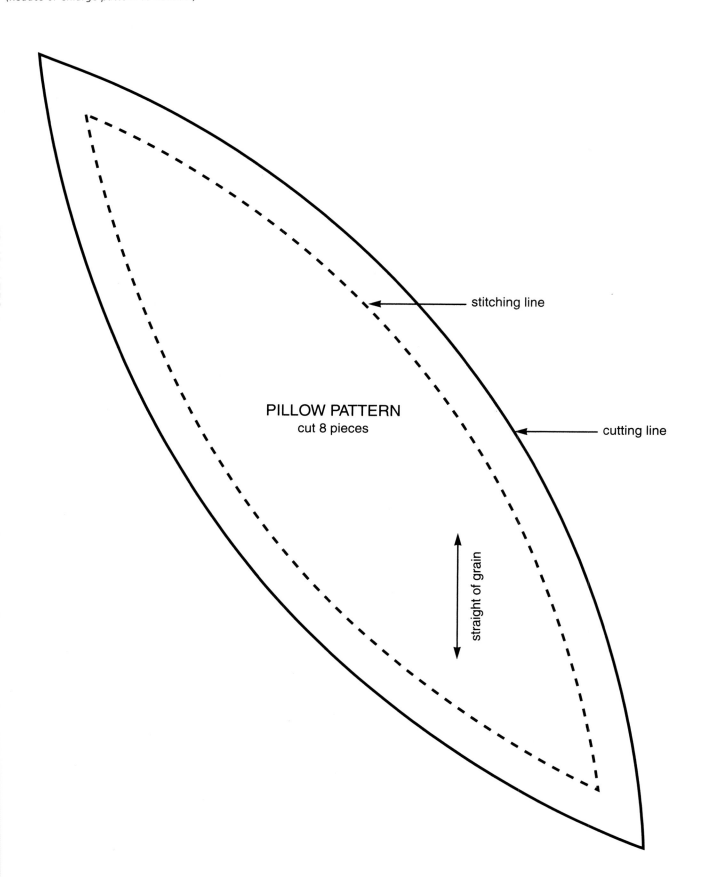

stitching line

cutting line

PILLOW PATTERN
cut 8 pieces

straight of grain

Fabric Art Dolls

(PAGE 202)

(Reduce or enlarge pattern as needed.)

Dragonfly Tray

(PAGE 234)

(Reduce or enlarge pattern as needed.)

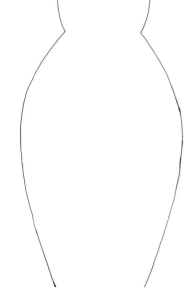

Pierced Metal Luminary

(PAGE 239)

(Reduce or enlarge pattern as needed.)

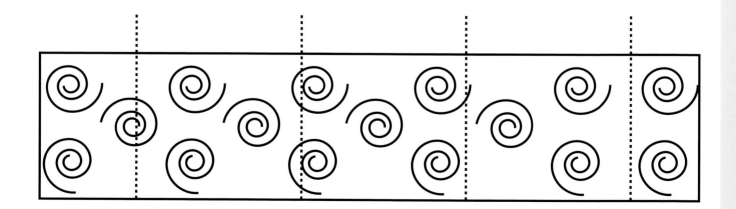

resources

ART STAMP COMPANIES

Above the Mark
P.O. Box 8307
Woodland, CA 95776, USA
T: 530.666.6648

Acey Deucy
P.O. Box 194
Ancram, NY 12502, USA
T: 518.398.5108
F: 518.398.6364

A La Art Stamp Crafters
37500 North Industrial Parkway
Willoughby, OH 44094, USA
T: 216.942.7885

Alice in Rubberland
519 East Pine Street
Seattle, WA 98122, USA

All Night Media
www.allnightmedia.com

A Lost Art
P.O. Box 1338
Baldwin Park, CA 91706, USA
T: 818.790.2125
F: 909.592.3067

Angelwings Enterprises
3065 North Sunnyside #101
Fresno, CA 93727, USA

Ann-ticipations
6507 Pacific Avenue
Stockton, CA 95207, USA
T: 209.952.5538
F: 209.952.4579

Art Impressions
6079 Trail Avenue N.E.
P.O. Box 20085
Salem, OR 97307, USA
T: 800.393.2014
F: 503.393.7956

Cherry Pie Art
Via Antica Romana
33A/4, 16166 Quinto al Mare
Genoa, Italy
www.cherrypie.theshoppe.com

Chronicle Books Stamps
85 2nd Street, 6th Floor
San Francisco, CA 94105, USA
T: 415.537.3730
www.chronbooks.com

Collections Rubber Stamps
6 Ailsa Court
Alexander Heights, Western
Australia 6064, Australia
T: + (61) 8 9342 0054
F: + (61) 8 9247 3665

Copper Leaf Creations
238 South Wall Street
Chandler, AZ 85225, USA
T: 480.821.2843

Curtis Uyeda Rubber Stamps
3326 Saint Michael Drive
Palo Alto, CA 94306, USA
T: 415.424.8840

DeNami Design Rubber Stamps
T: 253.437.1626
F: 253.437.1627
www.denamidesign.com

Distinctive Impressions
2883 Ygnacio Valley Road
Walnut Creek, CA 94598, USA
T: 925.930.7822
F: 925.930.7811
www.distinctive-impression.com

ERA Graphics
2476 Ottawa Way
San Jose, CA 95130, USA
T: 408.364.1124
F: 408.364.1126

Fred Mullett
Rubber Stamps from Nature Prints
2707 59th Southwest, Suite A
Seattle, WA 98116, USA
T: 206.932.9482
F: 206.932.8462

Fruit Basket Upset
1248 9th Avenue
San Francisco, CA 94122, USA
T: 415.566.1018
F: 415.566.6696
www.stampfrancisco.com

Gumbo Graphics
1320 N.W. Northrup Street
Portland, OR 97209, USA
T: 503.223.2824

Hero Arts
1343 Powell Street
Emeryville, CA 94608, USA
T: 800.822.4376
F: 800.441.3632
www.heroarts.com

Hot Potatoes
2805 Columbine Place
Nashville, TN 37204, USA
T: 615.269.8002
F: 615.269.8004
www.hotpotatoes.com

Impress
120 Andover Park
Tukwila, WA 98188, USA
T: 206.901.9101
www.impressrubberstamps.com

Impress Me Rubber Stamps
17116 Escalon Drive
Encino, CA 91436-4030, USA
T: 818.907.1486
E: impressme@earthlink.net

Inkadinkado
60 Cummings Park
Woburn, MA 01801,USA
T: 781.938.6100
F: 781.938.5585
www.inkadinkado.com

Ivory Coast Trading Poste
1248 9th Avenue
San Francisco, CA 94122, USA
T: 415.566.1018
F: 415.566.6696
www.stampfrancisco.com

Judi-Kins
17803 South Hobart Boulevard
Gardena, CA 90248, USA
T: 310.515.1115

Just for Fun
2620 State Road 590
Clearwater, FL 33759, USA
T: 727.669.4114
F: 727.791.6764
www.planetrubber.com

Kristin Powers Collection
12906 Barbezieux Drive
St. Louis, MO 63141, USA
T: 800.450.8586
F: 800.450.0185
www.glitzfinger.com

Krafty Lady
Rear 9 Edgewood Road
Dandenong, Victoria 3175, Australia
T/F: + (61) 3 9794 6064
www.kraftylady.com.au

Leavenworth Jackson
P.O. Box 9988
Berkeley, CA 94709, USA
www.ljackson.com

Limited Edition
1514 Stafford Street
Redwood City, CA 94063, USA
T: 650.299.9700
F: 650.261.9300

Lucy's Stamps
30 Macaranga Street
Marsden, Queensland 4132,
Australia
T: + (61) 7 3805 1115
F: + (61) 7 3805 9095

Magenta Rubber Stamps
351 Blain
Mont Saint-Hilaire,
Quebec J3H 3B4, Canada
T: 800.565.5254
F: 514.464.6353

Marks of Distinction
10 West North Avenue
Chicago, IL 60622-2553, USA
T: 312.335.9266
www.marksofdistinction.com

Modern Illuminator
P.O. Box 8555
Berkeley, CA 94707, USA
www.modernilluminator.com

Moon Rose
P.O. Box 833
Yaphank, NY 11980, USA
T: 516.549.0199
F: 516.924.7292

Non Sequitur
2602 Florence Avenue
Pasadena, TX 77502-3245, USA
F: 713.475.9506
www.nonsequiturstamps.com

OM Studio
P.O. Box 448
Seaside, OR 97138, USA
T: 800.738.6955

100 Proof Press
P.O. Box 299
Athens, OH 45701, USA
T: 740.594.2315
F: 800.511.2100

Ornamentum
32903 30th Avenue Southwest
Federal Way, WA 98023, USA
T: 206.838.3259

Our Lady of Rubber
P.O. Box 1892
Bisbee, AZ 85603, USA

Paper Inspirations
P.O. Box 7513
Kalispell, MT 59901, USA
T: 406.756.9677
F: 406.756.9678
www.stampgallery.com

Paper Parachute
P.O. Box 91385
Portland, OR 97291-0385, USA
T: 503.531.0385
E: raymond.werner@intel.com

Personal Stamp Exchange
360 Sutton Place
Santa Rosa, CA 95407, USA
T: 707.588.8058
F: 707.588.7476

Plaid Rubber Stamps
3225 Westech Drive
Norcross, GA 30092-350, USA
T: 800.842.4197
www.plaidonline.com

Postmodern Design
P.O. Box 720416
Norman, OK 73070, USA
T: 405.321.3176

Red Head Stamp
P.O. Box 3374
Bellevue, WA 98009, USA
T: 206.660.2028
F: 888.727.8267
E: redhead@aol.com

Red Pearl
P.O. Box 94502
Seattle, WA 98124, USA
T: 206.624.5723
F: 206.903.8202

River City Rubber Works
5555 South Meridian
Wichita, KS 67217, USA
T: 316.529.8656
F: 316.529.8940
www.rivercityrubberworks.com

Rubbermoon
P.O. Box 3258
Hayden Lake, ID 83835, USA
T: 208.772.9772
www.rubbermoon.com

Rubber Nature Art Stamps
7500 125th Avenue
Kenosha, WI 53142, USA
T: 414.857.3100
F: 414.857.2355

Rubber Poet
Box 218
Rockville, UT 84763, USA
T: 435.772.3441
F: 800.906.7638
www.wyoming.com/~cavenewt/pigs

Rubber Stampede
P.O. Box 246
Berkeley, CA 94701, USA
T: 800.632.8386
www.rubberstampede.com

Rubber Stamps of America
P.O. Box 576
Saxtons River, VT 05154, USA
T: 800.553.5031
F: 802.869.2262
www.stampusa.com

Rubberstiltzken
P.O. Box 1833
Fremont, CA 94538, USA

Saturdays Only
P.O. Box 4355
Albuquerque, NM 87196, USA
T: 505.232.4431

Simply Stamps
Plaid Rubber Stamps
3225 Westech Drive
Norcross, GA 30092-350, USA
T: 800.842.4197
www.plaidonline.com

Stampendous!
1357 South Lewis Street
Anaheim, CA 92805, USA
T: 714.563.9501
F: 714.563.9509
www.stampendous.com

Stampers Anonymous
20613 Center Ridge Road
Rocky River, OH 44116, USA
T: 440.333.7941
F: 440.333.7992
www.stampersanonymous.com

Stamp Francisco - Coco Stamp
1248 9th Avenue
San Francisco, CA 94122, USA
T: 415.566.1018
www.stampfrancisco.com

Stampington & Company
22992 Mill Creek, Suite B
Laguna Hills, CA 92653, USA
T: 949.380.7318
F: 949.380.9355
www.stampington.com

A Stamp in the Hand
20630 South Leapwood Avenue,
Suite B
Carson, CA 90746, USA
T: 310.329.8555
www.astampinthehand.com

Stampin' Up!
T: 800.782.6787
www.stampinup.com

Stamp-It Rubber Stamps
P.O. Box 653
Victoria Park, Western Australia
6979, Australia
T: + (61) 8 9470 5422
F: + (61) 8 9361 0547
www.stampit.com.au

Stamp Oasis
4750 West Sahara Avenue, Suite 17
Las Vegas, NV 89102, USA
T: 702.878.6474
F: 702.878.7824
www.stampoasis.com

Stamp Out Cute
7084 North Cedar, #137
Fresno, CA 93720, USA

Stampscapes
7451 Warner Avenue, Suite E #124
Huntington Beach, CA 92647, USA
T: 714.968.5541
www.stampscapes.com

Stamps Happen, Inc.
419 South Acacia Avenue
Fullerton, CA 92831, USA
T: 714.879.9894
F: 714.879.9896

Stamp Zia
29205 Elm Island
Waterford, WI 53185, USA
T: 414.534.6039
www.stampzia.com

Stephanie Olin's Stamps
6171 Foxshield Drive
Huntington Beach, CA 92647, USA
T: 714.848.1227
www.flash.net/~olinstmp

ThINKING Stamps
4/186 Main Road
Blackwood, South Australia
5051, Australia
T: + (61) 8 8370 3722

Tin Can Mail
60 Maxwell Court
Santa Rosa, CA 95401, USA
T: 800.554.5755
www.stamparosa.com

Too Much Fun Rubber Stamps
920 Trowbridge, Suite 345
East Lansing, MI 48823, USA
T: 517.646.7106
F: 517.347.1465
www.toomuchfunrubberstamps.com

Toybox Rubber Stamps
P.O. Box 1487
Healdsburg, CA 95448, USA
T: 707.431.1400
F: 707.431.2408

Uptown Rubber Stamps
315 West Hickory Street
Fort Collins, CO 80524-1100, USA
T: 800.888.3212
F: 800.466.9515
www.uptownrubberstamps.com

Zettiology
P.O. Box 2665
Renton, WA 98056, USA
T: 206.255.1543

ZimPrints
7121 Merrick Drive SW
Knoxville, TN 37919-8119, USA
T/F: 865.584.9430
www.zimprints.com

SUPPLIES

Aiko's Art Materials
3347 North Clark
Chicago, IL 60657, USA
T: 773.404.5600
paper

A Lost Art
P.O. Box 1338
Baldwin Park, CA 91706, USA
T: 818.790.2125
sealing wax and seals

Artistic Wire
752 North Larch Avenue
Elmhurst, IL 60126, USA
www.artisticwire.com
*colored copper wire, tools &
accessories*

Binney & Smith
1100 Church Lane
Easton, PA 18044, USA
www.binney-smith.com
*distributors of Crayola and Liquitex
products, Model Magic modeling
compound*

Cartoon Colour Company, Inc.
9024 Lindblade Street
Culver City, CA 90232, USA
T: 213.838.8467
cel-vinyl paint

Clearsnap, Inc.
Box 98
Anacortes, WA 98221, USA
T: 360.293.6634
F: 360.293.6699
www.clearsnap.com
ColorBox inks

Creative Paperclay
79 Daily Drive, Suite 101
Camarillo, CA 93010, USA
www.creativepaperclay.com
air-dry clay

Daniel Smith, Inc.
P.O. Box 84268
Seattle, WA 98124-5568, USA
T: 206.223.9599
F: 206.224.0404
art materials

DMD Industries
2300 South Old Missouri Rd.
Springdale, AR 72764, USA
www.dmdind.com
paper, journals, albums

Fascinating Folds
P.O. Box 10070
Glendale, AZ 85318, USA
T: 602.375.9978
F: 602.375.9979
www.fascinating-folds.com
papers

Fiskars, Inc.
7811 West Stewart Avenue
Wausau, WI 54401, USA
T: 715.842.2091
www.fiskars.com
*scissors, paper edgers, cutters,
accessories*

Greg Markim, Inc.
P.O. Box 13245
Milwaukee, WI 53213, USA
T: 414.453.1480
papermaking kits

Green Heron Book Arts
1928 21st Avenue, Suite A
Forest Grove, OR 97116, USA
T: 503.357.7263
www.green-heron-kits.com
bookmaking kits

The Japanese Paper Place
887 Queen Street West
Toronto, Ontario M6J 1G5, Canada
T: 416.703.0089
F: 416.703.0163

Loose Ends
P.O. Box 20310
Salem, OR 97307, USA
T: 503.390.4724
F: 503.390.4724
www.4loosends.com
papers

Marvy-Uchida
1027 East Burgrove Street
Carson, CA 90746, USA
T: 800.541.5877
markers

Paper Adventures
P.O. Box 04393
Milwaukee, WI 53204, USA
www.paperadventures.com
art and scrapbooking papers

Papers by Catherine
11328 South Post Oak Road, #108
Houston, TX 77035, USA
T: 713.723.3334
F: 713.723.4749

Quire Handmade Paper
P.O. Box 248
Belair, South Australia 5052,
Australia
T/F: + (61) 8 8295 2966

Ranger Industries
15 Park Road
Tinton Falls, NJ 07724, USA
T: 732.389.3535
F: 732.389.1102
ink

Speedball
Hunt Manufacturing Co.
Statesville, NC 28677, USA
T: 704.872.9511
opaque markers

Sunday International
5672 Buckingham Drive
Huntington Beach, CA 92649, USA
www.sundayint.com
rubber stamps & accessories

Suze Weinberg
39 Old Bridge Drive
Howell, NJ 07731, USA
T: 732.364.3136
F: 732.364.7244
www.schmoozewithsuze.com

mixed media
Tidy Crafts
1330 Enterprise
Idaho Falls, ID 83402, USA
www.tidycrafts.com
Tidy Trays and organizing accessories

Toner Plastics, Inc.
699 Silver Street
Agawam, MA 01001, USA
www.tonerplastics.com
colored plastic art wire

Tsukineko
15411 N.E. 95th Street
Redmond, WA 98052, USA
www.tsukineko.com
inks, inkpads, markers, pens

USArtQuest, Inc.
7800 Ann Arbor Road
Grass Lake, MI 49240, USA
www.usartquest.com
Perfect Paper adhesive

Walnut Hollow
1409 State Road 23
Dodgeville, WI 53533, USA
www.walnuthollow.com
*woodburners, unfinished wooden
albums, oil color pencils*

Xyron Inc.
15820 North 84th Street
Scottsdale, AZ 85260, USA
www.xyron.com
*laminating and sticker machines
and cartridges*

MAGAZINES

The Rubber Gazette
6 Ailsa Court
Alexander Heights, Western
Australia 6064, Australia
T: + (61) 8 9342 0054
F: + (61) 8 9247 3665

Rubberstampmadness
408 Southwest Monroe, #210
Corvallis, OR 97330, USA
T: 541.752.0075
F: 541.752.5475
www.rubberstampmadness.com

Somerset Studio
22992 Mill Creek, Suite B
Laguna Hills, CA 92653, USA
T: 949.380.7318
F: 949.380.9355
www.somersetstudio.com

The Stampers' Sampler
22992 Mill Creek, Suite B
Laguna Hills, CA 92653, USA
T: 949.380.7318
F: 949.380.9355
www.stampington.com

Stamping & Papercrafting
Express Publications Pty Ltd.
2 Stanley Street
Silverwater, New South Wales 2128,
Australia
T: + (61) 2 9748 0599

art stamp credits

Abstract Brooch
Impress Me Rubber Stamps

Accordion-Fold Book
Cherry Pie Art
Nature Journals
Alphabet stamps: Hero Arts

Artistamps
Collections Rubber Stamps

Asian Clock
Magenta Rubber Stamps

Asian Gift Box
Magenta Rubber Stamps

Block Printed Silk Scarf
Handcarved images (by Paula Grasdal)

Candles
Stampington & Company

Canvas Director's Chair
Plaid Rubber Stamps
Minwax Home Decor Blocking Patterns

Canvas Totebag
Magenta Rubber Stamps
Rubber Stampede

Canvas Wine Bottle Bag
Natural leaves

Clay Bowl
Copper Leaf Creations

Clay Jewelry
Copper Leaf Creations

Clay Picture Frames
All Night Media
A Stamp in the Hand
Judi-Kins
Just for Fun
PSX
Stampers Anonymous
Stampington & Company

Coffee Napkin
ZimPrints

Collage and Découpage
Acey Deucy

Collage Stamping
Cherry Pie Art

Copper Stamping
Hero Arts
Stamp Oasis
Stephanie Olin's Stamps

Deep Thermal Embossing
Acey Deucy

Double-Cover Bound Books
Impress Me Rubber Stamps

Dragonfly Tray
Handcarved images (Agatha Bell)

Elegant Brooches
Postmodern Design

"Ex Libris" Bookplates
Handcarved images (by Agatha Bell)

Fabric Art Dolls
A Stamp in the Hand
Hot Potatoes
Magenta Rubber Stamps
Moon Rose
Stamp Francisco
Toybox Rubber Stamps

Faux Finishes
Fred Mullett, Rubber Stamps From Nature Prints

Faux Fossil Necklace
Impress Me Rubber Stamps
Stampers Anonymous

Faux Postage
Stamp Out Cute

Finial Bookends
Inkadinkado
Just for Fun
Rubber Poet
Stampers Anonymous
Stampington & Company
Stampscapes

Floral Mirror
Rubber Stampede

Fortuny Velvet Pillows
Plaid Rubber Stamps
Rubber Stampede

Gift Bags & Tags
Hero Arts
Krystalvue

Gilded Slate Frame
Sponge stamp
Pencil eraser

Hawaiian Critters
Ivory Coast Trading Poste

Heat & Mold Stamping
Impress Me Rubber Stamps

Jewels in a Box
Alice in Rubberland

Jungle Shower Curtain
Rubber Stampede

Kiln-Fired Tiles
Chinese coins
Chinese stone seals (chops)
Chronicle Books stamps
Handcarved images (by the artist)
Handcarved images (by the artist)
Judi-Kins
Saturdays Only
Wood blocks from Nepal

Large-Format Art
Stamp Zia

Leaf-print Lamp Shade
Rubber Nature Art Stamps

Leather Journals
Above the Mark
Personal Stamp Exchange

Light Switch Plates
Judi-Kins
Magenta Rubber Stamps
Stampers Anonymous

Magnets
Fruit Basket Upset
Gumbo Graphics
Ivory Coast Trading Post
Leavenworth Jackson
Modern Illuminator
Rubberstiltzken

Mail Art
Acey Deucy
A Lost Art
Stampers Anonymous
Stampington & Company

Marbled Surfaces
Background stamp: Judi-Kins
Bird stamp: Paper Parachute

Masking, Layering, and Stenciling
Magenta Rubber Stamps

Metallic Accents
 Marble texture cube stamp: Stampendous!
 Spiral stamp and collage figure: Acey Deucy
 Papyrus background stamp: Judi-Kins

Miniature Books
Acey Deucy

Modeling Compound Beads & Buttons
Impress Me Rubber Stamps

Model Magic Stamps
Impress Me Rubber Stamps

Muslin Pillow
Rubber Stampede

Painted Glass Plate & Glasses
Rubber Moon

Painted Glass Vase
DeNami Rubber Stamps
Stampington & Company

Painted Tiles
Curtis Uyeda
Judi-Kins
Just for Fun
Personal Stamp Exchange
Rubber Moon
Rubber Poet
Stampers Anonymous
Stamp Francisco
Stampington & Company

Paper Art Dolls
A Lost Art
Art Impressions
A Stamp in the Hand
Inkadinkado
Kristin Powers Collection
Postmodern Design
Stampers Anonymous
Uptown Design (stamps and paper doll template)

Paperclay Jewelry
Found items

Paper Clock
Paper Inspirations

Paper Mobile
Hero Arts
Magenta Rubber Stamps
Our Lady of Rubber

Paper Placemat
Sponge stamps

Patterned Backgrounds
Magenta Rubber Stamps

Pierced Metal Luminary
Inkadinkado

Pillow Beads
Stampers Anonymous
Stampington & Company
Stamp Oasis

Pillow Bead Necklace
Impress Me Rubber Stamps

Placemats & Napkins
Plaid Rubber Stamps
Rubber Stampede
Simply Stamps by Plaid Enterprises

Reverse Stamping
Lotus stamp: Judi-Kins
Egyptian woman: Red Head Stamp

Ribbon
Stampin' Up!

Rollup Beads
Impress Me
Judi-Kins
Red Pearl

Round Wooden Bug Box
Leavenworth Jackson
Marks of Distinction
Rubber Stamps of America
Stamp Francisco

Seaglass Brooches
Stampers Anonymous
Fred Mullett

Seaglass Jewelry
Non Sequitur

Stamped Booklets
Impress Me Rubber Stamps

Stamping on Acetate
Magenta Rubber Stamps

Stamping on Candles
Stampington & Company

Stamping on Wood Charms
A Lost Art

Stamping with Foam Insulation
Handcarved images (by the artist)

Stamping with Model Magic
Impress Me Rubber Stamps

Star Fruit Coasters
Handmade images (Livia McRee)

Steno Pad Covers
Leavenworth Jackson
Magenta Rubber Stamps

Sunflower Box
Copper Leaf Creations

Tablecloth & Felt Table Topper
Plaid Rubber Stamps

Tag Art
Acey Deucy
All Night Media
A Stamp in the Hand
Hero Arts
Impress
Inkadinkado
Judi-Kins
Leavenworth Jackson
OM Studio
100 Proof Press
Personal Stamp Exchange
River City
Rubber Stamps of America
Stampers Anonymous
Tin Can Mail
Too Much Fun
Zettiology

Terra Cotta Pots
Stampin' Up!

Topiary Table Setting
Hero Arts